AF531753

AGRICULTURAL DRAINAGE AND WATER QUALITY

AGRICULTURAL DRAINAGE AND WATER QUALITY

By

Dr. Anupam Pandey

Diploma (i) Tourism, (ii) Creative Writing

M.A. (Geography) Ph.D. (Geomorphology)

Dr. R.M.L. Awadh University

Faizabad, (U.P.) (India)

(Writers & Editor of Numerous Books)

DISCOVERY PUBLISHING HOUSE PVT. LTD.

NEW DELHI-110 002

Published by:
Tilak Wasan
DISCOVERY PUBLISHING HOUSE PVT. LTD.
4383/4B, Ansari Road, Darya Ganj
New Delhi-110 002 (India)
Phone : +91-11-23279245, 43596064-65
Fax : +91-11-23253475
E-mail : parul.wasan@gmail.com
discoverypublishinghouse@gmail.com
web : www.discoverypublishinggroup.com

First Edition: **2013**

ISBN: 978-93-5056-234-5

Agricultural Drainage and Water Quality

© 2013, **Author**

All rights reserved. No part of this publication should be reproduced, stored in a retrieval system, or transmitted in any form or by any means: electronic, mechanical, photocopying, recording or otherwise, without the prior written permission of the author and the publisher.

This book has been published in good faith that the material provided by authors is original. Every effort is made to ensure accuracy of material, but the publisher and printer will not be held responsible for any inadvertent error(s). In case of any dispute, all legal matters are to be settled under Delhi jurisdiction only.

Printed at:
Aditi Fine Art Press
Delhi

PREFACE

Agricultural drainage is the checking of excess water from the soil surface by either gravity or artificial means. The purpose of this drainage is to remove excess water from the soil in order to enhance crop production. In some soils, the natural drainage processes are enough for growth and production of agricultural crops, but in many other soils, artificial drainage is needed for efficient agricultural production.

An agricultural drainage system is a system by which the water level on or in the soil is checked by human-beings to enhance agricultural crop production. It shows the field (or internal) and the main (or external) systems.

Draining systems that use pipes is good method for solving drainage problems. A trench system needs to be dug so that the pipes can be placed inside. One can determine where to dig these trenches by examining the water flow and deciding a suitable place for relocation. Another method of draining installation is a rain barrel. The rain barrel generally is installed where there is an excess of rain water, such as under a roof trough.

Drainage water can also be disposed of by injection to the deep groundwater. If drainage water is disposed of to large, open surface water systems with significant dilution or assimilative capacity, then water quality problems are minimized. However, water quality problems may develop with repeated re-use, disposal in closed basins and injection to deep wells.

This book is the outcome of long innings of research work in library and Internet. I also consulted foreign authors, book on this topic. The editorial staff of this publication along with publisher also helped me in every possible way. I am highly indebted to all these resources for publishing this book on scheduled time in eye-pleasing format.

—Author

CONTENTS

CHAPTER – 1

Understanding Agricultural Drainage

Agricultural land drainage usually consists of surface or sub-surface systems, or a combination of both. At the field scale, subsurface drain pipes and field ditches normally exit to an open main or collector drain. At the regional level, the latter then empties into a river or its tributaries. In some instances, depending on the character of the hydrological basin, main drains may dispose of drainage water to an evaporation pond, to a wetland, or to a saline agriculture/agriculture-forestry system. Not all of these management options will necessarily be used in a single watershed.

Most agricultural producers improve the drainage on their land to help create a healthier environment for plant growth and to provide drier field conditions so farm equipment can access the farm field throughout the crop production season. Healthy, productive plants have the potential to produce greater yields and more food.

Agricultural drainage is the removal of excess water from the soil surface and/or soil profile of cropland, by either gravity or artificial means. An agricultural drainage system is a system by which the water level on or in the soil is controlled to enhance agricultural crop production. It shows the field (or internal) and the main (or external) systems.

PURPOSE OF DRAINAGE SYSTEM

The function of the field drainage system is to control the water-table, whereas the function of the main drainage system is to collect, transport, and dispose of the water through an outfall or outlet. In some instances, one makes an additional distinction between collector and main drainage systems.

The two main reasons for improving the drainage on agricultural land are for soil conservation and enhancing crop production.

Agricultural research has shown that agricultural drainage improvement can help reduce the year-to-year variability in crop yield, which helps reduce the risks associated with the production of abundant, high quality, affordable food. Improved access of farm equipment to the field provides more time for field activities, can help extend the crop production season, and helps reduce crop damage at harvest.

Field drainage systems are differentiated in surface and subsurface field drainage systems. Sometimes in irrigated, submerged rice fields, a form of temporary drainage is required whereby the drainage system is allowed to function on certain occasions only during the harvest period.

If allowed to function continuously, excessive quantities of water would be lost. Such a system is therefore called a checked, or controlled, drainage system. More usually, however, the drainage system is meant to function as regularly as possible to prevent undue waterlogging at any time and one employs a regular drainage system. In literature, this is sometimes also called a "relief drainage system."

SURFACE DRAINAGE SYSTEMS

The regular surface drainage systems, which start functioning as soon as there is an excess of rainfall or irrigation, operate entirely by gravity. They consist of reshaped or reformed land surfaces and can be divided into:

1. Bedded systems, used in flat lands for crops other than rice.
2. Graded systems, used in sloping land for crops other than rice.

The bedded and graded systems may have ridges and furrows. The checked surface drainage systems consist of check gates placed in the embankments surrounding flat basins, such as those used for rice fields in flat lands. These fields are usually submerged and only need to be drained on certain occasions like at harvest time. Checked surface drainage systems are also found in terraced lands used for rice.

In literature, not much information can be found on the relations between the various regular surface field drainage systems, the reduction in the degree of waterlogging, and the agricultural or environmental effects. It is therefore difficult to develop sound agricultural criteria for the regular surface field drainage systems. Most of the known criteria for these systems concern the efficiency of the techniques of land leveling and earthmoving. Similarly, agricultural criteria for checked surface drainage systems are not very well known.

SUB-SURFACE DRAINAGE SYSTEMS

Like the surface field drainage systems, the subsurface field drainage systems can also be differentiated in regular systems and checked (controlled) systems. When the drain discharge takes place entirely by gravity, both types of subsurface systems have much in common, except that the checked systems have control gates that can be opened and closed according to need. They can save much irrigation water. A checked drainage system also reduces the discharge through the main drainage system, thereby reducing construction costs.

When the discharge takes place by pumping, the drainage can be checked simply by not operating the pumps or by reducing the pumping time. In northwestern India, this practice has increased the irrigation efficiency and reduced the quantity of irrigation water needed, and has not led to any undue salinization.

The sub-surface field drainage systems consist of horizontal or slightly sloping channels made in the soil; they can be open ditches, trenches, filled with brushwood and a soil cap, filled with stones and a soil cap, buried pipe drains, tile drains, or mole drains, but they can also consist of a series of wells.

Modern buried pipe drains often consist of corrugated, flexible, and perforated plastic (PE or PVC) pipe lines wrapped with an *envelope* or filter material to improve the permeability around the pipes and to prevent entry of soil particles, which is especially important in fine sandy and silty soils. The surround may consist of synthetic fibre (geotextile).

A subsoiler or mole plough is a tractor mounted implement used to loosen and break up soil at depths below the level of a traditional disk harrow or rototiller. Most tractor mounted cultivation tools will break up and turn over surface soil to a depth of 6″ to 8″ while a subsoiler will break up and loosen soil to twice those depths. Typically a subsoiler mounted to a Compact Utility Tractor will reach depths of about 12″ and typically have only one thin blade with a sharpened tip.

The subsoiler is a tillage tool which will improve growth in all crops where soil compaction is a problem. The design provides deep tillage, loosening soil deeper than a tiller or plough is capable of reaching. Agricultural subsoilers, according to the Unverferth Company, can disrupt hardpan ground down to 24″ depths.

Various manufacturer's brochures claim that crops perform well during hot and dry seasons because roots penetrate soil layers deeper to reach moisture and nutrients. Brochures further claim that in wet conditions, the water passes easier through the shattered areas, reducing the possibility of crops drowning.

Agricultural tractors will have multiple deeper reaching blades; each blade is called a scarifier or shank. Purdue University's Department of Agriculture indicates that common subsoilers for agricultural use are available with 3, 5 or 7 shanks. These units can be up to 15' wide, some models are towed behind tractors, others are tractor mounted to the 3pt hitch. A form of this implement with a single blade, a pipe-and-cable-laying plough, is used to lay buried cables or pipes, without the need to dig a deep trench and re-fill it.

FACTORS CONTRIBUTING TO EXCESS WATER PROBLEMS IN SOILS

The factors that contribute to excess soil water problems include: fine soil texture; massive soil structure; low soil permeability; topography; soil compaction; restrictive geologic layer; and excess precipitation.

Soil Texture

The sand, silt and clay composition of the solid mineral particles in a soil is called soil texture. For a loam soil texture, for instance, the mineral content might consist of 40 percent clay, 30 percent silt and 30 percent sand. Soil texture can have a dramatic effect on how well the soil holds water, and how easily water can move through the soil.

Fine-textured soils have a large percentage of clay and silt particles. These soils generally hold water well, but drain poorly. Coarse-textured soils have a large percentage of sand or gravel particles. These soils drain well, but have poor water-holding ability.

Soil Structure

The physical arrangement of the solid mineral particles of a soil is the soil structure. A granular structure helps promote the movement of water through a soil, but a structure that is massive lacking any distinct arrangement of soil particles usually decreases the movement of water.

Permeability

In general terms, the relative ease with which water can move through a block of soil is soil permeability. A soil's permeability can be affected by its texture, structure, human activities, and other factors.

Topography

The shape and slope of the land surface can cause wet soil conditions, especially around depressions where water tends to accumulate. Without an outlet, the water may drain away very slowly.

Geologic Formation

The geological formation underlying a soil can impact the drainage of water from that soil. For instance, a soil could have texture and structure properties that are beneficial to the movement of water. However, if the geologic formation underlying this soil consisted of dense clay or solid rock, it could restrict the downward movement of water, causing the soil above the formation to remain saturated during certain times of the year.

Compaction

Human activities may help create excess soil water problems. For example, operating equipment on a wet soil can compact the soil and destroy its structure. A soil layer that is compacted will generally have no structure, and most of the voids in this layer will have been eliminated.

Voids are open spaces between soil particles that can be filled with air, water, or a combination of both. Soil water will tend to accumulate above the compacted layer because movement of water through the compacted layer is severely restricted. If the compacted layer is located at the soil surface, very little water will enter the soil and much of the water will runoff, potentially creating a flooding and/or erosion hazard.

Precipitation

Ohio's average annual precipitation is 38 inches, based on a 50-year period of precipitation records. Even though the distribution of precipitation across the state varies, the state receives an abundant supply of precipitation in an average year. In an average month, most areas of the state receive two to four inches of precipitation.

This amount is adequate to sustain high crop yields. However, excessive rainfall, and/or winters with heavy snowfall, often produce excess soil water conditions. Furthermore, thunderstorms will frequently result in runoff because the rainfall rate is greater than the rate at which water can enter (infiltrate) into the soil.

The *field drains* (or *laterals*) discharge their water into the collector or main system either by *gravity* or by *pumping*. The wells (which may be open dug wells or *tubewells*) have normally to be pumped, but sometimes they are connected to drains for discharge by gravity.

Subsurface drainage by wells is often referred to as vertical drainage, and drainage by channels as horizontal drainage, but it is more clear to speak of "field drainage by wells" and "field drainage by ditches or pipes" respectively.

In some instances, subsurface drainage can be achieved simply by breaking up slowly permeable soil layers by *deep plowing* (*sub-soiling*), provided that the underground has sufficient natural drainage. In other instances, a combination of sub-soiling and subsurface drains may solve the problem.

A pipe-and-cable-laying plough is a trenchless method to bury cables or pipes. The machinery is a form of a subsoiler with a single blade. It is used to lay buried services of virtually any description, for drainage, water, electricity, tele-communications, gas supply etc.

A coil of the service pipe/cable is mounted on the tractor and is led down a guide behind the blade, and is left buried behind the plough, without the need to dig a deep trench and re-fill it. This process is normally used in rural areas where previously buried services will not be encountered and there are no hardened surfaces, e.g. tarmac concrete etc.

There are also specialised laying ploughs for cable laying behind traffic barriers, in stream or lake beds or even for the laying of submarine cables in deep sea, so-called sea ploughs. Sea ploughs are pulled behind cable ship and bury the cable in the sea bed. Burying submarine cables helps protect them from anchors, trawlers and other risks.

MAIN DRAINAGE SYSTEMS

The main drainage systems consist of deep or shallow collectors, and main drains or disposal drains. Deep collector drains are required for subsurface field drainage systems, whereas shallow collector drains are used for surface field drainage systems, but they can also be used for pumped subsurface systems. The deep collectors may consist of open ditches or buried pipe lines.

The terms 'deep collectors' and 'shallow collectors' refer rather to the depth of the water level in the collector below the soil surface than to the depth of the bottom of the collector. The bottom depth is determined both by the depth of the water level and by the required discharge capacity.

The deep collectors may either discharge their water into deep main drains (which are drains that do not receive water directly from field drains, but only from collectors), or their water may be pumped into a disposal drain.

Disposal drains are main drains in which the depth of the water level below the soil surface is not bound to a minimum, and the water level may even be above the soil surface, provided that embankments are made to prevent inundation. Disposal drains can serve both subsurface and surface field drainage systems.

Deep main drains can gradually become disposal drains if they are given a smaller gradient than the land slope along the drain. The technical criteria applicable to main drainage systems depend on the hydrological situation and on the type of system.

The final point of a main drainage system is the gravity outlet structure or the pumping station.

Applications

Surface drainage systems are usually applied in relatively flat lands that have soils with a low or medium infiltration capacity, or in lands with high-intensity rainfalls that exceed the normal infiltration capacity, so that frequent waterlogging occurs on the soil surface.

Subsurface drainage systems are used when the drainage problem is mainly that of shallow water tables. When both surface and subsurface waterlogging occur, a combined surface/subsurface drainage system is required.

Sometimes, a subsurface drainage system is installed in soils with a low infiltration capacity, where a surface drainage problem may improve the soil structure and the infiltration capacity so greatly that a surface drainage system is no longer required.

On the other hand, it can also happen that a surface drainage system diminishes the recharge of the groundwater to such an extent that the subsurface drainage problem is considerably reduced or even eliminated.

The choice between a subsurface drainage system by pipes and ditches or by tube wells is more a matter of technical criteria and costs than of agricultural criteria, because both types of systems can be designed to meet the same agricultural criteria and achieve the same benefits.

Usually, pipe drains or ditches are preferable to wells. However, when the soil consists of a poorly permeable top layer several meters thick, overlying a rapidly permeable and deep subsoil, wells may be a better option, because the drain spacing required for pipes or ditches would be considerably smaller than the spacing for wells.

When the land needs a subsurface drainage system, but saline groundwater is present at great depth, it is better to employ a shallow, closely spaced system of pipes or ditches instead of a deep, widely spaced system. The reason is that the deeper systems produce a more salty effluent than the shallow systems. Environmental criteria may then prohibit the use of the deeper systems.

Drainage Projects

In some drainage projects, one may find that only main drainage systems are envisaged. The agricultural land is then still likely to suffer from field drainage problems. In other cases, one may find that field drainage systems are ineffective because there is no adequate main drainage system. In either case, the installation of drainage systems is not recommended.

Reference: gives a general description of land drainage in the world and shows a paper on types of agricultural land drainage systems used in different parts of the world.

DRAINAGE SYSTEM DESIGN

The analysis of positive and negative (side) effects of drainage and the optimization of drainage design in accordance to the *drainage design procedures* is discussed in the article on Drainage research.

There are several concerns about the sustainability of irrigation and drainage projects, and there are water quality problems related to the disposal of drainage water. There are also problems with land degradation due to irrigation induced salinity and waterlogging. There have been instances where saline or high nutrient drainage water has damaged aquatic ecosystems.

Drainage continues to be a vital and necessary component of agricultural production systems. In order to enhance the net benefits of drainage systems, more attention will need to be given to the water quality impacts of drainage water disposal. This document identifies potential problems and management options in the development, production, treatment and disposal of agricultural drainage water.

Effects of Excess Water

Excess water in the crop root zone soil is injurious to plant growth. Crop yields are drastically reduced on poorly drained soils, and, in cases of prolonged waterlogging, plants eventually die due to a lack of oxygen in the root zone. Sources of excess soil water that result in high water tables include: high precipitation in humid regions; surplus irrigation water and canal seepage in the irrigated lands; and artesian pressure. Waterlogging in irrigated regions may result in excess soil salinity, i.e., the accumulation of salts in the plant root zone.

Artificial drainage is essential on poorly drained agricultural fields to provide optimum air and salt environments in the root zone. Drainage is regarded as an important water management practice, and as a component of efficient crop production systems.

World food supply and the productivity of existing agricultural lands can only be maintained and enhanced if drainage improvements are undertaken on cropland currently affected by excess water and high water tables.

Drainage (both surface and subsurface) is not simply the conversion of wetlands, but the improvement of naturally inadequately drained cropland. It is complementary to irrigation and is viewed as an essential component of irrigated agriculture. The objective is to increase production efficiency, crop yields and profitability on naturally poorly drained agricultural lands.

It is difficult to quantify the effectiveness of most drainage methods. Drainage is best used as a short-term stabilizing method, due to the fact that, in the long-term, the drains need much maintenance and repair, which is often difficult to perform, and expensive. Drainage methods are split into various categories:

Shallow/Surface Drains

- The aim of these is to reduce surface water and thereby reduce the porewater pressures at a much deeper level.
- These are the easiest drains to repair but get damaged easily.
- These drains will usually be either:
  - *(a)* lined or unlined ditches
  - *(b)* shallow, gravel-filled trenches
- Commonly a herringbone or chevron shape is used for the drains on the surface as this is most effective in catching run-off water.

Deep Drains

These perform the function of modifying the shape of the seepage flow in the slope material.

They can be:

- Deep trenches (although they are more commonly shallow),
- Vertical bored drains -filled with sand or gravel,
- Horizontal bored drains-lined with perforated pipes.

Drains to Eliminate Construction Porewater Pressures:

These fall into two types:

- *Drainage Blankets:* Thses are installed either between layers of the fill material (which allows low permeability material to be used), or between the fill and foundation material.

- *Vertical Drain Wells:* Sand filled vertical drains have been discussed above. Thesedrains may be constructed using geofabric materials, cardboard, or merely sand alone. Their aim is to "catch" horizontal water flow.

Benefits of Drainage

The primary benefits of drainage go beyond the control of excess soil water and accumulation of excess salts in the crop root zone. The coincident environmental and socio- economic benefits associated with disease vector control and public health must be fully recognized. One of the major environmental benefits of drainage is its positive impact on improving the health of humans, plants and farm animals.

Drainage of wet, swampy areas has led to a reduction in mosquito breeding sites in all parts of the world. The effect has been a drop in the incidence and prevalence of important water related and mosquito transmitted diseases, e.g., malaria, yellow fever and filariasis.

Furthermore, drainage of stagnant water can eliminate foot-rot in large animals and, to a certain extent, the breeding environment of aquatic and semi-aquatic snails, which are the intermediate host of schistosomiasis.

Drainage also reduces or eliminates mildew infections and various root rots of plants. The overall impact of improved drainage has been an improvement in hygienic conditions, in the health sector and in the productivity of human beings. By growing high value food crops in well-drained soils, the health, nutrition and economic status of rural populations can be improved. There are also increased opportunities for employment, as new industries may develop in prosperous areas.

Where drainage is used to reclaim salinized and waterlogged lands, it is an environmentally beneficial practice, because the land is returned to its full productive potential. The adaptation of subsurface drainage systems to serve as sub-irrigation or controlled drainage systems leads to other benefits, i.e., the reduction of nitrate pollution.

The field-scale benefits of drainage can be summarized as follows:

1. Drainage promotes beneficial soil bacteria activity and improves soil tilth.
2. There is less surface runoff and soil erosion on drained land.
3. Improved field machine trafficability reduces soil structural damage. Soil compaction is reduced and less energy is required for field machine operations. Drainage also allows for more timely field operations. Consequently, the growing season can be lengthened and crops can achieve full maturity.

4. Crop yields are increased because of improved water management and uptake of plant nutrients.
5. Higher value crops can be planted, and there is flexibility to introduce new and improved cropping systems.
6. In general, land value and productivity are increased.
7. Farm income is increased and income variability reduced.
8. Drainage maintains favourable salt and air environments in the crop root zone.

DRAINAGE INSTALLATION METHODS

There are many different types of drainage solutions and drainage installation methods. Choosing the right one often can help alleviate a drainage problem. Ascertaining the exact drainage problem usually is a good first step. This may give an idea of what type of drainage solution should be used. Employing the draining installation methods properly can be a subsequent crucial step in solving the problem.

Generally, the most common type of drainage problem is the collection of excess water in a yard which can lead to flooding of the home, such as in the basement. The buildup of water can be a result of the shape of the landscape. Inclines and slopes in the land make some spots more prone to collect water. By correctly identifying these problem areas, one can then usually begin to examine appropriate drainage installation methods.

French Drain

A French drain is basically a ditch lined with rocks or gravel that helps drain water away from an area. It is generally used in gardening or to protect the foundation of a house or other structure from ground and surface water. A French drain may also be used as backup for retaining walls or to drain water away from a septic tank.

A French drain works on the principle of gravity, being slightly sloped down from the area to be drained to the area where one wishes to redirect the water. It is typically lined with perforated clay pipe and surrounded with a landscaping textile to prevent dirt or plant roots from clogging the system. Excess ground and surface water percolates into the French drain and is directed away.

The French drain is named after Henry French, a judge and farmer, and discussed in his 1859 book on the subject, *Farm Drainage*. However, the French drain predates Henry French by many centuries, as a version was used in ancient Rome. The system continues to be one of the most efficient and widely used methods of redirecting water, though it has been improved upon over the years.

Modern French drains are often installed well underground and hidden from view, for example by being covered with sod. A French drain can lead to a dry well, a structure that returns excess water to the supply of groundwater, or to a rain garden, an environmentally friendly invention that uses wetland plants to absorb excess water and return it to the atmosphere through transpiration.

French drains are moderately simple for the gardener or homeowner to build. Keep in mind that many countries, including the United States and the United Kingdom, regulate the use of French drain systems to keep certain contaminants out of the water supply. City codes and effects on your neighbors' property should also be considered before installing a French drain.

French drains are a prevalent drainage solution. The method for making a French drain generally involves digging a trench-like structure in the ground that then usually is filled with gravel or sand. The installation of the French drain is generally made to best facilitate the distribution of water away from problem areas. In this regard, determining the slope is critical before any actual installation.

Typically, French drains have a depth of 7 to 12 inches (about 17.75 to 30.5 cm) and a width of approximately 5 inches (about 12.75 cm). This usually can be done by hand. Gravel occasionally is added to the completed trench, filling it almost to the surface. Sand some times can be placed on top of the gravel. As the French drainage installation method is fairly basic, it often can be an elegant and simple way to eliminate draining problems.

Selecting Pipes for Drainage

Draining systems that use pipes is another method for solving drainage problems. A trench system needs to be dug so that the pipes can be placed inside. One can determine where to dig these trenches by examining the water flow and deciding a suitable place for relocation.

Selecting the different pipes to use can be an important part of this method. Flexible perforated pipe, usually 3 or 4 inches (about 7.62 or 10.16 cm) in width, commonly is used in home gardens. The installation of pipe drainage system may also decrease the buildup of sub-surface water.

Another method of draining installation is a rain barrel. The rain barrel generally is installed where there is an excess of rain water, such as under a roof trough. Rain barrels store the rain water, rather than entirely redistributing it. The stored water then can be used as drinking water or for watering plants.

Many times, drainage installation methods can be complicated. In these cases, there are many professional companies that offer drainage solutions and installation. Such firms generally should be able to correctly identify the exact drainage problem and then find the appropriate drainage solution.

GROUNDWATER

Groundwater is water located beneath the ground surface in soil pore spaces and in the fractures of rock formations. A unit of rock or an unconsolidated deposit is called an aquifer when it can yield a usable quantity of water. The depth at which soil pore spaces or fractures and voids in rock become completely saturated with water is called the water table.

Groundwater is recharged from, and eventually flows to, the surface naturally; natural discharge often occurs at springs and seeps, and can form oases or wetlands. Groundwater is also often withdrawn for agricultural, municipal and industrial use by constructing and operating extraction wells. The study of the distribution and movement of groundwater is hydrogeology, also called groundwater hydrology.

Typically, groundwater is thought of as liquid water flowing through shallow aquifers, but technically it can also include soil moisture, permafrost (frozen soil), immobile water in very low permeability bedrock, and deep geothermal or oil formation water. Groundwater is hypothesized to provide lubrication that can possibly influence the movement of faults.

It is likely that much of the Earth's subsurface contains some water, which may be mixed with other fluids in some instances. Groundwater may not be confined only to the Earth. The formation of some of the landforms observed on Mars may have been influenced by groundwater. There is also evidence that liquid water may also exist in the subsurface of Jupiter's moon Europa.

The upper level of this saturated layer of an unconfined aquifer is called the water-table or phreatic surface. Below the water-table, where generally all pore spaces are saturated with water is the phreatic zone.

Substrate with low porosity that permits limited transmission of groundwater is known as an aquitard. An aquiclude is a substrate with porosity that is so low it is virtually impermeable to groundwater.

A confined aquifer is an aquifer that is overlain by a relatively impermeable layer of rock or substrate such as an aquiclude or aquitard. If a confined aquifer follows a downward grade from its recharge zone, groundwater can become pressurized as it flows. This can create artesian wells that flow freely without the need of a pump and rise to a higher elevation than the static water-table at the above, unconfined, aquifer.

The characteristics of aquifers vary with the geology and structure of the substrate and topography in which they occur. Generally, the more productive aquifers occur in sedimentary geologic formations. By comparison, weathered and fractured crystalline rocks yield smaller quantities of groundwater in many environments. Unconsolidated to poorly cemented alluvial materials that have accumulated as valley-filling sediments in major river valleys and geologically subsiding structural basins are included among the most productive sources of groundwater.

The high specific heat capacity of water and the insulating effect of soil and rock can mitigate the effects of climate and maintain groundwater at a relatively steady temperature. In some places where groundwater temperatures are maintained by this effect at about 50°F/10°C, groundwater can be used for controlling the temperature inside structures at the surface.

For example, during hot weather relatively cool groundwater can be pumped through radiators in a home and then returned to the ground in another well. During cold seasons, as it is relatively warm, the water can be used in the same way as a source of heat for heat pumps that is much more efficient than using air.

WATER CYCLE

Groundwater makes up about twenty percent of the world's fresh water supply, which is about 0.61% of the entire world's water, including oceans and permanent ice. Global groundwater storage is roughly equal to the total amount of freshwater stored in the snow and ice pack, including the north and south poles. This makes it an important resource which can act as a natural storage that can buffer against shortages of surface water, as in during times of drought.

Groundwater is naturally replenished by surface water from precipitation, streams, and rivers when this recharge reaches the water table. Groundwater can be a long-term 'reservoir' of the natural water cycle (with residence times from days to millennia), as opposed to short-term water reservoirs like the atmosphere and fresh surface water (which have residence times from minutes to years). The figure shows how deep groundwater (which is quite distant from the surface recharge) can take a very long time to complete its natural cycle.

The Great Artesian Basin in central and eastern Australia is one of the largest confined aquifer systems in the world, extending for almost two million km^2. By analysing the trace elements in water sourced from deep underground, hydrogeologists have been able to determine that water extracted from these aquifers can be more than one million years old.

By comparing the age of groundwater obtained from different parts of the Great Artesian Basin, hydrogeologists have found it increases in age across the basin. Where water recharges the aquifers along the Eastern Divide, ages are young.

As groundwater flows westward across the continent, it increases in age, with the oldest groundwater occurring in the western parts. This means that in order to have travelled almost 1000 km from the source of recharge in one million years, the groundwater flowing through the Great Artesian Basin travels at an average rate of about one metre per year.

ISSUES

Overview

Certain problems have beset the use of groundwater around the world. Just as river waters have been over-used and polluted in many parts of the world, so too have aquifers. The big difference is that aquifers are out of sight. The other major problem is that water management agencies, when calculating the 'sustainable yield' of aquifer and river water, have often counted the same water twice, once in the aquifer, and once in its connected river.

This problem, although understood for centuries, has persisted, partly through inertia within government agencies. In Australia, for example, prior to the statutory reforms initiated by the Council of Australian Government's Water Reform Framework in the 1990s, many Australian States managed groundwater and surface water through separate government agencies, an approach beset by rivalry and poor communication.

The time lags inherent in the dynamic response of groundwater to development have generally been ignored by water management agencies, decades after scientific understanding of the issue was consolidated. In brief, the effects of groundwater overdraft although undeniably real may take decades or centuries to manifest themselves.

In a classic study in 1982, researchers modelled a situation where groundwater extraction in an intermontane basin withdrew the entire annual recharge, leaving 'nothing' for the natural groundwater-dependent vegetation community. Even when the borefield was situated close to the vegetation, 30% of the original vegetation demand could still be met by the lag inherent in the system after 100 years. By year 500 this had reduced to 0%, signalling complete death of the groundwater-dependent vegetation.

The science has been available to make these calculations for decades; however water management agencies have generally ignored effects which will appear outside the rough timeframe of political elections (three to five years). Management agencies must define and use appropriate timeframes in groundwater planning. This will mean calculating groundwater withdrawal permits based on predicted effects decades, sometimes centuries in the future.

As water moves through the landscape it collects soluble salts, mainly sodium chloride. Where such water enters the atmosphere through evapotranspiration, these salts are left behind. In irrigation districts, poor drainage of soils and surface aquifers can result in water tables coming to the surface in low-lying areas. Major land degradation problems of soil salinity and waterlogging result, combined with increasing levels of salt in surface waters. As a consequence, major damage has occurred to local economies and environments.

Four important effects are worthy of brief mention. First, flood mitigation schemes, intended to protect infrastructure built on floodplains, have had the unintended consequence of reducing aquifer recharge associated with natural flooding. Second, prolonged depletion of groundwater in extensive aquifers can result in land subsidence, with associated infrastructure damage – as well as (thirdly) saline intrusion. Fourth, draining acid sulphate soils, often found in low-lying coastal plains, can result in acidification and pollution of formerly freshwater and estuarine streams.

Another cause for concern is that groundwater drawdown from over-allocated aquifers has the potential to cause severe damage to both terrestrial and aquatic ecosystems – in some cases very conspicuously but in others quite imperceptibly because of the extended period over which the damage occurs.

Overdraft

Groundwater is a highly useful and often abundant resource. However, over-use, or overdraft, can cause major problems to human users and to the environment. The most evident problem (as far as human groundwater use is concerned) is a lowering of the water table beyond the reach of existing wells. Wells must consequently be deepened to reach the groundwater; in some places (e.g., California, Texas and India) the water table has dropped hundreds of feet because of extensive well pumping.

In the Punjab region of India, for example, groundwater levels have dropped 10 meters since 1979, and the rate of depletion is accelerating. A lowered water table may, in turn, cause other problems such as groundwater-related subsidence and saltwater intrusion.

Groundwater is also ecologically important. The importance of groundwater to ecosystems is often overlooked, even by freshwater biologists and ecologists. Groundwaters sustain rivers, wetlands and lakes, as well as subterranean ecosystems within karst or alluvial aquifers.

Not all ecosystems need groundwater, of course. Some terrestrial ecosystems – for example, those of the open deserts and similar arid environments – exist on irregular rainfall and the moisture it delivers to the soil, supplemented by moisture in the air. While there are other terrestrial ecosystems in more hospitable environments where groundwater plays no central role, groundwater is in fact fundamental to many of the world's major ecosystems. Water flows between groundwaters and surface waters. Most rivers, lakes and wetlands are fed by, and (at other places or times) feed groundwater, to varying degrees.

Groundwater feeds soil moisture through percolation, and many terrestrial vegetation communities depend directly on either groundwater or the percolated soil moisture above the aquifer for at least part of each year. Hyporheic zones (the mixing zone of streamwater and groundwater) and riparian zones are examples of ecotones largely or totally dependent on groundwater.

Aquifer drawdown or overdrafting and the pumping of fossil water increases the total amount of water within the hydrosphere subject to transpiration and evaporation processes, thereby causing accretion in water vapour and cloud cover, the primary absorbers of infrared radiation in the Earth's atmosphere. Adding water to the system has a forcing effect on the whole earth system, an accurate estimate of which hydrogeological fact is yet to be quantified.

Solution to Over-use of Groundwater

Irrigated agriculture is a big business in Asia. It accounts for 70 per cent of the world's irrigated land and 73 per cent of water used each year by the farming industry. As ageing large-scale surface irrigation schemes have become increasingly inefficient, and farmers have begun growing a wider range of crops requiring water on demand, the number of groundwater wells in India has exploded.

In 1960, there were fewer than 100,000 such wells; by 2006 the figure had risen to nearly 12 million. In India, a possible solution to overuse of groundwater is emerging, known as 'groundwater recharge'. It involves capturing rainwater that would otherwise run-off, and using it to refill aquifers.

Since 2000, the International Water Management Institute (IWMI) has been working with the Indian authorities to help improve the availability of water for agriculture in India. In 2006, India's finance minister invited IWMI to submit policy recommendations based on its research on groundwater depletion. One of the key recommendations was to instigate a programme of recharging groundwater across the 65 per cent of India that has hard-rock aquifers.

As a result, the Indian government allocated Rs 1800 crore to fund dug-well recharge projects (a dug-well is a wide, shallow well, often lined with concrete) in 100 districts within seven states where water stored in hard-rock aquifers has been over-exploited. These geological formations have a much lower capacity to store rainwater than alluvial areas with porous sand or clay rocks, hence being given priority. The money is sufficient to fund seven million structures to be installed on dug-wells to divert monsoon runoff.

The structures include a de-siltation chamber, plus pipes to collect surplus rainwater and divert de-silted water from the chamber to the well. As of the end of November 2009, funds amounting to Rs. 216.98 crore including Rs. 199.98 crore as subsidy to beneficiaries and 17 crore for IEC/Capacity Building activities had been released to the concerned states. Subsidies had been released to 566,637 beneficiaries.

Subsidence

Subsidence occurs when too much water is pumped out from underground, deflating the space below the above-surface, and thus causing the ground to actually collapse. The result can look like craters on plots of land. This occurs because in its natural equilibrium state, the hydraulic pressure of groundwater in the pore spaces of the aquifer and the aquitard supports some of the weight of the overlying sediments.

When groundwater is removed from aquifers by excessive pumping, pore pressures in the aquifer drop and compression of the aquifer may occur. This compression may be partially recoverable if pressures rebound, but much of it is not. When the aquifer gets compressed it may cause land subsidence, a drop in the ground surface.

The city of New Orleans, Louisiana, is actually below sea level today, and its subsidence is partly caused by removal of groundwater from the various aquifer/aquitard systems beneath it. In the first half of the last century, the city of San Jose, California, dropped 13 feet from land subsidence caused by overpumping; this subsidence has been halted with improved groundwater management.

Seawater Intrusion

Generally, in very humid or undeveloped regions, the shape of the water table mimics the slope of the surface. The recharge zone of an aquifer near the seacoast is likely to be inland, often at considerable distance. In these coastal areas, a lowered water table may induce sea water to reverse the flow toward the land. Sea water moving inland is called a saltwater intrusion. Alternatively, salt from mineral beds may leach into the groundwater of its own accord.

Mining

Sometimes the water movement from the recharge zone to the place where it is withdrawn may take centuries (see figure above). When the usage of water is greater than the recharge, it is referred to as *mining* water (the water is often called fossil water because of its geologic age). Under those circumstances it is not a renewable resource.

Pollution

Water pollution of groundwater, from pollutants released to the ground that can work their way down into groundwater, can create a contaminant plume within an aquifer. Movement of water and dispersion within the aquifer spreads the pollutant over a wider area, its advancing boundary often called a plume edge, which can then intersect with groundwater wells or daylight into surface water such as seeps and springs, making the water supplies unsafe for humans and wildlife. The interaction of groundwater contamination with surface waters is analyzed by use of hydrology transport models.

The stratigraphy of the area plays an important role in the transport of these pollutants. An area can have layers of sandy soil, fractured bedrock, clay, or hardpan. Areas of karst topography on limestone bedrock are sometimes vulnerable to surface pollution from groundwater. Earthquake faults can also be entry routes for downward contaminant entry. Water table conditions are of great importance for drinking water supplies, agricultural irrigation, waste disposal including nuclear waste, wildlife habitat, and other ecological issues.

In the US, upon commercial real estate property transactions both groundwater and soil are the subjects of scrutiny, with a Phase I Environmental Site Assessment normally being prepared to investigate and disclose potential pollution issues. In the San Fernando Valley of California, Real estate contracts for property transfer below the Santa Susana Field Laboratory (SSFL) and eastward have clauses releasing the seller from liability for groundwater contamination consequences from existing or future water pollution of the Valley Aquifer.

Love Canal was one of the most widely known examples of groundwater pollution. In 1978, residents of the Love Canal neighbourhood in upstate

New York noticed high rates of cancer and an alarming number of birth defects. This was eventually traced to organic solvents and dioxins from an industrial landfill that the neighbourhood had been built over and around, which had then infiltrated into the water supply and evaporated in basements to further contaminate the air. Eight hundred families were reimbursed for their homes and moved, after extensive legal battles and media coverage.

Another example of widespread groundwater pollution is in the Ganges Plain of northern India and Bangladesh where severe contamination of groundwater by naturally occurring arsenic affects 25% of water wells in the shallower of two regional aquifers. The pollution occurs because aquifer sediments contain organic matter (dead plant material) that generates anaerobic (an environment without oxygen) conditions in the aquifer.

These conditions result in the microbial dissolution of iron oxides in the sediment and thus the release of the arsenic, normally strongly bound to iron oxides, into the water. As a consequence, arsenic-rich groundwater is often iron-rich, although secondary processes often obscure the association of dissolved arsenic and dissolved iron.

Groundwater Rule

In November 2006, the Environmental Protection Agency published the Ground Water Rule in the United States Federal Register. The EPA was worried that the ground water system would be vulnerable to contamination from fecal matter. The point of the rule was to keep microbial pathogens out of public water sources The 2006 Ground Water Rule was an amendment of the 1996 Safe Drinking Water Act.

Surface Drainage

In areas of heavy rainfall or low soil percolation, it is necessary to employ surface drainage systems to get rid of surplus surface water from the land. Commonly used surface drainage systems include shallow ditches, open channels, grassed waterways and sloped banks. These drainage systems drain away surface water quickly and efficiently, but do not make much of a difference to groundwater. If there are land drainage problems due to groundwater, they will need other solutions.

Surface drainage needs to be carefully planned by taking into account the land's topography, the amount of rainfall received, and the type of soil. In some cases, shallow ditches following the land contour may be enough, in others the ditches may need to be deeper or the land may need to be graded or sloped to facilitate soil drainage. The ditches may follow a random pattern or a parallel pattern.

Large fields with a good many depression areas do well with randomly patterned field ditches. These shallow ditches follow the land contours, do not impede the movement of farm machinery and drain away water from depressed areas. Parallel field ditches are excellent for agricultural drainage on flatter types of lands, and are also used as to prevent erosion on sloping farm lands. Water from the field ditches is drained away into side ditches. The side ditches then carry water to an outlet channel.

Surface drainage is often achieved by land forming and smoothing to remove isolated depressions, or by constructing parallel ditches. Ditches and furrow bottoms are gently graded and discharge into main drains at the field boundary. Although the ditches or furrows are intended primarily to convey excess surface runoff, there is some seepage through the soil to the ditches, depending on the water table position. This could be regarded as a form of shallow subsurface drainage. Surface drainage is especially important in humid regions on flat lands with limited hydraulic gradients to nearby rivers or other disposal points. There is also a need for good surface drainage in semi-arid regions which are affected by monsoons.

Subsurface Drainage

In this study, a two-dimensional numerical model for subsurface flow has been developed for the analysis of unsteady flow for subsurface drains. The governing equation is the two-dimensional Richard's equation in the mixed form. A strongly implicit finite-difference scheme has been used to solve the governing equation.

The model has been validated using the available analytical results of the one side drains. Validation of the model indicates good agreement between the results. It has been used to simulate a hypothetical case of subsurface drains with parallel drains. The present numerical model can be used to simulate the unsteady subsurface drainage problem having a side drain and parallel drains at both sides.

In areas with periodic irrigations or high intensity rainfall, the assumption of a steady recharge is no longer justified. Under these conditions, unsteady state solution of the flow problem must be applied. Therefore, knowledge of the water table and its fluctuations in the irrigated areas is essential in assessing the possibilities of waterlogging. In case a barrier is to be constructed to keep the polluted water on one side and fresh water on another, a lateral drainage can serve the purpose. The analysis of unsteady flow to subsurface drains has been carried out keeping this in view.

Surface drainage alone is seldom sufficient to remove excess water from the crop root zone. Deep ditches or subsurface pipe drainage systems enable a more rapid water table drawdown. The downstream ends of the laterals are normally connected to a collector drain. The required diameter of the pipe collectors increases with the area drained. Drain spacing is usually dependent on soil hydraulic conductivity and a design drainage rate coefficient. Depending on topography, land formation and proximity of a water receiving body, the collector may outlet by gravity to an open main drain or into a sump. In the latter case, the discharge is then pumped to another drain, or ultimately to a lake or stream.

In some flatter parts of eastern Canada, the eastern and mid-western United States, and parts of Europe, subsurface pipe drains are also used for sub-irrigation. In this case, in dry periods, surface water is introduced into the drain pipe system from an external source, and the water table is raised. Moisture then moves upward by capillary action to the root zone. Sub-irrigation is regarded as a highly energy and water efficient method of irrigation. In another process, known as controlled drainage, elevated water tables can be maintained with a control structure on the collector pipe.

Horizontal Subsurface Drainage Systems

These are used in irrigated arid and semi-arid regions to reclaim saline and waterlogged lands, and to maintain favourable long-term salt and water balances in the crop root zone. Salinity and waterlogging are caused by a build up of the water table due to deep percolation of normal excess water and canal seepage. Buried pipe drains are generally installed deeper in arid regions than in humid regions in order to control salinity.

Water in excess of plant evapotranspiration (ET) needs is always unavoidably applied during irrigation. This additional quantity of water applied is known as the leaching fraction. Naturally occurring as well as applied salts are then leached from the root zone by this water, and removed from the field via the pipe drains. Deeper drain installation ensures that salts do not rise too rapidly to the soil surface due to capillary action. Drainage also prevents waterlogging of the root zone.

The amount of irrigation water to be removed is generally less in arid than in humid regions. Vertical drainage by means of tube-wells is also used to control waterlogging and salinity in some parts of the world, e.g., India, Pakistan and central Asian republics. The primary purposes of tube-wells are the same as those of horizontal drains, and at the same time to extract groundwater for irrigation.

As a result of pumping, the water table is lowered, and salinization due to capillarity is minimized. This situation is ideal where the groundwater is not very brackish or saline, and is therefore suitable for irrigation. In areas where the groundwater is highly saline, the pumped water may be too saline for irrigation, unless mixed with fresher or less saline water.

Where the groundwater is too saline for crop production, it must be disposed of. Drainage does not have a direct impact on groundwater quality. It only serves to collect and transport excess water.

Improving Internal Drainage

Methods of improving the internal drainage of low permeability soils include: subsoiling, deep tillage, mole drainage, and biological practices, viz., cropping with deep rooted legumes (e.g., alfalfa) and crop rotations. In some parts of the world, deep rooted trees are used to lower the water table. There are usually no water quality hazards associated with these supplemental drainage practices.

Treating drainage water is normally one of the last drainage water management options to be considered. This is due to the high costs involved and to uncertainty about the treatment level achievable. The treatment of drainage water should be considered where all other drainage water management measures fail to guarantee safe disposal or where it is financially attractive. For subsurface drainage water containing very high levels of salinity, selenium and other trace elements, the treatment objectives are:

1. reduce salts and toxic constituents below hazardous levels;
2. meet agricultural water management goals;
3. meet water quality objectives in surface waters; and
4. reduce constituent levels below risk levels for wildlife.

The treatment of agricultural drainage water presents a challenge due to the complex chemical characteristics of most drainage waters. The drainage waters are saline and of the $NaCl$-Na_2SO_4-type water. The waters conveyed by the San Luis Drain came from a single site in Westlands Water District in contrast to the evaporation pond waters that came from 27 sites.

Table 1.1: Average Composition of Agricultural Tile Drainage Water in the San Luis Drain

(Drainage waters disposed into evaporation basins in parentheses)

Constituent	Concentration ppm	Constituent	Concentration ppb
(1)	(2)	(3)	(4)
Sodium	2 230	Boron	14 400 (25 000)
Calcium	554	Selenium	325 (16)
Magnesium	270	Arsenic	1 (101)
Potassium	6	Molybdenum	ND (2 817)

(Contd...)

(1)	(2)	(3)	(4)
Alkalinity as $CaCO_3$	196	Uranium	ND (308)
Sulphate	4 730	Vanadium	ND (22)
Chloride	1 480	Strontium	6 400
Nitrate	48	Total chromium	19
Silica	37	Cadmium	<1
TDS	9 820 (31 000)	Copper	4
Suspended solids	11	Lead	3
Total organic carbon	10.2	Manganese	25
COD	32	Iron	110
BOD	3.2	Mercury	<0.1
		Nickel	14
		Zinc	33

There are numerous wastewater treatment processes for industrial and urban wastewater and for the preparation of drinking-water. Many of them offer potential for the treatment of agricultural drainage water. Treatment processes for drainage water can be divided into processes that reduce the total salinity of the drainage water and processes that remove specific ions. Methods for the removal of trace elements can be biological, physical and chemical.

Most desalinization processes also remove trace elements but their costs are often prohibitive. Less costly methods for the removal of trace elements are being developed. Researchers have reviewed treatment technologies for drainage water and also reviewed treatment technologies for removing selenium from agricultural drainage water. The following is a brief summary of their findings.

Desalinization

There are numerous desalinization processes including ion exchange, distillation, electrodialysis and reverse osmosis. Of these processes, reverse osmosis is considered to be the most promising for the treatment of agricultural drainage water mainly due to its comparatively low cost.

Reverse osmosis (RO) is a process capable of removing different contaminants including dissolved salts and organics. In reverse osmosis, a semi-permeable membrane separates water from dissolved salts and other suspended solids. Pressure is applied to the feed-water, forcing the water through the membrane leaving behind salts and suspended materials in a brine stream.

The energy consumption of the process depends on the salt concentration of the feed-water and the salt concentration of the effluent. Depending on the quality of the water to be treated, pretreatment might be crucial to preventing fouling of the membrane. Other pretreatment steps could be lime treatment along with ion exchange.

Table 1.2: Results of a Trial-run for a Three-stage Reverse Osmosis System, Lime-soda Pretreatment

Description	TDS ppm	Sodium ppm	Chloride/ nitrateppm	Sulphate ppm	Boron ppm	Selenium ppb
Influent	9793	2919	1550	5010	14.5	325
Stage 1 Concentrate	19346	5721	3038	9970	23.4	650
Stage 1 Permeate	240	117	62	50	5.4	0
Stage 2 Concentrate	38 071	13 156	5 924	19 791	38	1 298
Stage 2 Permeate	614	286	152	150	8.8	1
Stage 3 Concentrate	73022	22107	15987	38650	62	2579
Stage 3 Permeate	1480	669	355	396	14.3	3
Overall Permeate	640	176	155	201	7.6	3

The California Department of Water Resources conducted pilot-plant-scale reverse osmosis of saline drainage using cellulose acetate membranes. The bacterial and chemical fouling of the membrane was a major problem.

The drainage water had to be treated with alum, and passed through a sedimentation pond and a chlorinated and filtration system. In spite of this level of pretreatment, the membranes tended to foul due to the precipitation of gypsum and calcite. The drainage waters are saturated with respect to calcite and gypsum. This same chemical fouling problem is being faced by the Yuma desalting plant off the Colorado River using drainage waters from the Wellton-Mohawk irrigation project.

The estimated cost of desalting is more than US\$ 0.81/m^3, too expensive for irrigated agriculture but possibly affordable for municipalities with freshwater shortages. This cost does not include the management and disposal of the brine water. However, a potential exists for partially treating the average 10-dS/m-drainage water to about 2-3 dS/m for use by agriculture and wildlife.

Trace Element Treatment

As the technology of reverse osmosis is experimental and expensive, cheaper methods of removing toxic trace elements are being pursued.

Biological Processes

Conventional column reactor systems have been utilized to remove selenium from drainage waters. Selenium is microbially reduced to elemental selenium under anoxic (anaerobic) conditions in the presence of organic carbon sources.

Se(+6) + bacteria + organic carbon → Se(+4) → Se(0)

(soluble selenate) (soluble selenite)
(elemental selenium particulates)

In the initial study, the biological reactor consisted of a two-stage upflow anaerobic sludge blanket reactor followed by a fluidized bed reactor. As selenium cannot be reduced while nitrates are present, a key treatment process is the reduction of nitrates prior to enhancing selenium reduction. The sludge blanket was seeded with inoculum from sludges from ordinary sewage treatment plants. This system yielded 30 ppb selenium product water.

A subsequent large-scale pilot study examined seven different reactor systems after upflow through a conical bottom liquid-gas-solid separator with the addition of methanol as the carbon source. The conical separator was seeded with granular sludge from a bread-making bakery. This first step reduced the average nitrate concentration from 45 to 3 ppm. The waters were then fed to a number of packed bed column reactors. The best sustained results were about a 90-percent removal of selenium from 500 to 50 ppb.

Biological treatment normally refers to the use of bacteria in engineered column reactor systems for the removal or transformation of certain constituents, e.g. organic compounds, trace elements and nutrients. However, biological treatment also includes algal-bacterial treatment processes and wetland systems.

Chemical Processes

Chemical treatment processes refer to the use of chemicals to remove trace elements from polluted wastewater. Chemicals are frequently used for industrial wastewater treatment but are not effective in agricultural drainage water due to their often complex chemical characteristics. Chemical processes have been developed for the reduction of selenate to elemental selenium by means of ferrous hydroxide.

Under laboratory conditions, ferrous hydroxide was able to reduce and precipitate selenium by 99 percent in 30 min. In field studies, although

90 percent of the selenate was reduced, the reactor time required was up to 6 h. It appeared that dissolved bicarbonate, oxygen and nitrate influenced the reduction process.

Physical processes involve the adsorption of ions on natural and synthetic surfaces of active materials, including ion exchange resins.

Flow-through Artificial Wetlands

Tile drainage effluent containing about 20-ppb selenium from an adjacent farm was passed through a sand bed filter system and metered into the cells (15.2 × 76 m) with a variety of substrates (vegetation). The inflow water was measured twice a week by a totalizing meter. The water depth in Cells 1-7 was maintained at about 20 cm, and outflow was measured by v-notch weir. Cells 8-10 had variable water depths of about 20 cm, 60 cm where widgeon grass (Ruppia) was grown.

The target residence time for the flowing waters was 7 days for Cells 1-7, 21 days in Cells 8 and 9, and 14 days in Cell 10. These residence times were selected after preliminary runs for optimal removal. A residence time of three days was too short for selenium removal and a residence time of more than twenty one days did not increase selenium removal. Seepage rates in the cells were about 1 cm/d and evapotranspiration slightly greater than ETo (annual value about 1 600 mm).

The residence times achieved were reasonably close to target values considering the variability in monthly ETo. The selenium concentration in the outflow waters varied from 4.6 to 12.3 ppb. The ratio of outflow to inflow selenium concentration ranged from 0.25 to 0.68 (a small ratio indicates high selenium removal).

The ratio of outflow to inflow selenium on a mass basis ranged from 0.07 to 0.57 or 93 to 43 removal. The cell with open water had reduced selenium because algae and microbes naturally populated the cell and contributed to some selenium removal.

In terms of performance, the ratio based on mass of selenium is a good indicator. However, in terms of potential impact on birds, the outflow concentration and ratio based on concentration are better indicators.

The remainder of the selenium accumulated in the cell as selenium present in the sediments, organic detrital matter, fallen litter, standing water and standing plants. The values reported are the mass of selenium found in the cells in September 2000. About 11 percent of the total selenium could not be accounted for due to errors in sampling and monitoring over a four-year period, and the difficulties of analysing for reduced forms of selenium.

The sink mechanisms removing selenium from the floodwater were: adsorption of selenite (Se+4) to the mineral sediments mainly in the top 10 cm or so; selenium immobilized into elemental selenium (Se0) due to reduced conditions in the organic detrital layer; and organic forms of selenium (Se-2) tied up with the detritus and fallen litter. The principal removal mechanisms were adsorption and immobilization into elemental selenium and organic selenium.

The recommended selenium water standard to protect waterbirds is 2 ppb. None of these cells achieved that level of remediation but many cells certainly will reduce selenium toxicity. However, outflow waters from these cells contain organic selenium (17-33% of the total selenium), which is more toxic than inorganic forms to wildlife. These and other results are currently being reviewed to determine whether selenium removal flow-through wetland cells is a viable treatment option.

Evaluation and Selection of Treatment Options

The first steps in the selection of any drainage treatment process are:

1. define the problem;
2. determine the reasons for the required treatment; and
3. determine what is to be achieved.

The main reason for opting for drainage water treatment is normally the desire to reuse the drainage effluent or to conform to regulatory disposal requirements. For both purposes, specific water quality criteria apply.

In order to make a preliminary selection of suitable treatment processes, it is necessary that sufficient data be available. These data consist of historical data on the chemical constituents of the drainage water, seasonal flow variations and variations in the concentrations of the constituents of concern. Once combined with information on the targeted quality of the treated effluent, it is then possible to shortlist drainage treatment processes that are theoretically suitable.

The technical capability of the treatment process is an important factor in the selection of a treatment technology. However, it is important to consider economic, financial, social and institutional criteria in order to ensure the sustainability of the treatment facilities.

Environmental Impact Assessment

Many institutions require an environmental impact assessment (EIA) prior to construction activities associated with new projects or the rehabilitation of existing projects. The objectives are to identify potential adverse environmental effects, the magnitude of these effects, and to develop mitigative measures.

Positive benefits are also identified. In cases where the adverse impacts far outweigh the expected benefits, the project may be completely redesigned or suspended. This is also the case where mitigative measures would be either too costly or technically not feasible. The EIA should be conducted in the earliest stages of decision making, when crucial decisions are still being deliberated.

The environmental effects can be classified as:

1. Direct and indirect, or first order and higher order. These are chain effects which are felt throughout, and possibly downstream of a catchment.
2. The primary activity of a drainage project may be extended to include secondary activities.
3. Synergistic effects include an increased threat to the survival of certain species of wildlife that are under pressure in several ways as a result of the same project.

The ICID has developed an 'Environmental Checklist to Identify Environmental Impacts of Irrigation, Drainage and Flood Control Projects'. The World Bank has prepared an Environmental Assessment Sourcebook. The FAO has produced a paper on the steps in the EIA process and the major environmental impacts of irrigation and drainage projects. The purpose of these documents is to enable detailed environmental impact assessments of irrigation and drainage projects to be conducted. The ICID checklist provides a comprehensive list of environmental parameters which must be evaluated in an EIA.

The main steps in the EIA process as:

1. *Scoping.* This is a public process, involving the participation of all parties. It results in specific guidelines for inclusion in the environmental impact study (EIS). (EIS refers to the document, whereas EIA refers to the entire process).
2. *Drawing up the EIS.* Potential adverse and beneficial impacts are identified. Proposed actions with alternatives are indicated and mitigative measures are presented.
3. *Submitting the EIS for public review.*
4. Receiving advice from the reviewing agency.
5. Accepting the EIS.
6. *Choosing project components.* The decision-maker chooses the project option to be implemented and the mitigative measures.

7. Implementing the project.
8. *Monitoring*. During and after project implementation, the actual environmental impacts are monitored and compared with the EIS predictions. This is useful for improving future predictions and project designs.

Matrices and checklists are some of the tools most commonly used in an EIA to assess the magnitude or relative weight of both positive and adverse environmental effects. It is hoped that the criteria on drainage water quality provided in the publication will further assist in the evaluation of EIA of irrigation and drainage projects.

Water Quality Impacts

The installation of drainage systems may result in changes to the associated ecosystem. These changes may be either beneficial or adverse.

However, there are potential adverse water quality impacts associated with drainage. The concentrations of salts, nutrients and other crop-related chemicals in drainage discharge vary with time and discharge rate. The use of fertilizers and pesticides in intensive agricultural production has sometimes led to damage to downstream aquatic ecosystems.

Drainage planners therefore need to analyse effluent for nutrients and pesticides. The nutrients of most concern are N and P. In addition, from time to time, natural trace elements from the soil itself may be harmful to the ecosystem. Effluent laden with N and P stimulates eutrophication in receiving water bodies. In addition to agricultural chemicals and trace elements, drainage water from irrigated areas frequently contains salts. The impact of salts on downstream users needs to be evaluated. Some soils are abundant in trace elements, and these could leach to the drainage system.

Small amounts of trace elements such as As, Cd, Hg, Pb, B, Cr and Se are harmful to aquatic species because of biological magnification. The environmental consequences of disposing of drainage water from California's irrigated San Joaquin Valley into the 470 ha Kesterson Reservoir are well known. The reservoir was a waterfowl habitat, and concentrating Se in the drainage water caused fish species to disappear, and resulted in deformities in waterbird embryos.

The failure to construct an adequate outfall drain to the sea, the use of a waterfowl habitat for drainage water disposal, and the lack of proper water quality monitoring were the major reasons for these negative environmental impacts. Care must be taken to ensure that the disposal of drainage water does not interfere with the ecosystem's aquatic and terrestrial species. Concern has been expressed about damage by agricultural drainage water to estuarine fisheries in some countries.

Drainage water can be disposed directly to open surface water bodies, e.g., rivers, lakes, outfall drains, seas or oceans. Wetlands, evaporation ponds and solar evaporators are used as discharge points where there is no direct outlet to one of the open surface water bodies mentioned above.

This is generally the situation in hydrologically closed drainage basins. Some re-use of drainage water for irrigation is another management option, where sequential irrigation of increasingly salt-tolerant plants, ending with Salicornia, occurs. Drainage water can also be disposed of by injection to the deep groundwater.

If drainage water is disposed of to large, open surface water systems with significant dilution or assimilative capacity, then water quality problems are minimized. However, water quality problems may develop with repeated re-use, disposal in closed basins and injection to deep wells. In this last case, the concern is that if the drainage water contains sufficient amounts of salts, nitrates, bacteria and trace elements, the groundwater could become contaminated. The problem may be especially severe if the aquifer is also used for drinking water supplies downslope.

Minimizing Environmental Problems

The most efficient method of minimizing environmental problems is to implement source control practices at the farm level. In irrigated areas, this can be achieved by improved irrigation water management.

Higher irrigation efficiencies and lined irrigation conveyance structures will reduce the amount of drainage water which needs to be removed. Furthermore, timely and efficient applications of fertilizers and pesticides, used only when necessary, will reduce chemical leaching. Research shows that intercropping corn with a legume or ryegrass reduces the amount of nitrates found in drainage water.

In many regions where irrigation water is scarce, drainage water is used to meet crop water requirements. Re-use is only sustainable if the drainage water is of sufficiently good quality. Some of the water quality concerns about drainage water re-use with plants of increasing salt tolerance are that: the effluent may be high in salt content (in irrigated lands); the drainage water can be contaminated with trace elements, toxic organic substances, industrial waste and municipal waste in open main drains.

Contaminated drainage water could lead to various problems including: impairment of soil physical and chemical properties, water-related health problems, and possible contamination of food products.

Ultimate disposal of drainage water to a river or sea is not always possible. Closed drainage basins present a unique environmental or water quality challenge. In such situations, evaporation ponds may be an appropriate means for disposing of drainage water.

However, these ponds may eventually lead to other environmental problems. For example, toxic substances could accumulate in the ponds. Furthermore, in arid climates, as pure water evaporates from the pond, the concentration of the remaining water approaches that of brine.

The health of waterfowl, fish and other aquatic biota which use the pond could be negatively affected. Other environmental problems associated with evaporation ponds include: use of the pond to collect wastewater from homes; human health problems caused by consuming water from the ponds; and the need to ultimately dispose of the accumulated concentrated chemicals in the ponds.

In some cases, dry toxic materials may be spread by the wind. Furthermore, these ponds could become habitats for snails and mosquitoes, thereby causing malaria and schistosomiasis epidemics. In addition, if not properly managed, new waterlogged and saline areas will develop adjacent to the ponds.

Managing Drainage Water

There is now increasing interest in the utilization of natural and constructed wetlands to manage drainage water. Wetlands are particularly effective for removing sediment, N and P. Plant, soil and hydrologic parameters interact in a complex way to filter and trap pollutants, and to recycle nutrients. Certain tree and plant species have the potential to absorb pollutants.

Residence time, flow rate, hydraulic roughness and wetland size and shape are some of the factors which influence treatment efficiency. The water supply to the wetland must be sufficient to provide an excess to discharge and prevent salt accumulation.

In areas where soils, geologic and hydrologic conditions do not permit constructed wetlands, the saline agriculture/agriculture-forestry system may be appropriate for the disposal of drainage water. The operating principle is to successively re-use saline drainage water to irrigate crops and trees of increasing salt tolerance, and to discharge the final much reduced volume of water into a solar evaporator for salt crystallization.

The depth of water ponded in the evaporator is regulated to match the daily evaporation rate. The goal is to make the crystallization pond unattractive to flora and fauna. Another challenge of evaporation ponds is that evaporation is reduced as the ponds become more concentrated. This necessitates the use of additional land to maintain disposal (evaporation) capacity.

While there are instances where ecosystems have been damaged by poor quality drainage water, it is also possible to use subsurface drainage systems beneficially to improve water quality. By managing the water table, through controlled drainage or sub-irrigation, nitrate concentrations in drainage effluent can be significantly reduced. Downstream flood flows can also be reduced. Water table management could therefore be viewed as a best management practice. Researchers have shown that sub-irrigation and controlled drainage not only increase crop yields, but also enhance denitrification. Water-table management is best suited to flat lands, and can be achieved by a simple modification to the outlet of subsurface drainage systems.

It is important to recognize that while technologies may be available to minimize water quality impacts from drainage effluent, institutional mechanisms must also be put in place to ensure that the technologies can be implemented. Policies and programmes, including legal and monitoring aspects, require an institutional framework.

It is recognized that, in some instances, there may be insufficient data in the project design and planning stages to enable precise conclusions to be drawn about possible environmental impacts. For this reason, most chapters contain sections on environmental monitoring, so that project planners and designers can elicit the information required for proper decision making. For more detailed information on water quality monitoring, the reader is referred to the United States Environmental Protection Agency (EPA).

CHAPTER – 2

Water Quality for Agriculture

Agricultural wastewater treatment relates to the treatment of wastewaters produced in the course of agricultural activities. Agriculture is a highly intensified industry in many parts of the world, producing a range of wastewaters requiring a variety of treatment technologies and management practices.

Non-point source pollution from farms is caused by surface runoff from fields during rain storms. Agricultural runoff is a major source of pollution, in some cases, the only source, in many watersheds.

Soil washed off fields is the largest source of agricultural pollution in the United States. Excess sediment causes high levels of turbidity in water bodies, which can inhibit growth of aquatic plants, clog fish gills and smother animal larvae.

Farmers may utilize erosion controls to reduce runoff flows and retain soil on their fields. Common techniques includes :

- contour plowing;
- crop mulching;
- crop rotation;
- planting perennial crops; and
- installing riparian buffers.

Nitrogen and phosphorus are key pollutants found in runoff, and they are applied to farmland in several ways:

- commercial fertilizer;
- animal manure; and
- municipal or industrial wastewater (effluent) or sludge.

These chemicals may also enter runoff from crop residues, irrigation water, wildlife, and atmospheric deposition.

- Knowledge of irrigation water quality is critical to understanding management for long-term productivity.
- Irrigation water quality is evaluated based upon total salt content, sodium and specific ion toxicities.
- In many areas of Colorado, irrigation water quality can influence crop productivity more than soil fertility, hybrid, weed control and other factors.

Corn Plant Damaged by Saline Sprinkler Water

Salt-affected soils develop from a wide range of factors including: soil type, field slope and drainage, irrigation system type and management, fertilizer and manuring practices, and other soil and water management practices.

In Colorado, perhaps the most critical factor in predicting, managing, and reducing salt-affected soils is the quality of irrigation water being used. Besides affecting crop yield and soil physical conditions, irrigation water quality can affect fertility needs, irrigation system performance and longevity, and how the water can be applied. Therefore, knowledge of irrigation water quality is critical to understanding what management changes are necessary for long-term productivity.

IRRIGATION WATER AND CROP

Soil scientists use the following categories to describe irrigation water effects on crop production and soil quality:

- *Salinity hazard* – total soluble salt content

- *Sodium hazard* – relative proportion of sodium to calcium and magnesium ions
- *pH* – acid or basic
- *Alkalinity* – carbonate and bicarbonate
- *Specific ions* – chloride, sulfate, boron, and nitrate.

Another potential irrigation water quality impairment that may affect suitability for cropping systems is microbial pathogens.

Table 2.1: General Guidelines for Salinity Hazard of Irrigation water based Upon Conductivity

Limitations for Use	Electrical Conductivity (dS/m)*
None	>0.75
Some	0.76 - 1.5
Moderate[1]	1.51 - 3.00
Severe[2]	>3.00

* dS/m at 25°C = mmhos/cm

1. Leaching required at higher range.
2. Good drainage needed and sensitive plants may have difficulty at germination.

Salinity Hazard

The most influential water quality guideline on crop productivity is the water salinity hazard as measured by electrical conductivity (EC_w). The primary effect of high EC_w water on crop productivity is the inability of the plant to compete with ions in the soil solution for water (physiological drought). The higher the EC, the less water is available to plants, even though the soil may appear wet. Because plants can only transpire "pure" water, usable plant water in the soil solution decreases dramatically as EC increases.

Actual yield reductions from irrigating with high EC water varies substantially. Factors influencing yield reductions include soil type, drainage, salt type, irrigation system and management.

The amount of water transpired through a crop is directly related to yield; therefore, irrigation water with high EC_w reduces yield potential (Table 2.2). Beyond effects on the immediate crop is the long term impact of salt loading through the irrigation water. Water with an EC_w of only 1.15 dS/m contains approximately 2,000 pounds of salt for every acre foot of water. One can use conversion factors in Table 2.3 to make this calculation for other water EC levels.

Table 2.2: Potential Yield Reduction from Saline Water for Selected Irrigated Crops[1]

	% Yield Reduction			
Crop	0%	10% EC_w[2]	25%	50%
Barley	5.3	6.7	8.7	12.0
Wheat	4.0	4.9	6.4	8.7
Sugarbeet[3]	4.7	5.8	7.5	10.0
Alfalfa	1.3	2.2	3.6	5.9
Potato	1.1	1.7	2.5	3.9
Corn (grain)	1.1	1.7	2.5	3.9
Corn (silage)	1.2	2.1	3.5	5.7
Onion	0.8	1.2	1.8	2.9
Dry Beans	0.7	1.0	1.5	2.4

1. Adapted from "Quality of Water for Irrigation." R.S. Ayers. Jour. of the Irrig. and Drain. Div., ASCE. Vol 103, No. IR2, June 1977, p. 140.
2. EC_w = electrical conductivity of the irrigation water in dS/m at 25°C. Sensitive during germination.
3. EC_w should not exceed 3 dS/m for garden beets and sugarbeets.

Other terms that laboratories and literature sources use to report salinity hazard are: salts, salinity, electrical conductivity (EC_w), or total dissolved solids (TDS). These terms are all comparable and all quantify the amount of dissolved "salts" (or ions, charged particles) in a water sample. However, TDS is a direct measurement of dissolved ions and EC is an indirect measurement of ions by an electrode.

Although people frequently confuse the term "salinity" with common table salt or sodium chloride (NaCl), EC measures salinity from all the ions dissolved in a sample. This includes negatively charged ions (e.g., Cl^-, NO_3^-) and positively charged ions (e.g., Ca^{++}, Na^+). Another common source of confusion is the variety of unit systems used with EC_w. The preferred unit is deciSiemens per meter (dS/m), however millimhos per centimeter (mmho/cm) and micromhos per centimeter (µmho/cm) are still frequently used. Conversions to help you change between unit systems are provided in Table 2.3.

Table 2.3: Conversion factors for irrigation water quality laboratory reports.

Component	To Convert	Multiply by	To Obtain
Water nutrient or TDS	mg/L	1.0	ppm
Water salinity hazard	1 dS/m	1.0	1mmho/cm
Water salinity hazard	1 mmho/cm	1,000	1 µmho/cm
Water salinity hazard	EC_w (dS/m) for EC <5 dS/m	640	TDS (mg/L)
Water salinity hazard	EC_w (dS/m) for EC >5 dS/m	800	TDS (mg/L)
Water NO_3N, SO_4-S,B applied	ppm	0.23	lb per acre inch of water
Irrigation water	acre inch	27,150	gallons of water

mg/L = milligrams per litre
meq/L = milliequivalents per litre
ppm = parts per million
dS/m = deciSiemens per metre
µS/cm = microSiemens per centimetre
mmho/cm = millimhos per centimetre
TDS = total dissolved solids

SODIUM HAZARD

Salinity Level

Although plant growth is primarily limited by the salinity (EC_w) level of the irrigation water, the application of water with a sodium imbalance can further reduce yield under certain soil texture conditions. Reductions in water infiltration can occur when irrigation water contains high sodium relative to the calcium and magnesium contents. This condition, termed "sodicity", results from excessive soil accumulation of sodium. Sodic water is not the same as saline water. Sodicity causes swelling and dispersion of soil clays, surface crusting and pore plugging. This degraded soil structure condition in turn obstructs infiltration and may increase runoff. Sodicity causes a decrease in the downward movement of water into and through the soil, and actively growing plants roots may not get adequate water, despite pooling of water on the soil surface after irrigation.

The most common measure to assess sodicity in water and soil is called the Sodium Adsorption Ratio (SAR). The SAR defines sodicity in terms of the relative concentration of sodium (Na) compared to the sum of calcium (Ca) and magnesium (Mg) ions in a sample. The SAR assesses the potential for infiltration problems due to a sodium imbalance in irrigation water. The SAR is mathematically written below, where Na, Ca and Mg are the concentrations of these ions in milliequivalents per liter (meq/L). Concentrations of these ions in water samples are typically provided in milligrams per liter (mg/L). To convert Na, Ca, and Mg from mg/L to meq/L, you should divide the concentration by 22.9, 20, and 12.15 respectively.

For most irrigation waters encountered in Colorado the standard SAR formula provided above is suitable to express the potential sodium hazard. However, for irrigation water with high bicarbonate (HCO_3) content, an "adjusted" SAR (SAR_{ADJ}) can be calculated. In this case, the amount of calcium is adjusted for the water's alkalinity, is recommended in place of the standard SAR. Your laboratory may calculate an adjusted SAR in situations where the HCO_3 is greater than 200 mg/L or pH is greater than 8.5.

The potential soil infiltration and permeability problems created from applications of irrigation water with high "sodicity" cannot be adequately assessed on the basis of the SAR alone. This is because the swelling potential of low salinity (EC_w) water is greater than high EC_w waters at the same sodium content (Table 4). Therefore, a more accurate evaluation of the infiltration/permeability hazard requires using the electrical conductivity (EC_w) together with the SAR.

Many factors including soil texture, organic matter, cropping system, irrigation system and management affect how sodium in irrigation water affects soils. Soils most likely to show reduced infiltration and crusting from water with elevated SAR (greater than 6) are those containing more than 30% expansive (smectite) clay. Soils containing more than 30% clay include most soils in the clay loam, silty clay loam textural classes and finer and some sandy clay loams. In Colorado, smectite clays are common in areas with agricultural production.

Acidity of Irrigation Water

The acidity or basicity of irrigation water is expressed as pH (< 7.0 acidic; > 7.0 basic). The normal pH range for irrigation water is from 6.5 to 8.4. Abnormally low pH's are not common in Colorado, but may cause accelerated irrigation system corrosion where they occur. High pH's above 8.5 are often caused by high bicarbonate (HCO_3^-) and carbonate (CO_3^{2-}) concentrations, known as alkalinity. High carbonates cause calcium and magnesium ions to form insoluble minerals leaving sodium as the dominant ion in solution. This alkaline water could intensify the impact of high SAR water on sodic soil conditions. Excessive bicarbonate concentrates can also be problematic for drip or micro-spray irrigation systems when calcite or scale build up causes reduced flow rates through orifices or emitters. In these situations, correction by injecting sulfuric or other acidic materials into the system may be required.

Chloride

Chloride is a common ion in Colorado irrigation waters. Although chloride is essential to plants in very low amounts, it can cause toxicity to sensitive crops at high concentrations. Like sodium, high chloride concentrations cause more problems when applied with sprinkler irrigation. Leaf burn under sprinkler from both sodium and chloride can be reduced by night time irrigation or application on cool, cloudy days. Drop nozzles and drag hoses are also recommended when applying any saline irrigation water through a sprinkler system to avoid direct contact with leaf surfaces.

Boron

Boron is another element that is essential in low amounts, but toxic at higher concentrations (Table 7). In fact, toxicity can occur on sensitive crops at concentrations less than 1.0 ppm. Colorado soils and irrigation waters contain enough B that additional B fertilizer is not required in most situations. Because B toxicity can occur at such low concentrations, an irrigation water analysis is advised for ground water before applying additional B to crops.

Sulfate

The sulfate ion is a major contributor to salinity in many of Colorado irrigation waters. As with boron, sulfate in irrigation water has fertility benefits, and irrigation water in Colorado often has enough sulfate for maximum production for most crops. Exceptions are sandy fields with less than 1 percent organic matter and <10 ppm SO^4-S in irrigation water.

Nitrogen

Nitrogen in irrigation water (N) is largely a fertility issue, and nitrate-nitrogen (NO_3-N) can be a significant N source in the South Platte, San Luis Valley, and parts of the Arkansas River basins. The nitrate ion often occurs at higher concentrations than ammonium in irrigation water. Waters high in N can cause quality problems in crops such as barley and sugar beets and excessive vegetative growth in some vegetables.

However, these problems can usually be overcome by good fertilizer and irrigation management. Regardless of the crop, nitrate should be credited toward the fertilizer rate especially when the concentration exceeds 10 ppm NO_3-N (45 ppm NO_3^-).

IMPLEMENTING NUTRIENT MANAGEMENT

Farmers can develop and implement nutrient management plans to mitigate impacts on water quality:

- map and document fields, crop types, soil types, water bodies
- develop realistic crop yield projections
- conduct soil tests and nutrient analyses of manures and/or sludges applied
- identify other significant nutrient sources (e.g. irrigation water)
- evaluate significant field features such as highly erodible soils, subsurface drains, and shallow aquifers
- apply fertilizers, manures, and/or sludges based on realistic yield goals and using precision agriculture techniques.

Pesticides

Pesticides are widely used by farmers to control plant pests and enhance production, but chemical pesticides can also cause water quality problems. Pesticides may appear in surface water due to:

- direct application (e.g. aerial spraying or broadcasting over water bodies)
- runoff during rain storms
- aerial drift (from adjacent fields).:p.2-22

Some pesticides have also been detected in groundwater.

Farmers may use Integrated Pest Management (IPM) techniques (which can include biological pest control) to maintain control over pests, reduce reliance on chemical pesticides, and protect water quality.

There are few safe ways of disposing of pesticide surpluses other than through containment in well managed landfills or by incineration. In some parts of the world, spraying on land is a permitted method of disposal.

Farms with large livestock and poultry operations, such as factory farms, can be a major source of point source wastewater. In the United States, these facilities are called concentrated animal feeding operations or confined animal feeding operations and are being subject to increasing government regulation.

Animal Wastes

The constituents of animal wastewater typically contain:

- Strong organic content — much stronger than human sewage.

- High solids concentration.
- High nitrate and phosphorus content.
- Antibiotics.
- Synthetic hormones.
- Often high concentrations of parasites and their eggs.
- Spores of Cryptosporidum (a protozoan) resistant to drinking water treatment processes.
- Spores of Giardia.
- Human pathogenic bacteria such as Brucella and Salmonella.

Animal wastes from cattle can be produced as solid or semisolid manure or as a liquid slurry. The production of slurry is especially common in housed dairy cattle.

Treatment

Whilst solid manure heaps outdoors can give rise to polluting wastewaters from runoff, this type of waste is usually relatively easy to treat by containment and/or covering of the heap.

Animal slurries require special handling and are usually treated by containment in lagoons before disposal by spray or trickle application to grassland. Constructed wetlands are sometimes used to facilitate treatment of animal wastes, as are anaerobic lagoons.

Excessive application or application to sodden land or insufficient land area can result in direct runoff to watercourses, with the potential for causing severe pollution. Application of slurries to land overlying aquifers can result in direct contamination or, more commonly, elevation of nitrogen levels as nitrite or nitrate.

The disposal of any wastewater containing animal waste upstream of a drinking water intake can pose serious health problems to those drinking the water because of the highly resistant spores present in many animals that are capable of causing disabling disease in humans. This risk exists even for very low-level seepage via shallow surface drains or from rainfall run-off.

Some animal slurries are treated by mixing with straws and composted at high temperature to produce a bacteri-ologically sterile and friable manure for soil improvement.

Piggery Waste

Piggery waste is comparable to other animal wastes except that many piggery wastes contain elevated levels of copper that can be toxic in the natural environment. Ascarid worms and their eggs are also common and can infect humans if wastewater treatment is ineffective.

Treatment

As for general animal waste, although the liquid fraction of the waste is frequently separated off and re-used in the piggery to avoid the prohibitively expensive costs of disposing of a copper-rich liquor.

Silage Liquor

Fresh or wilted grass or other green crops can be made into the semi-fermented product called silage which can be stored and used as winter forage for cattle and sheep. The production of silage often involves the use of an acid conditioner such as sulfuric acid or formic acid.

The process of silage making frequently produces a yellow-brown strongly smelling liquid which is very rich in simple sugars, alcohol, short-chain organic acids and silage conditioner. This liquor is one of the most polluting organic substances known. The volume of silage liquor produced is generally in proportion to the moisture content of the ensiled material.

Treatment

Silage liquor is best treated through prevention by wilting crops well before silage making. Any silage liquor that is produced can be used as part of the food for pigs. The most effective treatment is by containment in a slurry lagoon and by subsequent spreading on land following substantial dilution with slurry. Containment of silage liquor on its own can cause structural problems in concrete pits because of the acidic nature of silage liquor.

Milking Parlour (dairy farming) Wastes

Although milk has a deserved reputation as an important and valuable food product, its presence in wastewaters is highly polluting because of its organic strength, which can lead to very rapid de-oxygenation of receiving waters. Milking parlour wastes also contain large volumes of wash-down water, some animal waste together with cleaning and disinfection chemicals.

Treatment

Milking parlour wastes are often treated in admixture with human sewage in a local sewage treatment plant. This ensures that disinfectants and cleaning agents are sufficiently diluted and amenable to treatment. Running milking wastewaters into a farm slurry lagoon is a possible option although this tends to consume lagoon capacity very quickly. Land spreading is also a treatment option.

Slaughtering Waste

Wastewater from slaughtering activities is similar to milking parlour waste although considerably stronger in its organic composition and therefore potentially much more polluting.

Treatment

As for milking parlour waste.

Vegetable Washing Water

Washing of vegetables produces large volumes of water contaminated by soil and vegetable pieces. Low levels of pesticides used to treat the vegetables may also be present together with moderate levels of disinfectants such as chlorine.

Treatment

Most vegetable washing waters are extensively recycled with the solids removed by settlement and filtration. The recovered soil can be returned to the land.

Firewater

Although few farms plan for fires, fires are nevertheless more common on farms than on many other industrial premises. Stores of pesticides, herbicides, fuel oil for farm machinery and fertilizers can all help promote fire and can all be present in environmentally lethal quantities in firewater from fire fighting at farms.

Treatment

All farm environmental management plans should allow for containment of substantial quantities of firewater and for its subsequent recovery and disposal by specialist disposal companies. The concentration and mixture of contaminants in firewater make them unsuited to any treatment method available on the farm. Even land spreading has produced severe taste and odour problems for downstream water supply companies in the past.

Pollution by agricultural run-offs has too main effects on the environment. Pesticides may be responsible for poisoning. They are specially difficult to remove from freshwater, and thus, can be found in municipal or bottled water, even after conventional treatment. A study from the CSE recently drew the alarm about the concentration in pesticides such as organochlorines and organophosphaters that was exceeding the WHO standards in almost all the Indian brands of bottled water.

As for the fertlisers, they have an indirect adverse impact on the water resources. Indeed, by increasing the nutritional content of the water courses, fertilisers allow organisms to proliferate. These organisms may be disease vectors, or algae.

The proliferation of algae may slower the flow in the water courses, thus increasing again the proliferation of organisms and sedimentation. In spite of these well known adverse effects, and the worrying growth of fertiliser and pesticide use in the India agricultural sector, these products are still subsidised by the government.

The following table shows the increasing use of fertiliser and pesticide in the country.

Table 2.4: Evolution of Fertiliser and Pesticide use in India

Fertiliser Use	(Million of Tonnes)
1984	7.7
1995-96	13.9 (80 % increase)
Pesticide Use	(Tonnes)
1971	24305
1994-95	85030 (240% increase)

Source: Central Statistical Organisation, 1999 (reported in IGIDR, 2000)

The World Health Organization (WHO) has defined a permissible limit of concentration of Nitrates of 45 mg/L of NO_3, which is also accepted by the Indian Council of Medical Research (ICMR).

It can be observed that in states such as Haryana, the NO3 concentration was already exceeding by far the permissible limits in 1986. The increase in fertilisers consumption reported in the right part of the chart leads us to assume that those concentrations are now exceeding the limits in several other states.

IRRIGATION SYSTEM

Irrigation may be defined as the science of artificial application of water to the land or soil. It is used to assist in the growing of agricultural crops, maintenance of landscapes, and revegetation of disturbed soils in dry areas and during periods of inadequate rainfall. Additionally, irrigation also has a few other uses in crop production, which includes protecting plants against frost, suppressing weed growing in grain fields and helping in preventing soil consolidation. In contrast, agriculture that relies only on direct rainfall is referred to as rain-fed or dryland farming.

Irrigation systems are also used for dust suppression, disposal of sewage, and in mining. Irrigation is often studied together with drainage, which is the natural or artificial removal of surface and sub-surface water from a given area. Irrigation is also a term used in medical/dental fields to refer to flushing and washing out anything with water or another liquid.

Archaeological investigation has identified evidence of irrigation where the natural rainfall was insufficient to support crops. Perennial irrigation was practised in the Mesopotamian plain wherby crops were regularly watered throughout the growing season by coaxing water through a matrix of small channels formed in the field.

Ancient Egyptians practised Basin irrigation using the flooding of the Nile to inundate land plots which had been surrounded by dykes. The flood water was held until the fertile sediment had settled before the surplus was returned to the watercourse. There is evidence of the ancient Egyptian pharaoh Amenemhet III in the twelfth dynasty (about 1800 BCE) using the natural lake of the Faiyum Oasis as a reservoir to store surpluses of water for use during the dry seasons, the lake swelled annually from flooding of the Nile.

Terrace irrigation is evidenced in pre-Columbian America, early Syria India and China. In the Zana Valley of the Andes Mountains in Peru, archaeologists found remains of three irrigation canals radiocarbon dated from the 4th millennium BCE, the 3rd millennium BCE and the 9th century CE. These canals are the earliest record of irrigation in the New World. Traces of a canal possibly dating from the 5th millennium BCE were found under the fourth millennium canal.

Sophisticated irrigation and storage systems were developed by the Indus Valley Civilization in present-day Pakistan and North India, including the reservoirs at Girnar in 3000 BCE and an early canal irrigation system from circa 2600 BCE. Large scale agriculture was practiced and an extensive network of canals was used for the purpose of irrigation.

Ancient Persia (now Iran) as far back as the 6th millennium BCE, where barley was grown in areas where the natural rainfall was insufficient to support such a crop. The Qanats, developed in ancient Persia in about 800 BCE, are among the oldest known irrigation methods still in use today. They are now found in Asia, the Middle East and North Africa.

The system comprises a network of vertical wells and gently sloping tunnels driven into the sides of cliffs and steep hills to tap groundwater. The noria, a water wheel with clay pots around the rim powered by the flow of the stream (or by animals where the water source was still), was first brought into use at about this time, by Roman settlers in North Africa. By 150 BCE, the pots were fitted with valves to allow smoother filling as they were forced into the water.

The irrigation works of ancient Sri Lanka, the earliest dating from about 300 BCE, in the reign of King Pandukabhaya and under continuous development for the next thousand years, were one of the most complex irrigation systems of the ancient world. In addition to underground canals, the Sinhalese were the first to build completely artificial reservoirs to store water.

Due to their engineering superiority in this sector, they were often called 'masters of irrigation'. Most of these irrigation systems still exist undamaged up to now, in Anuradhapura and Polonnaruwa, because of the advanced and precise engineering. The system was extensively restored and further extended during the reign of King Parakrama Bahu (1153–1186 CE).

The oldest known hydraulic engineers of China were Sunshu Ao (6th century BCE) of the Spring and Autumn Period and Ximen Bao (5th century BCE) of the Warring States period, both of whom worked on large irrigation projects. In the Szechwan region belonging to the State of Qin of ancient China, the Dujiangyan Irrigation System was built in 256 BCE to irrigate an enormous area of farmland that today still supplies water.

By the second century AD, during the Han Dynasty, the Chinese also used chain pumps that lifted water from lower elevation to higher elevation. These were powered by manual foot pedal, hydraulic waterwheels, or rotating mechanical wheels pulled by oxen. The water was used for public works of providing water for urban residential quarters and palace gardens, but mostly for irrigation of farmland canals and channels in the fields.

In fifteen century Korea, the world's first water gauge, uryanggye was invented in 1441. The inventor was Jang Yeong-sil, a Korean engineer of the Joseon Dynasty, under the active direction of the king, Sejong the Great. It was installed in irrigation tanks as part of a nationwide system to measure and collect rainfall for agricultural applications. With this instrument, planners and farmers could make better use of the information gathered in the survey.

In the Americas, extensive irrigation systems were created by numerous groups in prehistoric times. One example is seen in the recent archaeological excavations near the Santa Cruz River in Tucson, Arizona. They have located a village site dating from 4,000 years ago. The floodplain of the Santa Cruz River was extensively farmed during the Early Agricultural period, circa 1200 BC to AD 150. These people constructed irrigation canals and grew corn, beans, and other crops while gathering wild plants and hunting animals.

In the middle of the last century, the advent of diesel and electric motors led for the first time to systems that could pump groundwater out of major aquifers faster than it was recharged. This can lead to permanent loss of aquifer capacity, decreased water quality, ground subsidence, and other problems. The future of food production in such areas as the North China Plain, the Punjab, and the Great Plains of the US is threatened.

IRRIGATION INFRASTRUCTURE

At the global scale 2,788,000 km^2 (689 million acres) of agricultural land was equipped with irrigation infrastructure around the year 2000. About 68% of the area equipped for irrigation is located in Asia, 17% in America, 9% in Europe, 5% in Africa and 1% in Oceania. The largest contiguous areas of high irrigation density are found in North India and Pakistan along the rivers Ganges and Indus, in the Hai He, Huang He and Yangtze basins in China, along the Nile river in Egypt and Sudan, in the Mississippi-Missouri river basin and in parts of California. Smaller irrigation areas are spread across almost all populated parts of the world.

TYPES OF IRRIGATION

Various types of irrigation techniques differ in how the water obtained from the source is distributed within the field. In general, the goal is to supply the entire field uniformly with water, so that each plant has the amount of water it needs, neither too much nor too little.The modern methods are efficient enough to achieve this goal.

Surface

In surface irrigation systems, water moves over and across the land by simple gravity flow in order to wet it and to infiltrate into the soil. Surface irrigation can be subdivided into furrow, borderstrip or basin irrigation. It is often called flood irrigation when the irrigation results in flooding or near flooding of the cultivated land. Historically, this has been the most common method of irrigating agricultural land.

Where water levels from the irrigation source permit, the levels are controlled by dikes, usually plugged by soil. This is often seen in terraced rice fields (rice paddies), where the method is used to flood or control the level of water in each distinct field. In some cases, the water is pumped, or lifted by human or animal power to the level of the land!

Localized

Localized irrigation is a system where water is distributed under low pressure through a piped network, in a pre-determined pattern, and applied as a small discharge to each plant or adjacent to it. Drip irrigation, spray or micro-sprinkler irrigation and bubbler irrigation belong to this category of irrigation methods.

Drip

Drip irrigation, also known as trickle irrigation, functions as its name suggests.in this system water falls drop by drop just at the position of roots.Water is delivered at or near the root zone of plants, drop by drop. This method can be the most water-efficient method of irrigation, if managed properly, since evaporation and runoff are minimized. In modern agriculture, drip irrigation is often combined with plastic mulch, further reducing evaporation, and is also the means of delivery of fertilizer. The process is known as fertigation.

Deep percolation, where water moves below the root zone, can occur if a drip system is operated for too long or if the delivery rate is too high. Drip irrigation methods range from very high-tech and computerized to low-tech and labor-intensive.

Lower water pressures are usually needed than for most other types of systems, with the exception of low energy center pivot systems and surface irrigation systems, and the system can be designed for uniformity throughout a field or for precise water delivery to individual plants in a landscape containing a mix of plant species.

Although, it is difficult to regulate pressure on steep slopes, pressure compensating emitters are available, so the field does not have to be level. High-tech solutions involve precisely calibrated emitters located along lines of tubing that extend from a computerized set of valves.

Sprinkler

In sprinkler or overhead irrigation, water is piped to one or more central locations within the field and distributed by overhead high-pressure sprinklers or guns. A system utilizing sprinklers, sprays, or guns mounted overhead on permanently installed risers is often referred to as a solid-set irrigation system. Higher pressure sprinklers that rotate are called rotors and are driven by a ball drive, gear drive, or impact mechanism. Rotors can be designed to rotate in a full or partial circle.

Guns are similar to rotors, except that they generally operate at very high pressures of 40 to 130 lbf/in^2 (275 to 900 kPa) and flows of 50 to 1200 US gal/min (3 to 76 L/s), usually with nozzle diameters in the range of 0.5 to 1.9 inches (10 to 50 mm). Guns are used not only for irrigation, but also for industrial applications such as dust suppression and logging.

Sprinklers can also be mounted on moving platforms connected to the water source by a hose. Automatically moving wheeled systems known as traveling sprinklers may irrigate areas such as small farms, sports fields, parks, pastures, and cemeteries unattended. Most of these utilize a length of polyethylene tubing wound on a steel drum.

As the tubing is wound on the drum powered by the irrigation water or a small gas engine, the sprinkler is pulled across the field. When the sprinkler arrives back at the reel the system shuts off. This type of system is known to most people as a "waterreel" travelling irrigation sprinkler and they are used extensively for dust suppression, irrigation, and land application of waste water. Other travelers use a flat rubber hose that is dragged along behind while the sprinkler platform is pulled by a cable. These cable-type travelers are definitely old technology and their use is limited in today's modern irrigation projects.

Centre Pivot

Centre pivot irrigation is a form of sprinkler irrigation consisting of several segments of pipe (usually galvanized steel or aluminum) joined together and supported by trusses, mounted on wheeled towers with sprinklers positioned along its length. The system moves in a circular pattern and is fed with water from the pivot point at the center of the arc. These systems are found and used in all parts of the world and allow irrigation of all types of terrain. Newer systems have drop sprinkler heads as shown in the image that follows.

Most centre pivot systems now have drops hanging from a u-shaped pipe attached at the top of the pipe with sprinkler heads that are positioned a few feet (at most) above the crop, thus limiting evaporative losses. Drops can also be used with drag hoses or bubblers that deposit the water directly on the ground between crops. Crops are often planted in a circle to conform to the center pivot.

This type of system is known as LEPA (Low Energy Precision Application). Originally, most center pivots were water powered. These were replaced by hydraulic systems (T-L Irrigation) and electric motor driven systems. Many modern sprinklers features GPS devices.

Lateral Move

A series of pipes, each with a wheel of about 1.5 m diameter permanently affixed to its midpoint and sprinklers along its length, are coupled together at one edge of a field. Water is supplied at one end using a large hose. After sufficient water has been applied, the hose is removed and the remaining assembly rotated either by hand or with a purpose-built mechanism, so that the sprinklers move 10 m across the field. The hose is reconnected. The process is repeated until the opposite edge of the field is reached.

This system is less expensive to install than a center pivot, but much more labor intensive to operate, and it is limited in the amount of water it can carry. Most systems utilize four or five-inch (130 mm) diameter aluminum pipe. One feature of a lateral move system is that it consists of sections that can be easily disconnected. They are most often used for small or oddly shaped fields, such as those found in hilly or mountainous regions, or in regions where labor is inexpensive.

SUB-IRRIGATION

Sub-irrigation also sometimes called seepage irrigation has been used for many years in field crops in areas with high water-tables. It is a method of artificially raising the water table to allow the soil to be moistened from below the plants' root zone. Often those systems are located on permanent grasslands in lowlands or river valleys and combined with drainage infrastructure. A system of pumping stations, canals, weirs and gates allows it to increase or decrease the water level in a network of ditches and thereby control the water table.

Sub-irrigation is also used in commercial greenhouse production, usually for potted plants. Water is delivered from below, absorbed upwards, and the excess collected for recycling. Typically, a solution of water and nutrients floods a container or flows through a trough for a short period of time, 10–20 minutes, and is then pumped back into a holding tank for reuse.

Sub-irrigation in greenhouses requires fairly sophisticated, expensive equipment and management. Advantages are water and nutrient conservation, and labor-saving through lowered system maintenance and automation. It is similar in principle and action to subsurface drip irrigation.

These systems have low requirements for infrastructure and technical equipment but need high labor inputs. Irrigation using watering cans is to be found for example in peri-urban agriculture around large cities in some African countries.

Besides the common manual watering by bucket, an automated, natural version of this also exist. Using plain polyester ropes combined with a prepared ground mixture can be used to water plants from a vessel filled with water.

The ground mixture would need to be made depending on the plant itself, yet would mostly consist of black potting soil, vermiculite and perlite. This system would (with certain crops) allow to save expenses as it does not consume any electricity and only little water unlike sprinklers, water timers.

However, it may only be used with certain crops probably mostly larger crops that do not need a humid environment; perhaps e.g. paprikas.

In countries where at night, humid air sweeps the countryside, water can be obtained from the humid air by condensation onto cold surfaces. This is for example practiced in the vineyards at Lanzarote using stones to condense water or with various fog collectors based on canvas or foil sheets.

Sources of Irrigation Water

It can be groundwater extracted from springs or by using wells, surface water withdrawn from rivers, lakes or reservoirs or non-conventional sources like treated wastewater, desalinated water or drainage water.

A special form of irrigation using surface water is spate irrigation, also called floodwater harvesting. In case of a flood (*spate*) water is diverted to normally dry river beds (*wadis*) using a network of dams, gates and channels and spread over large areas. The moisture stored in the soil will be used thereafter to grow crops.

Spate irrigation areas are in particular located in semi-arid or arid, mountainous regions. While floodwater harvesting belongs to the accepted irrigation methods, rainwater harvesting is usually not considered as a form of irrigation. Rainwater harvesting is the collection of runoff water from roofs or unused land and the concentration of this. Some of Ancient India's water systems were pulled by oxen.

Water Scarcity

Fifty years ago, the common perception was that water was an infinite resource. At that time, there were fewer than half the current number of people on the planet. People were not as wealthy as today, consumed fewer calories and ate less meat, so less water was needed to produce their food. They required a third of the volume of water we presently take from rivers.

Today, the competition for water resources is much more intense. This is because there are now nearly seven billion people on the planet, their consumption of water-thirsty meat and vegetables is rising, and there is increasing competition for water from industry, urbanisation and biofuel crops. To avoid a global water crisis, farmers will have to strive to increase productivity to meet growing demands for food, while industry and cities find ways to use water more efficiently.

Successful agriculture is dependent upon farmers having sufficient access to water. However, water scarcity is already a critical constraint to farming in many parts of the world. Physical water scarcity is where there is not enough water to meet all demands, including that needed for ecosystems to function effectively.

Arid regions frequently suffer from physical water scarcity. It also occurs where water seems abundant but where resources are over-committed. This can happen where there is overdevelopment of hydraulic infrastructure, usually for irrigation. Symptoms of physical water scarcity include environmental degradation and declining groundwater.

Economic scarcity, meanwhile, is caused by a lack of investment in water or insufficient human capacity to satisfy the demand for water. Symptoms of economic water scarcity include a lack of infrastructure, with people often having to fetch water from rivers for domestic and agricultural uses. Some 2.8 billion people currently live in water-scarce areas.

How An In-ground Irrigation System Works

Most commercial and residential irrigation systems are "in ground" systems, which means that everything is buried in the ground. With the pipes, sprinklers, emitters (drippers), and irrigation valves being hidden, it makes for a cleaner, more presentable landscape without garden hoses or other items having to be moved around manually. This does, however, create some drawbacks in the maintenance of a completely buried system.

Controllers, Zones, and Valves

Most irrigation systems are divided into zones. A zone is a single irrigation valve and one or a group of drippers or sprinklers that are connected by pipes or tubes. Irrigation systems are divided into zones because there is usually not enough pressure and available flow to run sprinklers for an entire yard or sports field at once. Each zone has a solenoid valve on it that is controlled via wire by an irrigation controller.

The irrigation controller is either a mechanical (now the "dinosaur" type) or electrical device that signals a zone to turn on at a specific time and keeps it on for a specified amount of time. "Smart Controller" is a recent term used to describe a controller that is capable of adjusting the watering time by itself in response to current environmental conditions.

The smart controller determines current conditions by means of historic weather data for the local area, a soil moisture sensors (water potential or water content), rain sensor, or in more sophisticated systems satellite feed weather station, or a combination of these.

Emitters and Sprinklers

When a zone comes on, the water flows through the lateral lines and ultimately ends up at the irrigation emitter (drip) or sprinkler heads. Many sprinklers have pipe thread inlets on the bottom of them which allows a fitting and the pipe to be attached to them. The sprinklers are usually installed with the top of the head flush with the ground surface.

When the water is pressurized, the head will pop up out of the ground and water the desired area until the valve closes and shuts off that zone. Once there is no more water pressure in the lateral line, the sprinkler head will retract back into the ground. Emitters are generally laid on the soil surface or buried a few inches to reduce evaporation losses.

Problems in Irrigation

Irrigation can lead to a number of problems:

- Competition for surface water rights.
- Depletion of underground aquifers.
- Ground subsidence (e.g. New Orleans, Louisiana)
- Underirrigation or irrigation giving only just enough water for the plant (e.g. in drip line irrigation) gives poor soil salinity control which leads to increased soil salinity with consequent build up of toxic salts on soil surface in areas with high evaporation. This requires either leaching to remove these salts and a method of drainage to carry the salts away. When using drip lines, the leaching is best done regularly at certain intervals (with only a slight excess of water), so that the salt is flushed back under the plant's roots.
- Overirrigation because of poor distribution uniformity or management wastes water, chemicals, and may lead to water pollution.
- Deep drainage (from over-irrigation) may result in rising water tables which in some instances will lead to problems of irrigation salinity requiring watertable control by some form of subsurface land drainage.
- Irrigation with saline or high-sodium water may damage soil structure owing to the formation of alkaline soil

The quality of irrigation water available to farmers and other irrigators has a considerable impact on what plants can be successfully grown, the productivity of these plants, and water infiltration and other soil physical conditions.

CHAPTER – 3

Soil Conservation and Rain-water Harvesting

Soil conservation is important because with the erosion of the topsoil layer, valuable nutrients are lost and crop yields diminish, which means less food is produced per acre. Soil conservation is a set of management strategies for prevention of soil being eroded from the Earth's surface or becoming chemically altered by overuse, acidification, salinization or other chemical soil contamination. It is a component of environmental soil science.

Decisions regarding appropriate crop rotation, cover crops, and planted windbreaks are central to the ability of surface soils to retain their integrity, both with respect to erosive forces and chemical change from nutrient depletion. Crop rotation is simply the conventional alternation of crops on a given field, so that nutrient depletion is avoided from repetitive chemical uptake/deposition of single crop growth.

Cover crops serve the function of protecting the soil from erosion, weed establishment or excess evapotranspiration; however, they may also serve vital soil chemistry functions. For example, legumes can be ploughed under to augment soil nitrates, and other plants have the ability to metabolize soil contaminants or alter adverse pH.

The cover crop Mucuna pruriens (velvet bean) has been used in Nigeria to increase phosphorus availability after application of rock phosphate. Some of these same precepts are applicable to urban landscaping, especially with respect to ground-cover selection for erosion control and weed suppression. Soil is one of the three main natural resources alongside with water and air.

Soil erosion affects farming in detrimental ways. Physical damage is the most visible form of soil loss, and most likely to be remedied. Gravity pulls constantly at soil, nudging it down hill, causing soil slips, earth clips, cracks, creep and slumps. Ironically, the most damaging of rainfall is the impact with which water droplets hit the soil. From there on, the flow of water causes sheet-wash, rilling, surface gullying, tunneling and in rivers it scours banks. In dry climates, wind blow is the main cause of erosion.

METHODOLOGY OF SOIL CONSERVATION

The main methodology of soil conservation are improvement of the choice of vegetative cover, soil erosion prevention, salinity management, to augment the health of beneficial soil organisms and stopping of soil contamination. Soil conservation is a set of methods and procedures which are adopted for prevention of soil being eroded from the earth's surface or becoming chemically altered by overuse or salinization or acidification.

Soil conservation if of utmost importance for a country like India which is mainly has an agricultural economy. A large part of India's population depends on the soil for their livelihood and hence soil erosion and the measures of soil conservation taken up to prevent. Soil erosion are of key concern for the Indian government

Windbreaks are created by planting sufficiently dense rows or stands of trees at the windward exposure of an agricultural field subject to wind erosion. Evergreen species are preferred to achieve year-round protection; however, as long as foliage is present in the seasons of bare soil surfaces, the effect of deciduous trees may also be adequate.

Conventional Practices

There are also conventional practices that farmers have invoked for centuries. These fall into two main categories: contour farming and terracing, standard methods recommended by the U.S. Natural Resources Conservation Service , whose Code 330 is the common standard. Contour farming was practised by the ancient Phoenicians, and is known to be effective for slopes between two and ten per cent. Contour plowing can increase crop yields from 10 to 50 per cent, partially as a result from greater soil retention.

There are many erosion control methods that can be used such as conservation tillage systems and crop rotation. Keyline design is an enhancement of contour farming, where the total watershed properties are taken into account in forming the contour lines. Terracing is the practice of creating benches or nearly level layers on a hillside setting. Terraced farming is more common on small farms and in under-developed countries, since mechanized equipment is difficult to deploy in this setting.

Human overpopulation is leading to destruction of tropical forests due to widening practices of slash-and-burn and other methods of subsistence farming necessitated by famines in lesser developed countries. A sequel to the deforestation is typically large scale erosion, loss of soil nutrients and sometimes total desertification.

Soil erosion lead to degradation of soils' physical property and loss of plant nutrients. Hence proper care should be taken to ensure soil conservation. Soil erosion if left unchecked leads to the formation of gullies and ravines and can reduce the fertility of the soil .

Perimeter Runoff Control

Trees, shrubs and groundcovers are also effective perimeter treatment for soil erosion prevention, by insuring any surface flows are impeded. A special form of this perimeter or inter-row treatment is the use of a "grassway" that both channels and dissipates runoff through surface friction, impeding surface runoff, and encouraging infiltration of the slowed surface water.

SALINITY MANAGEMENT

Salinity in soil is caused by irrigating the crops by salty water during the evaporation the water from the soil evaporates leaving the soil behind causing salinization. Salinization causes the soil structure to break down causing infertility and the plants cannot grow.

The ions responsible for salination are: Na^+, K^+, Ca^{2+}, Mg^{2+} and Cl^-. Salinity is estimated to affect about one third of all the earth's arable land. Soil salinity adversely affects the metabolism of most crops, and erosion effects usually follow vegetation failure. Salinity occurs on drylands from overirrigation and in areas with shallow saline water tables. In the case of over-irrigation, salts are deposited in upper soil layers as a byproduct of most soil infiltration; excessive irrigation merely increases the rate of salt deposition.

The best-known case of shallow saline water table capillary action occurred in Egypt after the 1970 construction of the Aswan Dam. The change in the groundwater level due to dam construction led to high concentration of salts in the water table. After the construction, the continuous high level of the water table led to soil salination of previously arable land.

The mechanism involved is that humic acids can fix both anions and cations and eliminate them from root zones. In some cases it may be valuable to find plants that can tolerate saline conditions to use as surface cover until salinity can be reduced; there are a number of such saline-tolerant plants, such as saltbush, a plant found in much of North America and in the mediterranean regions of Europe.

SOIL pH

Soil pH levels adverse to crop growth can occur naturally in some regions; it can also be induced by acid rain or soil contamination from acids or bases. The role of soil pH is to control nutrient availability to vegetation. The principal macronutrients (calcium, phosphorus, nitrogen, potassium, magnesium, sulfur) prefer neutral to slightly alkaline soils. Calcium, magnesium and potassium are usually made available to plants via cation exchange surfaces of organic material and clay soil surface particles.

While acidification increases the initial availability of these cations, the residual soil moisture concentrations of nutrient cations can fall to alarmingly low levels after initial nutrient uptake. Moreover, there is no simple relationship of pH to nutrient availability because of the complex combination of soil types, soil moisture regimes and meteorological factors.

SOIL ORGANISMS

Promoting the viability of beneficial soil organisms is an element of soil conservation; moreover this includes macroscopic species, notably the earthworm, as well as microorganisms. Positive effects of the earthworm are known well, as to aeration and promotion of macronutrient availability. When worms excrete egesta in the form of casts, a balanced selection of minerals and plant nutrients is made into a form accessible for root uptake.

US research shows that earthworm casts are five times richer in available nitrogen, seven times richer in available phosphates and eleven times richer in available potash than the surrounding upper150 mm of soil. The weight of casts produced may be greater than 4.5 kg per worm per year. By burrowing, the earthworm is of value in creating soil porosity, creating channels enhancing the processes of aeration and drainage.

Microorganisms

Soil micro-organisms play a vital role in macronutrient wildlife. For example, nitrogen fixation is carried out by free-living or symbiotic bacteria. These bacteria have the nitrogenase enzyme that combines gaseous nitrogen with hydrogen to produce ammonia, which is then further converted by the bacteria to make other organic compounds. Some nitrogen fixing bacteria such as rhizobia live in the root nodules of legumes.

Here they form a mutualistic relationship with the plant, producing ammonia in exchange for carbohydrates. In the case of the carbon cycle, carbon is transferred within the biosphere as heterotrophs feed on other organisms. This process includes the uptake of dead organic material (detritus) by fungi and bacteria in the form of fermentation or decay phenomena.

Mycorrhizae are symbiotic associations between soil-dwelling fungi and the roots of vascular plants. Fungi helps increase the availability of minerals, water, and organic nutrients to the plant, while extracting sugars and amino acids from the plant. There are two main types, endomycorrhizae which penetrate the roots and ectomy-corrhizae which resemble 'socks', forming a sheath around the roots. They were discovered when scientists observed that certain seedlings failed to grow or prosper without soil from their native environment.

Some soil micro-organisms known as extremophiles have remarkable properties of adaptation to extreme environ-mental conditions including temperature, pH and water deprivation.

Use of Insecticides and Herbicides

The viability of soil organisms can be compromised when insecticides and herbicides are applied to planting regimes. Often there are unforeseen and unintended consequences of such chemical use in the form of death of impaired functioning of soil organisms. Thus any use of pesticides should only be undertaken after thorough understanding of residual toxicities on soil organisms as well as terrestrial ecological components.

Killing soil micro-organisms is a deleterious impact of slash and burn agricultural methods. With the surface temperatures generated, virtual annilation of soil and vegetative cover organisms are destroyed, and in many environments these effects can be virtually irreversible (at least for generations of mankind). Shifting cultivation is also a farming system that often employs slash and burn as one of its elements.

Systems, most of which have an adverse effect upon soil quality and plant metabolism. While the role of pH has been discussed above, heavy metals, solvents, petroleum hydrocarbons, herbicides and pesticides also contribute soil residues that are of potential concern.

Some of these chemicals are totally extraneous to the agricultural landscape, but others notably herbicides and pesticides are intentionally introduced to serve a short term function. Many of these added chemicals have long half-lives in soil, and others degrade to produce derivative chemicals that may be either persistent or pernicious.

One alternative to chemicals in agriculture is soil steaming. Steam sterilizes the soil by killing almost all beneficial and harmful micro organisms. However no harmful remains are left. Soil health may even increase since steam unlocks nutrients in the soil which may lead to better plant growth after the thermal treatment.

Typically the expense of soil contamination remediation cannot be justified in an agricultural economic analysis, since cleanup costs are generally quite high; often remediation is mandated by state and county environmental health agencies based on human health risk issues.

MINERALIZATION

To allow plants full realization of their phytonutrient potential, active mineralization of the soil is sometimes undertaken. This can be in the natural form of adding crushed rock or can take the form of chemical soil supplement. In either case the purpose is to combat mineral depletion of the soil.

There are a broad range of minerals that can be added including common substances such as phosphorus and more exotic substances such as zinc and selenium. There is extensive research on the phase transitions of minerals in soil with aqueous contact. The process of flooding can bring significant bedload sediment to an alluvial plain.

While this effect may not be desirable if floods endanger life or if the eroded sediment originates from productive land, this process of addition to a floodplain is a natural process that can rejuvenate soil chemistry through mineralization and macronutrient addition.

RAINWATER HARVESTING

Rainwater harvesting (RH) is defined as a method for inducing, collecting, storing and conserving local surface runoff for agriculture in arid and semi-arid regions. Rainfall has four facets. Rainfall induces surface flow on the runoff area. At the lower end of the slope, runoff collects in the basin area, where a major portion infiltrates and is stored in the root zone. After infiltration has ceased, then follows the conservation of the stored soil water.

It is the accumulating and storing, of rainwater for reuse, before it reaches the aquifer. It has been used to provide drinking water, water for livestock, water for irrigation, as well as other typical uses given to water. Rainwater collected from the roofs of houses, tents and local institutions, can make an important contribution to the availability of drinking water.

It can supplement the sub-soil water level and decrease urban greenery. Water collected from the ground, sometimes from areas which are especially prepared for this purpose, is called 'stormwater harvesting'.

In some cases, rainwater may be the only available, or economical, water source. Rainwater harvesting systems can be simple to construct from inexpensive local materials, and are potentially successful in most habitable locations. Roof rainwater can't be of good quality and may require treatment before consumption. As rainwater rushes from your roof it may carry pollutants in it such as the tiniest bit of mercury from coal burning buildings to bird feces.

Although, some rooftop materials may produce rainwater that is harmful to human health, it can be useful in flushing toilets, washing clothes, watering the garden and washing cars; these uses alone halve the amount of water used by a typical home. Household rainfall catchment systems are appropriate in areas with an average rainfall greater than 200 mm (7.9 in) per year, and no other accessible water sources. Overflow from rainwater harvesting tank systems can be used to refill aquifers in a process called 'groundwater recharge', though this is a related process, it must not be confused with rainwater harvesting.

There are a number of types of systems to harvest rainwater ranging from very simple to the complex industrial systems. The rate at which water can be collected from either system is dependent on the plan area of the system, its efficiency, and the intensity of rainfall (i.e. annual precipitation (mm per annum) x square meter of catchment area = litres per annum yield) ... a 200 square metre roof catchment catching 1,000 mm PA yields 200 kLPA.

Basic Configuration

Rainwater is harvesting systems channel rainwater that falls on to a roof into storage via a system of gutters and pipes. The first flush of rainwater after a dry season should be allowed to run to waste as it will be contaminated with dust, bird droppings etc.

Roof gutters should have enough, and large enough to carry peak flows. Storage tanks should be covered to prevent mosquito breeding and to reduce evaporation losses, contamination and algal growth. Rainwater harvesting systems require regular maintenance and cleaning to keep the system hygienic.

Subsurface Dyke

A subsurface dyke is built in an aquifer to obstruct the natural flow of groundwater, thereby raising the groundwater level and increasing the amount of water stored in the aquifer. The subsurface dyke at Krishi Vigyan Kendra, Kannur under Kerala Agricultural University with the support of ICAR, has become an effective method for ground water conservation by means of rain water harvesting technologies.

The sub-surface dyke has demonstrated that it is a feasible method for conserving and exploiting the groundwater resources of the Kerala state of India. The dyke is now the largest rainwater harvesting system in that region.

Groundwater Recharge

Rainwater may also be used for groundwater recharge, where the runoff on the ground is collected and allowed to be absorbed, adding to the groundwater. In the US, rooftop rainwater is collected and stored in sump.

Advantages in Urban Areas

Rainwater harvesting can:

(*a*) assure an independent water supply during water restrictions, that is though somewhat dependent on end use and maintenance;

(*b*) usually of acceptable quality for household needs; and

(*c*) renewable at acceptable volumes despite forecast climate change.

It produces beneficial externalities by reducing peak storm water runoff and processing costs. In municipalities with combined sewer systems, reducing storm runoff is especially important, because excess runoff during heavy storms leads to the discharge of raw sewage from outfalls when treatment plant capacity cannot handle the combined flow.

The RH systems are simple to install and operate. Running costs are negligible, and they provide water at the point of consumption. Rainwater harvesting in urban communities has been made possible by companies such as Living Rainwater Tanks. Tanks such as this provide an attractive yet effective solution to rainwater catchment.

Rain water harvesting law Some states have water law in favor of land owners, and some states own all water rights, leaving you only water rights they are willing to grant through permits. For example, in Colorado you may not catch, collect or harvest rain water from your roof unless you first buy a permit.

Precipitation in arid and semi-arid zones results largely from convective cloud mechanisms producing storms typically of short duration, relatively high intensity and limited areal extent. However, low intensity frontal-type rains are also experienced, usually in the winter season. When most precipitation occurs during winter, as in Jordan and in the Negev, relatively low-intensity rainfall may represent the greater part of annual rainfall.

Rainfall intensity is defined as the ratio of the total amount of rain (rainfall depth) falling during a given period to the duration of the period It is expressed in depth units per unit time, usually as mm per hour (mm/h).

The statistical characteristics of high-intensity, short-duration, convective rainfall are essentially independent of locations within a region and are similar in many parts of the world. Analysis of short-term rainfall data suggests that there is a reasonably stable relationship governing the intensity characteristics of this type of rainfall.

Studies carried out in Saudi Arabia suggest that, an average, around 50 per cent of all rain occurs at intensities in excess of 20 mm/hour and 20-30 per cent occurs at intensities in excess of 40 mm/hour. This relationship appears to be independent of the long-term average rainfall at a particular location.

Water harvesting planning and management in arid and semi-arid zones present difficulties which are due less to the limited amount of rainfall than to the inherent degree of variability associated with it.

In temperate climates, the standard deviation of annual rainfall is about 10-20 per cent and in 13 years out of 20, annual amounts are between 75 and 125 per cent of the mean. In arid and semi-arid climates the ratio of maximum to minimum annual amounts is much greater and the annual rainfall distribution becomes increasingly skewed with increasing aridity.

With mean annual rainfalls of 200-300 mm, the rainfall in 19 years out of 20 typically ranges from 40 to 200 per cent of the mean and for 100 mm/year, 30 to 350 per cent of the mean. At more arid locations it is not uncommon to experience several consecutive years with no rainfall. For a water harvesting planner, the most difficult task is therefore to select the appropriate "design" rainfall according to which the ratio of catchment to cultivated area will be determined.

Design rainfall is defined as the total amount of rain during the cropping season at which or above which the catchment area will provide sufficient runoff to satisfy the crop water requirements. If the actual rainfall in the cropping season is below the design rainfall, there will be moisture stress in the plants; if the actual rainfall exceeds the design rainfall, there will be surplus runoff which may result in a damage to the structures.

The design rainfall is usually assigned to a certain probability of occurrence or exceedance. If, for example, the design rainfall with a 67 per cent probability of exceedance is selected, this means that on average this value will be reached or exceeded in two years out of three and therefore the crop water requirements would also be met in two years out of three.

Quality

As rainwater may be contaminated due to pollutants like microscopic germs etc., it is often not considered suitable for drinking without treatment. However, there are many examples of rainwater being used for all purposes including drinking following suitable treatment.

Rainwater harvested from roofs can contain human, animal and bird faeces, mosses and lichens, windblown dust, particulates from urban pollution, pesticides, and inorganic ions from the sea (Ca, Mg, Na, K, Cl, SO_4), and dissolved gases (CO_2, NO_x, SO_x).

High levels of pesticide have been found in rainwater in Europe with the highest concentrations occurring in the first rain immediately after a dry spell; the concentration of these and other contaminants are reduced significantly by diverting the initial flow of water to waste as described above. The water may need to be analysed properly, and used in a way appropriate to its safety.

In the Gansu province for example, harvested rainwater is boiled in parabolic solar cookers before being used for drinking. In Brazil alum and chlorine is added to disinfect water before consumption. So-called "appropriate technology" methods, such as solar water disinfection, provide low-cost disinfection options for treatment of stored rainwater for drinking.

Probability Analysis

A rather simple, graphical method to determine the probability or frequency of occurrence of yearly or seasonal rainfall will be described in this chapter. For the design of water harvesting schemes, this method is as valid as any analytical method described in statistical textbooks.

The first step is to obtain annual rainfall totals for the cropping season from the area of concern. In locations where rainfall records do not exist, figures from stations nearby may be used with caution. It is important to obtain long-term records. The variability of rainfall in arid and semi-arid areas is considerable. An analysis of only five or six years of observations is inadequate as these 5 or 6 values may belong to a particularly dry or wet period and hence may not be representative for the long term rainfall pattern.

As the rain continues, water reaching the ground surface infiltrates into the soil until it reaches a stage where the rate of rainfall (intensity) exceeds the infiltration capacity of the soil. Thereafter, surface puddles, ditches, and other depressions are filled (depression storage), after which runoff is generated.

The infiltration capacity of the soil depends on its texture and structure, as well as on the antecedent soil moisture content (previous rainfall or dry season). The initial capacity (of a dry soil) is high but, as the storm continues, it decreases until it reaches a steady value termed as final infiltration rate.

The process of runoff generation continues as long as the rainfall intensity exceeds the actual infiltration capacity of the soil but it stops as soon as the rate of rainfall drops below the actual rate of infiltration.

The rainfall runoff process is well described in the literature. Numerous papers on the subject have been published and many computer simulation models have been developed. All these models, however, require detailed knowledge of a number of factors and initial boundary conditions in a catchment area which in most cases are not readily available.

For a better understanding of the difficulties of accurately predicting the amount of runoff resulting from a rainfall event, the major factors which influence the rainfall-runoff process are described below.

Factors Affecting Runoff

Apart from rainfall characteristics such as intensity, duration and distribution, there are a number of site (or catchment) specific factors which have a direct bearing on the occurrence and volume of runoff.

Soil Type

The infiltration capacity is among others dependent on the porosity of a soil which determines the water storage capacity and affects the resistance of water to flow into deeper layers.

Porosity differs from one soil type to the other. The highest infiltration capacities are observed in loose, sandy soils while heavy clay or loamy soils have considerable smaller infiltration capacities.

System Sizing

It is important that the system is sized to meet the water demand throughout the dry season. Generally speaking, the size of the storage tank should be big enough to meet the daily water requirement throughout the dry season. In addition, the size of the catchment area or roof should be large enough to fill the tank.

Around the World

- Currently in China and Brazil, rooftop rainwater harvesting is being practiced for providing drinking water, domestic water, water for livestock, water for small irrigation and a way to replenish ground water levels. Gansu province in China and semi-arid north east Brazil have the largest rooftop rainwater harvesting projects ongoing.
- In Rajasthan, India rainwater harvesting has traditionally been practiced by the people of the Thar Desert. There are many ancient water harvesting systems in Rajasthan which have now been revived.
- In Bermuda, the law requires all new construction to include rainwater harvesting adequate for the residents.
- The U.S. Virgin Islands have a similar law.
- In the indus valley civilization, Elephanta Caves and Kanheri Caves in Mumbai rainwater harvesting alone has been used to supply in their water requirements.
- In Senegal and Guinea-Bissau, the houses of the Diola-people are frequently equipped with homebrew rainwater harvesters made from local, organic materials.

- In the United Kingdom water butts are often found in domestic gardens to collect rainwater which is then used to water the garden. However, the British government's Code For Sustainable Homes encourages fitting large underground tanks to new-build homes to collect rainwater for flushing toilets, washing clothes, watering the garden and washing cars. This reduces by 50% the amount of mains water used by the home.
- In the Irrawaddy Delta of Myanmar, the groundwater is saline and communities rely on mud-lined rainwater ponds to meet their drinking water needs throughout the dry season. Some of these ponds are centuries old and are treated with great reverence and respect.
- Until 2009 in Colorado, water rights laws almost completely restricted rainwater harvesting; a property owner who captured rainwater was deemed to be stealing it from those who have rights to take water from the watershed. Now, residential well owners that meet certain criteria may obtain a permit to install a rooftop precipitation collection system (SB 09-080). Up to 10 large scale pilot studies may also be permitted (HB 09-1129). The main factor in persuading the Colorado Legislature to change the law was a 2007 study that found that in an average year, 97% of the precipitation that fell in Douglas County, in the southern suburbs of Denver, never reached a stream—it was used by plants or evaporated on the ground. In colorado you cannot even drill a water well unless you have at least 35 acres. In New Mexico, rainwater catchment is mandatory for new dwellings in Santa Fe.
- In Australia rainwater harvesting is typically used to supplement the reticulated mains supply. In south east Queensland, households that harvested rainwater doubled each year from 2005 to 2008, reaching 40% penetration at that time (White, 2009 (PhD)).
- In Beijing, some housing societies are now adding rain water in their main water sources after proper treatment.

CLEAN WATER ACT

It is the primary federal law in the United States governing water pollution. Commonly abbreviated as the CWA, the act established the goals of eliminating releases of high amounts of toxic substances into water, eliminating additional water pollution by 1985, and ensuring that surface waters would meet standards necessary for human sports and recreation by 1983.

The principal body of law currently in effect is based on the Federal Water Pollution Control Amendments of 1972 and was significantly expanded from the Federal Water Pollution Control Amendments of 1948. Major amendments were enacted in the Clean Water Act of 1977 and the Water Quality Act of 1987.

This Act does not directly address groundwater contamination. Groundwater protection provisions are included in the Safe Drinking Water Act, Resource Conservation and Recovery Act, and the Superfund Act.

WATERS PROTECTED UNDER THE CWA

All waters with a "significant nexus" to "navigable waters" are covered under the CWA; however, the phrase "significant nexus" remains open to judicial interpretation and considerable controversy.

The 1972 statute frequently uses the term "navigable waters," but also defines the term as "waters of the United States, including the territorial seas." Some regulations interpreting the 1972 law have included water features such as intermittent streams, playa lakes, prairie potholes, sloughs and wetlands as "waters of the United States"

In 2006, a plurality of the Supreme Court held that the term "waters of the United States":

> . . . includes only those relatively permanent, standing or continuously flowing bodies of water "forming geographic features" that are described in ordinary parlance as "streams[,] . . . oceans, rivers, [and] lakes."

POLLUTION CONTROL STRATEGY IN THE CWA

Point Sources

The 1972 act introduced the National Pollutant Discharge Elimination System (NPDES), which is a permit system for regulating point sources of pollution. Point sources include:

- Industrial facilities (including manufacturing, mining, oil and gas extraction, and service industries);
- Municipal governments and other government facilities (such as military bases); and
- Some agricultural facilities, such as animal feedlots.

Point sources may not discharge pollutants to surface waters without a permit from the National Pollutant Discharge Elimination System (NPDES). This system is managed by the United States Environmental Protection Agency (EPA) in partnership with state environmental agencies.

EPA has authorized 46 states to issue permits directly to the discharging facilities. The CWA also allows tribes to issue permits, but no tribes have been authorized by EPA. In the remaining states and territories, the permits are issued by an EPA regional office.

In previous legislation, Congress had authorized states to develop water quality standards, which would limit discharges from facilities based on the characteristics of individual water bodies.

However, these standards were only to be developed for interstate waters, and the science to support this process (i.e. data, methodology) was in the early stages of development. This system was not effective and there was no permit system in place to enforce the requirements. In the 1972, CWA Congress added the permit system and a requirement for technology-based effluent limitations.

Technology-based Standards

The 1972 CWA created a new requirement for technology-based standards for point source discharges. EPA develops these standards for categories of dischargers, based on the performance of pollution control technologies without regard to the conditions of a particular receiving water body.

The intent of Congress was to create a "level playing field" by establishing a basic national discharge standard for all facilities within a category, using a "Best Available Technology." The standard becomes the minimum regulatory requirement in a permit. If the national standard is not sufficiently protective at a particular location, then water quality standards may be employed.

Water Quality Standards

The 1972 act authorized continued use of the water quality-based approach, but in coordination with the technology-based standards. After application of technology-based standards to a permit, if water quality is still impaired for the particular water body, then the permit agency (state or EPA) may add water quality-based limitations to that permit. The additional limitations are to be more stringent than the technology-based limitations and would require the permittee to install additional controls.

Non-point Sources

Congress exempted some water pollution sources from the point source definition in the 1972 CWA, and was unclear on the status of some other sources. These sources were therefore considered to be nonpoint sources that were not subject to the permit programme.

Agricultural stormwater discharges and irrigation return flows were specifically exempted from permit requirements. Congress, however, provided support for research, technical and financial assistance programmes at the U.S. Department of Agriculture to improve runoff management practices on farms.

Stormwater runoff from industrial sources, municipal storm drains, and other sources were not specifically addressed in the 1972 law. The EPA declined to include urban runoff and industrial stormwater discharges in the NPDES programme and consequently was sued by an environmental group. The courts ruled that stormwater discharges must be covered by the permit programme.

A growing body of water research during the late 1970s and 1980s indicated that stormwater runoff was a significant cause of water quality impairment in many parts of the U.S. In the early 1980s EPA conducted the Nationwide Urban Runoff Programme (NURP) to document the extent of the urban stormwater problem.

The agency began to develop regulations for stormwater permit coverage, but encountered resistance from industry and municipalities, and there were additional rounds of litigation. This litigation was pending when Congress considered further amendments to the Act in 1986.

In the Water Quality Act of 1987 (1987 WQA) Congress responded to the stormwater problem by requiring that industrial stormwater dischargers and municipal separate storm sewer systems (often called "MS4") obtain NPDES permits, by specific deadlines. The permit exemption for agricultural discharges continued, but Congress created a nonpoint source pollution demonstration grant programme at EPA to expand the research and development of nonpoint controls and management practices.

To combat nonpoint source pollution, EPA initiated numerous programmes and grants to aid the public in improving their local water quality. These programmes are described at an EPA website, Watershed Central.

Financing of Pollution Controls

Congress created a major public works financing programme for municipal sewage treatment in the 1972 CWA. A system of grants for construction of municipal sewage treatment plants was authorized and funded in Title II. In the initial programme the federal portion of each grant was up to 75 per cent of a facility's capital cost, with the remainder financed by the state. In subsequent amendments Congress reduced the federal proportion of the grants and in the 1987 WQA transitioned to a revolving loan programme in Title VI. Industrial and other private facilities are required to finance their own treatment improvements on the "polluter pays" principle.

MAJOR STATUTORY PROVISIONS

The Act has six different titles.

Title I - Research and Related Programmes

Title I includes a Declaration of Goals and Policy and various grant authorizations for research programmes and pollution control programmes. Some of the programmes authorized by the 1972 law are ongoing (e.g. section 104 research programmes, section 106 pollution control programmes, section 117 Chesapeake Bay Programme) while other programmes no longer receive funds from Congress and have been discontinued.

Title II - Grants for Construction of Treatment Works

To assist municipalities in creating or expanding sewage treatment plants, also known as publicly owned treatment works (POTW), Title II established a system of construction grants. This was replaced by the Clean Water State Revolving Fund in the 1987 WQA.

Title III - Standards and enforcement

Discharge Permits Required

Section 301 of the Act prohibits discharges to waters of the U.S. except with a permit.

Technology-Based Standards Programme

Under the 1972 Act EPA began to issue technology-based standards for municipal and industrial sources.

- Municipal sewage treatment plants (POTW) are required to meet secondary treatment standards.
- Effluent guidelines (for existing sources) and New Source Performance Standards are issued for categories of industrial facilities discharging directly to surface waters.
- Categorical Pretreatment Standards are issued to industrial users (also called "indirect dischargers") contributing wastes to POTW. These standards are developed in conjunction with the effluent guidelines programme.

To date, the effluent guidelines and categorical pretreatment standards regulations have been published for 56 categories and apply to between 35,000 and 45,000 facilities that discharge directly to the nation's waters. These regulations are responsible for preventing the discharge of almost 700 billion pounds of pollutants each year. EPA has updated some categories since their initial promulgation and has added new categories.

The secondary treatment standards for POTWs and the effluent guidelines are implemented through NPDES permits. The categorical pretreatment standards are typically implemented by POTWs through permits that they issue to their industrial users.

Water Quality Standards Programme

Water quality standards (WQS) are risk-based (also called hazard-based) requirements which set site-specific allowable pollutant levels for individual water bodies, such as rivers, lakes, streams and wetlands. States set WQS by designating uses for the water body (e.g., recreation, water supply, aquatic life, agriculture) and applying water quality criteria (numeric pollutant concentrations and narrative requirements) to protect the designated uses. An antidegradation policy is also issued by each state to maintain and protect existing uses and high quality waters.

Water bodies that do not meet applicable water quality standards with technology-based controls alone are placed on the section 303(d) list of water bodies not meeting standards. Water bodies on the 303(d) list require development of a Total Maximum Daily Load (TMDL). A TMDL is a calculation of the maximum amount of a pollutant that a water body can receive and still meet WQS.

The TMDL is determined after study of the specific properties of the water body and the pollutant sources that contribute to the non-compliant status. Generally, the TMDL determines load based on a Waste Load Allocation (WLA), Load Allocation (LA), and Margin of Safety (MOS). Once the TMDL assessment is completed and the maximum pollutant loading capacity defined, an implementation plan is developed that outlines the measures needed to reduce pollutant loading to the non-compliant water body, and bring it into compliance. Over 60,000 TMDLs are proposed or in development for U.S. waters in the next decade and a half.

Following the issuance of a TMDL for a water body, implementation of the requirements involves modification to NPDES permits for facilities discharging to the water body to meet the WLA allocated to the water body.

As of 2007, approximately half of the rivers, lakes, and bays under EPA oversight were not safe enough for fishing and swimming. The development of WQS and TMDL is a complex process, both scientifically and legally, and it is a resource-intensive process for state agencies.

National Water Quality Inventory

Section 305(b) requires EPA and the states to compile a biennial Report to Congress on the nation's water quality.

Enforcement

Under section 309, EPA can issue administrative orders against violators, and seek civil or criminal penalties when necessary.

- For a first offense of criminal negligence, the minimum fine is $2,500, with a maximum of $25,000 fine per day of violation. A violator may also receive up to a year in jail. On a second offense, a maximum fine of $50,000 per day may be issued.
- For a knowing endangerment violation, i.e. placing another person in imminent danger of death or serious bodily injury, a fine may be issued up to $250,000 and/or imprisonment up to 15 years for an individual, or up to $1,000,000 for an organization.

States that are authorized by EPA to administer the NPDES programme must have authority to enforce permit requirements under their respective state laws.

Federal Facilities

Military bases, national parks and other federal facilities must comply with CWA provisions.

Thermal Pollution

Section 316 requires standards for thermal pollution discharges, as well as standards for cooling water intake structures. These standards are applicable to power plants and other industrial facilities.

Nonpoint Source Management Programme

The 1987 amendments created the Nonpoint Source Management Programme under CWA section 319. This programme provides grants to states, territories and Indian tribes to support demonstration projects, technology transfer, education, training, technical assistance and related activities designed to reduce nonpoint source pollution. Grant funding for the programme averaged $210 million annually for Fiscal Years 2004 through 2008.

Title IV - Permits and Licences

State Certification of Compliance

States are required to certify that discharges authorized by federal permits will not violate the state's water quality standards.

NPDES Permits for Point Sources

The NPDES permit programme is authorized by CWA section 402. The initial permits issued in the 1970s and early 1980s focused on POTWs and industrial wastewater—typically "process" wastewater and cooling water where applicable, and in some cases, industrial stormwater. The 1987 WQA expanded the programme to cover stormwater discharges explicitly, both from municipal separate storm sewer systems (MS4) and industrial sources. The MS4 NPDES permits require regulated municipalities to use Best Management Practices to reduce pollutants to the "Maximum Extent Practicable."

Non-stormwater permits typically include numeric effluent limitations for specific pollutants. A numeric limitation quantifies the maximum pollutant load or concentration allowed in the discharge, e.g. 30 mg/L of biochemical oxygen demand. Exceeding a numeric limitation constitutes a violation of the permit, and the discharger is subject to fines as laid out in section 309. Facilities must periodically monitor their effluent (i.e. collect and analyze wastewater samples), and submit Discharge Monitoring Reports to the appropriate agency, to demonstrate compliance.

Stormwater permits typically require facilities to prepare a Stormwater Pollution Prevention Plan and implement best management practices, but do not specify numeric effluent limits and may not include regular monitoring requirements. Some permits cover both stormwater and non-stormwater discharges. NPDES permits must be reissued every five years. Permit agencies (EPA, states, tribes) must provide notice to the public of pending permits and provide an opportunity for public comment.

As of 2001, over 400,000 facilities were subject to NPDES permit requirements.

Dredge and Fill Exemptions

After passage of the CWA in 1972, a controversy arose as to its application to agriculture and certain other activities. The Act was interpreted by some to place restrictions on virtually all placement of dredged materials in wetlands and other waters of the United States, raising concern that the federal government was about to place all agricultural activities under the jurisdiction of the U.S. Army Corps of Engineers (USACE). For opponents of the Act, section 404 had, as a result of this concern, become a symbol of dramatic over-regulation.

When Congress considered the 1977 CWA Amendments, a significant issue was to assure that certain agricultural activities and other selected activities, could continue without the government's supervision—in other words, completely outside the regulatory or permit jurisdiction of any federal agency.

The 1977 amendments included a set of six section 404 exemptions. For example, totally new activities such as construction of farm roads, Sec. 1344(f)(1)(E), construction of farm or stock ponds or irrigation ditches, and minor agricultural drainage, Sec. 1344(f)(1)(A), all are exempted by Statute.

Section 1344(f)(1)(C), which exempts discharge of dredged material "for the purpose of. . . the maintenance of drainage ditches." All of these exemptions were envisioned to be self-executing, that is not technically requiring an administrative no-jurisdiction determination. One such example was the maintenance of agricultural drainage ditches.

Throughout the hearing process, Congressmen of every environmental persuasion repeatedly stated that the over $5 Billion invested in drainage facilities could be maintained without government regulation of any kind. Senator Edmund Muskie, for example, explained that exempt activities such as agricultural drainage would be entirely unregulated. Other exemptions were granted as well, including exemptions for normal farming activities.

Importance of No-Jurisdiction Determinations

Despite the fact that Congress envisioned a set of self-executing exemptions, it has become common for landowners to seek no-jurisdiction determinations from the USACE. A landowner who intends to make substantial investments in acquisition or improvement of land might lawfully proceed with exempt activity, a permit not being required. The problem is that should the activity later be determined not exempt, the agency will issue a cease and desist order. Obtaining an advanced ruling provides some level of comfort that the activities will have been deemed conducted in good faith.

Recapture of Exemptions

Because some of the six exemptions involved new activities, such as minor drainage and silviculture (the clearing of forests by the timber industry), Congress recognized the need to impose some limitations on exemptions. Consequently, Congress placed the so-called recapture clause limitation on these new project exemptions. Under section 404(f)(2), such new projects would be deprived of their exemption if all of the following three characteristics could be shown:

1. A discharge of dredge or fill material in the navigable waters of the United States;
2. The discharge is incidental to an activity having as its purpose the bringing of an area of navigable waters into a use to which it was not previously subject; and

3. Where the flow or circulation of navigable waters may be impaired or the reach of such waters may be reduced.

To remove the exemption, all of these requirements must be fulfilled—the discharge, the project purpose of bringing an area into a use to which it was not previously subject, and the impairment or reduction of navigable waters.

Dredge and Fill Permits (Wetlands)

Under sections 301 and 502 of the Clean Water Act, any discharge of dredged or fill materials into "waters of the United States," including wetlands, is forbidden unless authorized by a permit issued by the USACE pursuant to section 404. Essentially, all discharges of fill or dredged material affecting the bottom elevation of a jurisdictional water of the U.S. require a permit from USACE.

These permits are an essential part of protecting wetlands, which are often filled by land developers. Wetlands are vital to the ecosystem in filtering streams and rivers and providing habitat for wildlife. Mountaintop removal mining requires a section 404 permit when soil and rock from the mining operation is placed in streams and wetlands commonly called a "valley fill". Pollutant discharges from valley fills to streams also requires an NPDES permit.

There are two main types of wetlands permits: general permits and individual permits. General permits change periodically and cover broad categories of activities, and require the user to comply with all stated conditions. General permits (such as the Nationwide Permits) are issued for fill activities that will result in minimal adverse effects to the environment.

Individual permits are utilized for actions that are not addressed by a general permit, or that do not meet the conditions of a General Permit. In addition, individual permits typically require more analysis than do the general permits, and usually require much more time to prepare the application and to process the permit.

When the USACE processes an application for an Individual Permit, it must publish/issue a public notice (typically in the Federal Register) describing the proposed action described in the permit application. The public notice must be issued no later than fifteen days after the Corps determines the application to be complete. Although the Corps District Engineer makes the decision to grant a permit, the EPA Administrator may veto a permit if it is not reasonable. Before making such a decision, however, EPA must consult with the USACE. A wetlands permit expires after five years.

When a state wants a permit, they make sure that all other states being affected are aware they will be sent a copy of the request and the state is able to write a recommendation. A state permit also expires after five years.

POTW Biosolids Management Programme

The 1987 WQA created a programme for management of biosolids (sludge) generated by POTWs.

Title V - General Provisions

Citizen Suits

Any U.S. citizen may file a citizen suit against any person who has allegedly violated an effluent limitation regulation or against the EPA Administrator if the EPA Administrator failed to perform any non-discretionary act or duty required by the CWA.

Employee Protection

The CWA includes an employee ("whistleblower") protection provision. Employees in the U.S. who believe they were fired or suffered adverse action related to enforcement of the CWA may file a written complaint with the Occupational Safety and Health Administration.

Title VI - State Water Pollution Control Revolving Funds

The Clean Water State Revolving Fund (CWSRF) programme was authorized by the 1987 WQA. This replaced the municipal construction grants programme, which was authorized in the 1972 law under Title II. In the CWSRF, federal funds are provided to the states and Puerto Rico to capitalize their respective revolving funds, which are used to provide financial assistance (loans or grants) to local governments for wastewater treatment, nonpoint source pollution control and estuary protection.

The fund provides loans to municipalities at lower-than-market rates. As of 2007 the average rate was 2.1 per cent nationwide, compared to an average market rate of 4.3 per cent. In 2006, CWSRF assistance totaling $5 billion was provided to 1858 local projects across the country.

Earlier Legislation

During the 1880s and 1890s, Congress directed USACE to prevent dumping and filling in the nation's harbors, and the programme was vigorously enforced. Congress first addressed water pollution issues in the Rivers and Harbors Act of 1899, giving the Corps the authority to regulate most kinds of obstructions to navigation, including hazards resulting from effluents. Portions of this law remain in effect, including Section 13, the so-called Refuse Act.

In 1910, USACE used the act to object to a proposed sewer in New York City, but the judge ruled that pollution control was a matter left to the states alone. Speaking to the 1911 National Rivers and Harbors Congress, the chief of the Corps, Brigadier General William H. Bixby, suggested that modern treatment facilities and prohibitions on dumping "should either be made compulsory or at least encouraged everywhere in the United States."

Some sections of the 1899 act have been superseded by various amendments, including the 1972 CWA, while other notable legislative predecessors include:

- Public Health Service Act of 1912. Expanded the mission of the United States Public Health Service to study problems of sanitation, sewage and pollution.
- Oil Pollution Act of 1924. Prohibited the intentional discharge of fuel oil into tidal waters, authorizing USACE to apprehend violators. This was repealed by the 1972 CWA, reducing the Corps' role in pollution control to the discharge of dredged or fill material.
- Federal Water Pollution Control Act of 1948. Created a comprehensive set of water quality programmes that also provided some financing for state and local governments. Enforcement was limited to interstate waters. The Public Health Service provided financial and technical assistance.
- Water Quality Act of 1965. Required states to issue water quality standards for interstate waters, and authorized the newly created Federal Water Pollution Control Administration to set standards where states failed to do so.

Recent Developments

Representative Frank Pallone introduced H.R. 1310, the Clean Water Protection Act, on March 4, 2009. The bill would amend the CWA by redefining the term, "fill material" to exclude "any pollutant discharged into the water primarily to dispose of waste." This amendment is intended to restrict the practice of mountaintop removal mining.

Senator Russell Feingold introduced S. 787, the "Clean Water Restoration Act," on April 2, 2009, to amend the CWA and clarify the jurisdiction of "waters of the United States." The intent of the bill is to restore protections for rivers, streams and wetlands that may be subject to question due to the recent Supreme Court rulings in SWANCC and Rapanos.

On December 3, 2009, Representative Donna Edwards introduced H.R. 4202, the "Green Infrastructure for Clean Water Act of 2009." The bill would create "Centers of Excellence" for green infrastructure (GI) research, establish a GI programme at EPA and authorize issuance of grants for GI projects. GI projects are designed to improve water quality through better management of stormwater runoff.

Representative James Oberstar introduced H.R. 5088, "America's Commitment to Clean Water Act," on April 21, 2010. The bill would restore the definition of "waters of the United States" to that in place before the SWANCC and Rapanos court decisions.

CHAPTER – 4

Purpose of Agricultural Drainage

The purpose of agricultural drainage is to remove excess water from the soil in order to enhance crop production. In some soils, the natural drainage processes are sufficient for growth and production of agricultural crops, but in many other soils, artificial drainage is needed for efficient agricultural production.

Surface drainage is the removal of water that collects on the land surface. Many fields have low spots or depressions where water ponds. Surface drainage techniques such as land levelling, constructing surface inlets to subsurface drains, and the construction of shallow ditches or waterways can allow the water to leave the field rather than causing prolonged wet areas.

Subsurface drainage removes excess water from the soil profile, usually through a network of perforated tubes installed two to four feet below the soil surface. These tubes are commonly called "tiles" because they were originally made from short lengths of clay pipes known as tiles. Water would seep into the small spaces between the tiles and drains away.

The most common type of "tile" is corrugated plastic tubing with small perforations to allow water entry. When the water table in the soil is higher than the tile, water flows into the tubing, either through holes in the plastic tube or through the small cracks between adjacent clay tiles. This lowers the water-table to the depth of the tile over the course of several days. Drain tiles allow excess water to leave the field, but once the water-table has been lowered to the elevation of the tiles, no more water flows through the tiles. In most years, drain tiles are not flowing between June and October.

Drain Tile Outlet to a Drainage Ditch

A drain tile is a specialized pipe used in a drain tile drainage system. This type of drainage system is used to pull water away from the footings and foundation of a structure so that the water cannot penetrate the foundation. Water seepage can damage a structure over time, in addition to being inconvenient if the water ends up in a location such as a basement. Many hardware and home supply stores sell several styles of drain tile, and it can also be ordered directly from manufacturers.

The installation of a drain tile system starts with digging a trench around the footings of a home. A filter barrier is laid in the trench, and a drain tile is laid inside before being covered with gravel and covered with another filter. The filters prevent dirt and silt from entering the trench and clogging it, while the gravel provides a filter for water. Water will naturally drawn to the gravel because it is easier for water to flow through the gravel than it is for water to move through the surrounding soil. Perforations in the drain tile allow water to enter the pipe.

The system also has an outlet, allowing the water which collects in the drain tile to disperse. The outlet may be connected to a sump pump if a structure is on level ground or it is lower than the surrounding ground, or it may simply drain freely if a house is built on high ground, allowing the water to flow into storm drains or to trickle harmlessly downhill.

This type of drainage system is used to control the water table. As long as the water table lies below the drain tile, the drainage system is not needed, because the water is too low to enter the structure. If the water table starts to rise as a result of an event such as heavy rain, the drain tile quickly brings the water level back down, keeping water away from the foundations and footers of a home. Drain tile is usually installed as part of the process involved in building the foundation, although it may require periodic maintenance and replacement.

It is important to confirm that the trench and outlet are not clogged with dirt and silt. If the gravel becomes packed with dirt, it will be harder for the water to move through, which will result in less water reaching the pipe, and water may start to pool around a home. This can result in water seepage.

A silt trap is a designated area where water that is contaminated with suspended sediment as a result of construction activity or water runoff is contained. While the water is in a silt trap, the sediment can settle to the bottom of the trap until it can be removed. Silt traps can be made using silt curtains, silt fences or a series of shallow ponds to naturally filter the sediment from the water before it reaches a stream or clean body of water.

Environmental protection efforts, such as the silt trap, are often seen in conjunction with mining or construction. Activity from these industries can result in the production of grain-size particles, stone dust and other components that create suspended sediment when caught up in water runoff during rainfall. As the rainwater carries these particles and other pollutants to streams, rivers and lakes, the suspended sediment can cause a serious issue for the fish and other wildlife that inhabit these waters.

The silt trap is designed to prevent the ecological disaster that could follow if these waterways were suddenly to become filled with suspended sediment as a result of mining or construction activity. Using the laws of gravity and the physics associated with liquid suspensions, the silt trap allows the denser, heavy particles of the suspended sediment to drop out of the suspension by creating an artificial break in the current. These particles are easily picked up by water runoff moving with a certain amount of speed, but when the water's current is slowed or completely eliminated by the silt trap, the heavier particles of sediment naturally drop to the bottom of the trap.

If left unchecked, silty soil and suspended sediment could travel long distances in fast-moving water. The potential for damage to aquatic wildlife is very great. By incorporating the silt trap into a mining or construction site, these industries can prevent unnecessary pollution or damage to the local watershed, thus helping the environment.

In some cases, the silt trap might also serve an additional purpose. Particularly in the mining industry, the silt trap becomes the last opportunity to reclaim precious metal ores that otherwise might have been lost. Settling tables, sluices and gold pans are time-tested methods of reclaiming gold, and these methods all work on the same principles as the silt trap. Many mining companies that produce ore in areas where precious metals are found might also regularly remove the accumulated sediment in their silt traps and process it to reclaim the precious metals that can be found.

DRAINAGE DITCH: PATHWAY FOR WATER TO FLOW

Excess water can erode landscaping, damage home foundation and create a very muddy and messy situation for a homeowner. To prevent water buildup and collection in a yard, create a drainage ditch that will naturally allow excess water to flow away from the yard and home.

A drainage ditch creates an avenue or pathway for water to flow, which corrects the issue of standing or collecting water. To create the best flow of water, the best angle for a drainage ditch is downhill or sloping to create a gravitational pull to flow the water away from the yard. A drainage ditch can be left with a gravel or stone bottom or can be planted with grass to disguise the ditch if desired.

Digging a Drainage Ditch

Remove grass, plants and vegetation from the path of the drainage ditch. Use the shovel to clear the top of the ground or a hoe to help remove tough rooted grass or plants.

Dig the drainage ditch using the shovel. When digging, place the removed soil into the wheelbarrow for use later, do not discard the soil. The ditch needs to be 1 foot wide and starting at 1 foot deep at the highest point of the ditch. As one progress in digging the ditch, it must slightly slope downward. Remember to keep the ditch sloping downward for proper drainage of water.

Line the bottom of the ditch with the large stones or large-sized gravel. If using gravel, make certain the gravel is big enough that the water can't move it and create a blockage. The stones or gravel will prevent the water from eroding the bottom of the ditch and enlarging or deepening the ditch.

Planting Over Ditch

Lay a flat, thin layer of landscaping cloth over the stone or gravel bottom of the drainage ditch. This step is only required if you plan to plant grass over the ditch to disguise its appearance.

Create a 1-inch layer of soil over the landscaping cloth. This soil can be new potting soil or can simply be soil that was removed when digging the ditch.

Seed the soil with grass seeds and water. The grass will grow over the drainage ditch. Because the ditch still has pitch and slope, water will flow away from the yard and home, but the drainage ditch will be less obvious in the yard.

OPERATIONS AND TIMING

On average, about two-thirds of annual precipitation is used by crops in the eastern Corn Belt. The rest falls at a time when it does not meet crop needs. Monthly precipitation remains fairly constant throughout the year, while evapotranspiration (a combination of evaporation from soil and transpiration from the crop), is much higher from June to September.

From January to May, and from October to December, precipitation is greater than evapotranspiration, creating a water surplus. The surplus results in excess water in the crop root zone and the need for drainage. Drainage is primarily a concern in the periods prior to the growing season (January to April) so that crops can be planted at the optimum time.

Even in humid areas, crop water needs often exceed precipitation in July, August and September. Although some of the moisture deficiency is met by stored soil moisture, irrigation can often increase yields.

Equipment Used

Designing and installing a drainage system is a complex process. Every field is unique and usually requires an individual design. Drainage depends on topography, crops that will be grown on the field, and soil type. Every soil type has different properties that affect its drainage. Agronomists and engineers have developed recommendations for drainage depth and spacing in specific soil types based on years of experience and knowledge of soil properties. Drainage contractors use these recommendations to design drainage systems that economically and effectively drain a particular field.

Equipment Used in Drainage System

Drainage plows that can be pulled by farm tractors are becoming more popular. But most farmers hire contractors to design and install their tile drainage systems because of the knowledge, skills and experience needed to install a successful system.

Potential Environmental Concerns

The major concerns related to drainage are:

- Loss of wetlands; and
- Increased loss of nitrate through tile drains.

Wetlands

Much of the Midwest landscape consisted of wetlands before large-scale drainage began in the 19th century. Although enormous public health and economic benefits have resulted from the draining of these wetlands over the last 150 years, there have also been negative impacts on the environment. Wetlands have an important hydrologic function in regulating water flow and maintaining water quality, as well as providing habitat for water-based wildlife. Recognition of their value has changed the way our society thinks about and protects wetlands.

Drainage improvements today are rarely for the purpose of converting existing wetlands to agricultural production. Improved drainage is usually aimed at making existing agricultural land more productive. Some fields have drain tiles that were installed 100 or more years ago, and are broken or plugged.

In many fields, only a few of the wettest spots were originally drained, while the entire field would benefit from improved drainage. More tiles are often added to improve drainage efficiency, with the goal of increasing production.

Poor Drainage

Water Quality

Drainage has both positive and negative effects on water quality. In general, less surface runoff, erosion, and phosphorus is lost from land that has good subsurface drainage than from land without drainage improvements or with only surface drainage.

Nitrate loss can be quite high from drained land. Because nitrate is very soluble, it flows easily through the soil and into tile lines. Nitrate flow from subsurface drains is one of the main sources of nitrate in streams and rivers in the Midwest. Concern about hypoxia, or low oxygen levels, in the Gulf of Mexico has increased concern about this nitrate source. Concentrations of nitrate in tile drains are usually quite high (10-40 mg/l).

Pesticides can also flow into subsurface drains, but usually only in very low concentrations. Pesticides move more easily in flow over the soil surface than through the soil, so the highest concentrations of pesticides in tiles are often in fields that have surface inlets into the drains. In fact, subsurface drainage may actually reduce pesticide loss to rivers and streams because it reduces surface runoff.

Best Management Practices

Traditionally, the goals of drainage were to:

1. Maximise crop yield and
2. Minimise costs of drainage installation.

Reducing water quality effects of drainage is becoming a third objective in drainage design.

Nitrate loss is the biggest water quality concern related to tile drainage. Several new technologies can reduce nitrate loss. Controlled drainage keeps the water table high during the off-season when crops are not growing. The high water table increases the rate of denitrification (a process that converts nitrate to harmless nitrogen gas (N_2) as soon as the saturated soil warms up in the spring) and reduces nitrate loss to the environment.

Controlled drainage can be combined with subirrigation to improve yields while protecting water quality. Subirrigation is irrigation back through the subsurface drain tiles. Subirrigation may be economical when fields are relatively level and need to be drained anyway, since additional infrastructure consists mainly of increased numbers of tiles the pumping system.

One system being developed in Ohio combines a wetland for water treatment and a pond serving as a reservoir for subirrigation with a drainage system. This system has been shown to increase yields and reduce water quality impacts of drainage, although it is costly.

TILE DRAINAGE

Tile drainage is an agriculture practice that removes excess water from soil subsurface. Whereas irrigation is the practice of adding additional water when the soil is naturally too dry, drainage brings soil moisture levels down for optimal crop growth. While surface water can be drained via pumping and/or open ditches, tile drainage is often the best recourse for subsurface water. Too much subsurface water can be counterproductive to agriculture by preventing root development, and inhibiting the growth of crops. Too much water also can limit access to the land, particularly by farm machinery.

In terms of access, most modern agriculture depends on the usage of large machinery—tractors and implements—to prepare the seedbed, plant the crop, carry out any cultivation and applications during the growing season, and ultimately, to harvest the crop. Operating most machinery in excessively wet conditions may result in soil degradation because of excessive soil compaction, and inhibit the operation of the machinery (i.e., "getting stuck").

INCREASED CROP YIELDS

Most crops require specific soil moisture conditions and do not grow well in wet, "mucky" soil. Even in soil that isn't "mucky" the roots of most plants will not grow much deeper than the water table. Early in the growing season when water is in ample supply, plants are small and don't require much water. During this time, the plants do not need to develop their roots to "reach" for the water.

As the plants grow and use more water during the growing season water becomes more scarce. During this time, the water table starts to fall. Plants suddenly need to start developing roots to reach to the water. During dry times, the water table can fall faster than the plants can develop roots to "reach" for the water. This can seriously stress the plants.

By adding drain tile, the water table is effectively lowered, and plants can properly develop their roots. The lack of water saturation allows oxygen to exist in the soil around the roots. Drain tile prevents the roots from being under the water table during wet periods that could cause excessive plant stress. By removing excessive water, crops use water they have more effectively.

An increase in crop yield can be simply summarized by the following: Simply by forcing the plants to have more developed roots, the plants can more effectively absorb more nutrients and water.

The same principal is employed by containers that hold house plants: they have drain holes in the bottom to allow oxygen to the roots, and prevent soil saturation. By placing drain tile under a field in a grid style layout, the same effect can be employed on a several hundred acre field.

PLUMBING OF DRAIN TILE

In a tile drainage system, a sort of "plumbing" is installed below the surface of agricultural fields, effectively consisting of a network of below-ground pipes that allow subsurface water to move out from between soil particles and into the tile line. Water flowing through tile lines is often ultimately deposited into surface water points—lakes, streams, and rivers—located at a lower elevation than the source. Water enters the tile line either via the gaps between tile sections, in the case of older tile designs, or through small perforations in modern plastic tile.

Soil type greatly affects the efficacy of tile systems, and dictates the extent to which the area must be tiled to ensure sufficient drainage. Sandier soils will need little, if any, additional drainage, whereas soils with high clay contents will hold their water tighter, requiring tile lines to be placed closer together.

Both Cato and Pliny have described tile drainage systems, in 200 BC and the first century AD, respectively. According to the Johnston Farm website, tile drainage was first introduced to the United States in 1838, when John Johnston brought the practice from his native Scotland to his farm in Seneca County, New York. Johnston labored to lay 72 miles (116 km) worth of clay tile on 320 acres (1.3 km^2). The effort paid off by increasing his wheat yield from 12 bushels per acre to 60 bu/acre. Johnston, "Father of American Tile Drainage", continued to advocate tile drainage throughout his life, attributing his success as a farmer to the formula "D, C, and D" (dung, credit and drainage).

The expansion of drainage networks was an important technical aspect of Westward Expansion in the 19th century. Although land in the United States was parceled out in accordance with the Public Land Survey System as established by the Land Ordinance of 1785, development, especially of agricultural land, was often limited by the rate at which it was made capable for cultivation. For example, although Iowa was made a state in 1846, maps depicting land ownership show below-average population densities in the northwestern region as late as the 1870s, a corner of the state that today is still noted for its high water table and numerous lakes, marshes, and wetlands.

States thoughout the region faced similar limits to agricultural intensification. Many states offered government incentives to improve land for farming. For example, legislation in Indiana prompted an Act of Congress in 1850 that provided for swamplands to be sold at a discount to farmers on the condition that they drain the land and bring it into agricultural productivity. To facilitate this process, most states set up government agencies to oversee and regulate the installation of tile drainage systems. Even today, ballots for elections in rural America often include candidates for local drainage supervisory boards.

The decades following the American Civil War saw rapid expansion of drainage systems. For example, historical literature from Ohio notes that in the year of 1882, the number of acres drained was about equal to the area of land drained in all previous years. In the 1930s, the Civilian Conservation Corps contributed to the tile network throughout the Midwest, much of which is still in use.

Advances in Drainage Technology

Throughout the twentieth century, the technology of tile installation remained similar to the methods first used in 1838. Although, cement sections later replaced the original clay tiles, and machines were used to dig the trenches for the tile lines, the process remained quite labor-intensive and limited to specialized contractors.

The introduction of plastic tile served to reduce both the cost of tile installation, as well as the amount of labor involved. Rather than set individual sections of cement tile end-to-end in the trench, tile installers had only to unroll a continuous section of lightweight, flexible tile line. Towards the end of the twentieth century, when large, four-wheel-drive tractors became more common on American farms, do-it-yourself tile implements appeared on the market.

By making tile installation cheaper and allowing it to be done on the landowner's schedule, farmers are capable of draining localized wet spots that may not create enough of a problem to merit more costly operations. In this way, farmers may enjoy increases in crop yield while saving on the capital costs of tile installation.

Perhaps the most useful implement in drainage history was James B. Hill's Buckeye Traction Ditcher, which laid drainage tiles at a record pace. Hill's ditching machine drained the Great Black Swamp in Ohio, vast stretches of Louisiana and Florida's swampland.

Effects of Tile Drainage

Unfortunately, the ability for farmers to install their own tile can be problematic. First of all, private installations may reduce the ability of local drainage supervisory boards to regulate tile installation, which in some areas of the country requires proper documentation before a contractor can continue. This leads to the second potential conflict, the unintentional interruption of existing tile networks.

Most "do-it-yourself" tile plows do not dig trenches but rather split the soil enough to squeeze the tile line in; thus, a farmer would not be aware if he breaks a line of tile that might serve his neighbors, as well Mutual tile lines are often dictated by topography rather than land ownership, and the location of many old, but still effective, tile lines are unknown. The potential for across-the-fence disputes are obvious.

Ecologically, the expansion of drainage systems has had tremendous negative effects. Hundreds of thousands of wetland species experienced significant population declines as their habitat was increasingly fragmented and destroyed. Although market hunting within the Central Flyway was a contributing factor in the decline of many waterfowl species' numbers in the early decades of the twentieth century, loss of breeding habitat to agricultural expansion is certainly the most significant. Early maps of midwestern states depict many lakes and marshes that are either nonexistent or significantly reduced in area today. Channelization, a related process of concentrating and facilitating the flow of water from agricultural areas, also contributed to this degradation.

In bypassing the natural flow of water from the surface to the water table, drainage systems often prevent the natural filtration of water provided by soils and wetlands. Thus, drainage systems pose a threat to surface water sources by directly depositing water laden with fertilizers, eroded soil, agrochemicals, and other types of agricultural runoff pollutants. In very flat areas, where the natural topography does not provide the gradient necessary for water flow, "agricultural wells" can be dug to provide tile lines sufficient outlet. In these cases, it is the groundwater that stands to be polluted by unfiltered tile output.

Intensive Livestock Operations (ILO) have led to challenges of livestock effluent disposal. Livestock effluent contains valuable nutrients, but the misapplication of these materials can lead to serious ecological problems, such as nutrient loading. Injecting effluent directly into the ground is one method employed by manure applicators to improve nutrient uptake. Drainage tiles may increase injected manure seepage into surface waterways from manure injection because liquid manure seeps through soils and then drains out of the field and into waterways via drainage tiles.

Today, a number of state and federal initiatives serve to reverse habitat loss. Many programmes encourage and even reimburse farmers for interrupting the drainage of localized wetholes on their property, often by breaking tile intakes or removing the tile completely. Land-owners are often partially or fully compensated for forfeiting the ability to grow crops on this land. Such programmes and the cooperation of land-owners across the country have had significant positive effects on the populations of a wide variety of waterfowl.

DRAINAGE RESEARCH

Drainage research is the study of agricultural drainage systems and their effects to arrive at optimal system design. Agricultural land drainage has agricultural, environmental, hydrological, engineering, economical, social and socio-political aspects.

All these aspects can be subject of drainage research.

The aim (objective, target) of agricultural land drainage is the optimized agricultural production related to:

1. Reclamation of agricultural land.
2. Conservation of agricultural land.
3. Optimization of crop yield.
4. Crop diversification.
5. Cropping intensification.
6. Optimization of farm operations.

Systems Analysis

1. A drainage system influences this depth; the relation between drainage system design and depth of water table is mainly physical and can be described by drainage equations, in which the drainage requirements are to be found from a water balance.
2. The depth of the water-table as a criterion factor needs to be translated into a criterion index to be given a numerical value that represents the behavior of the water table on the one hand and that can be related to the target (e.g. crop production) on the other hand.
3. The relation between criterion index and target can often be optimized, the maximum value providing the ultimate aim while the corresponding value of the criterion index can be used as an agricultural drainage criterion in the design procedure.

Crop Response Processes

The underlying processes in the optimization are manifold. The processes can be grouped into mutually dependent soil physical, soil chemical/biological, and hydrological processes:

- The soil physical processes include soil aeration, soil structure, soil stability, and soil temperature

- The chemical processes include soil salinity, soil acidity and soil alkalinity.
- The hydrological processes include evaporation, runoff, and soil salinity.

Examples of processes can be found in.

Field Data

In drainage research the collection and analysis of field data is important. In dealing with field data one must expect considerable random variation owing to the large number of natural processes involved and the large variability of plant and soil properties and hydrological conditions.

An example of a relation between crop yield and depth of water table subject to random natural variation is shown in the attached graph. The graph was made with the SegReg programme.

When analysing field data with random variation a proper application of statistical principles like in regression and frequency analysis is necessary.

Preventing Soil Salination

In irrigated lands, subsurface drainage may be required to leach the salts brought into the soil with the irrigation water to prevent soil salination.

Agro-hydro-salinity and leaching models like SaltMod may be helpful to determine the drainage requirement.

Groundwater Energy Balance

The groundwater energy balance is the energy balance of a groundwater body in terms of incoming hydraulic energy associated with groundwater inflow into the body, energy associated with the outflow, energy conversion into heat due to friction of flow, and the resulting change of energy status and groundwater level.

When multiplying the horizontal velocity of groundwater (dimension, for example, m^3/day per m^2 cross-sectional area) with the groundwater potential (dimension energy per m^3 water, or E/m^3) one obtains an energy flow (flux) in E/day per m^2 cross-sectional area.

Summation or integration of the energy flux in a vertical cross-section of unit width (say 1 m) from the lower flow boundary (the impermeable layer or base) up to the water table in an unconfined aquifer gives the energy flow Fe through the cross-section in E/day per m width of the aquifer.

While flowing, the groundwater loses energy due to friction of flow, i.e. hydraulic energy is converted into heat. At the same time, energy may be added with the recharge of water coming into the aquifer through the water table. Thus one can make an hydraulic energy balance of a block of soil between two nearby cross-sections.

In steady state, i.e. without change in energy status and without accumulation or depletion of water stored in the soil body, the energy flow in the first section plus the energy added by groundwater recharge between the sections minus the energy flow in the second section must equal the energy loss due to friction of flow.

In mathematical terms this balance can be obtained by differentiating the cross-sectional integral of Fe in the direction of flow using the Leibniz rule, taking into account that the level of the water table may change in the direction of flow. The mathematics is simplified using the Dupuit assumption.

The hydraulic friction losses can be described in analogy to Joule's law in electricity (see Joule's law#Hydraulic equivalent), where the friction losses are proportional to the square value of the current (flow) and the electrical resistance of the material through which the current occurs. In groundwater hydraulics (fluid dynamics, hydrodynamics) one often works with hydraulic conductivity (i.e. permeability of the soil for water), which is inversely proportional to the hydraulic resistance.

The resulting equation of the energy balance of groundwater flow can be used, for example, to calculate the shape of the water table between drains under specific aquifer conditions. For this a numerical solution can be used, taking small steps along the impermeable base.

The drainage equation is to be solved by trial and error (iterations), because the hydraulic potential is taken with respect to a reference level taken as the level of the water table at the water divide midway between the drains. When calculating the shape of the water table, its level at the water divide is initially not known.

Therefore, this level is to be assumed before the calculations on the shape of the water table can be started. According to the findings of the calculation procedure, the initial assumption is to be adjusted and the calculations are to be restarted until the level of the water table at the divide does not differ significantly from the assumed level. The trial and error procedure is cumbersome and therefore computer programmes may be developed to aid in the calculations.

Application

The energy balance of groundwater flow can be applied to flow of groundwater to subsurface drains. The computer programme EnDrain compares the outcome of the traditional drain spacing equation, based on

Darcy's law cum continuity equation (i.e. conservation of mass), with the solution obtained by the energy balance and it can be seen that drain spacings are wider in the latter case. This is owing to the introduction of the energy supplied by the incoming recharge.

Groundwater Discharge

Groundwater discharge is the volumetric flow rate of groundwater through an aquifer.

Total groundwater discharge, as reported through a specified area, is similarly expressed as:

$$Q = \frac{dh}{dl} KA$$

where:

Q is the total groundwater discharge ($[L^3 \cdot T''^{-1}]$; m^3/s),

K is the hydraulic conductivity of the aquifer ($[L \cdot T''^{-1}]$; m/s);

dh/dl is the hydraulic gradient ($[L \cdot L''^{-1}]$; unitless) and

A is the area which the groundwater is flowing through ($[L^2]$; m^2)

For example, this can be used to determine the flow rate of water flowing along a plane with known geometry.

CHAPTER – 5

Re-use of Drainage Water

Re-use is an important and natural method of managing drainage water. In order to develop the maximum benefit from a water supply and to help dispose of drainage waters, strategies for water re-use have evolved. Water re-use must be balanced against both short and long-term needs, with consideration for both local and off-site effects.

When talking about subsurface drainage it usually refers to lowering the water table in areas where rising water table brings salinity problems. You can either plant lots of trees to use up the excess water or dig deep drainage ditches to lower the water table. When talking about catching and treating surface run off water this refers to run off from Feed lots, animal pens/sheds, Silage heaps etc. This water is best disposed of through either evaporation ponds or special built wetlands where the nutrient load is removed by plants.

In regions where irrigation water supplies are limited, drainage water can be used to supplement them. However, the quality of the drainage water determines which crops can be irrigated. Highly saline drainage water cannot be used to irrigate salt-sensitive crops. It could, however, be re-used on tolerant forages or in a saline agriculture-forestry system.

Saline drainage water is being successively re-used for the irrigation of salt-tolerant crops and trees. Where an irrigation project is located near a natural wetland, the drainage water can be re-used in the wetland. However, precautions will have to be taken to ensure that the quality of the drainage water does not harm fish, waterfowl or other wildlife in the wetland and that the amount of water passing through the wetland is sufficient to prevent toxic concentrations from developing.

The major degradation factor of re-used waters is the high concentration of ions. Waters with low ionic concentrations provide plants with an adequate supply of many of the essential nutrients needed for growth. However, as salinity increases, specific ions may become toxic or interfere with the uptake of other nutrients. In soils, the accumulation of ions increases the osmotic potential against which plants extract water. It can also degrade soil structure.

Drainage and leaching of salts from the root zone are key factors in the management of salinity in agriculture. Another management factor is control of the range of salt tolerance expressed in crop species. Water re-use for agricultural crops has distinct economic incentives and a number of crops are known to be highly tolerant to salinity. However, as salinity increases in the irrigation water, there is a greater need to monitor and manage irrigation and drainage practices and to consider the sustainability of the system.

It is possible to safely re-use agricultural drainage water if the characteristics of the water, soil, and the intended crop plants are known and can be economically managed. Poor quality water requires selection of crops with appropriate salt tolerances, improvements in water management, and maintenance of soil structure and permeability tilth, hydraulic conductivity.

When sensitive crop growth stages such as germination and early growth are excluded, the temporal weighted mean root zone salinity has been found to be a valid measure for evaluating crop response to salt. The arithmetic mean root zone salinity within the rooting depth integrated over the time of exposure is an effective approximation for estimating crop response. Plants respond to the weighted mean salinity within a specific growth period.

EFFECTS OF SALINITY ON CROP GROWTH AND YIELD

Salinity in water or soil is an environmental factor that, in general, reduces crop growth. At relatively low salinity, especially among crop species such as cotton or the halophytic sugar beet, some salinity may actually improve crop production. This effect has been attributed in some instances to an improvement in water use efficiency of the plant. However, as salinity increases beyond some threshold tolerance, yield decline is inevitable. Usually, at low to moderate salinities, plant growth is simply reduced and there is a slight darkening in leaf colour.

These effects are difficult to detect without comparisons with non-saline controls. When salt concentrations in the soil water reach toxic levels, leaves or shoots may exhibit visible symptoms of tip or edge burning or scorching due to high internal concentrations of salts. Other visible symptoms may be associated with nutrient imbalances caused by competitive interactions between Na^+ and Ca^{2+} or K^{4+}, or between Cl^- and nitrate.

Interactions of salinity with nutrients such as PO_4^{3-}, Mg and micronutrients have also been reported, but these observations seem to be specific to certain crops and waters of specific ionic composition. Depending upon crop species and salinity concentration, salt in the crop root zone may also influence the rate of plant development by increasing or decreasing the time to crop maturity. In most crops, there are some notable differences in root/shoot ratio, a response that would not be identifiable in the field. In some crops, salinity changes plant growth habit or increases succulence.

There is a wide range in plant species response to salinity. Sugar beet, sugar cane, dates, cotton and barley are among the most salt tolerant; whereas beans, carrots, onions, strawberries and almonds are considered sensitive. In general, salinity decreases both yield and quality in crops, and previous research has led to the development of large data bases on the salt tolerances of many crop species and varieties.

Salt tolerance can be represented most simply based on two parameters: the threshold salinity (t) which is expected to cause an initial significant reduction in the maximum expected yield (Y); and the slope (s) of the yield decline. Slope is simply the rate that yield is expected to be reduced by for each unit of added salinity beyond the threshold value. The formula to calculate relative yields is:

$$YR = Y - s\,(EC_e - t) \text{ where } EC_e > t$$

The threshold value and the slope of the yield decline line for beans, corn, wheat and barley are shown to illustrate different crop responses in each of the broad tolerance classifications.

Usually, salinity is measured in units of electrical conductivity of a saturated soil paste extract (EC_e) taken from the root zone of the plant as averaged over time and depth. Soil paste extracts are water taken from soil samples which are brought up to their water saturation points.

Electrical conductivities are measured on the filtered water extracts from these samples in units of deciSiemens per metre (dS/m). For most natural waters, 1 dS/m is equivalent to about 640 mg/litre salts. New methods use electronic probes or electromagnetic pulses to estimate EC_e with less time and effort.

Where there is uncertainty in the determination of the t and s parameters in Equation 1, crops have been classified in a general range from sensitive to tolerant based upon available data. Crop salt-tolerance values and classifications are extremely useful in predicting the effects of re-using a water of a specific salinity on a particular crop.

Most salt-tolerance data are based upon the effects of saline waters predominated by sodium chloride, sometimes with varied amounts of calcium as needed to avoid the development of soil permeability problems associated with soil sodicity. Drainage waters or waters re-used from agricultural processing or manufacturing operations may predominate in other chemical species and/or have high concentrations of B, Se, As or other ions that may be environmental hazards..

AGRICULTURAL MANAGEMENT PRACTICES

Irrigation Systems and Scheduling

Traditionally, the goal of agriculture has been to maximize yield and profit, defined by the net difference between inputs and outputs. To maximize yields, soil salinity is reduced by leaching. The kind of management directed toward this goal is mediated by costs of water, drainage, applied nutrients and amendments to soils and waters.

Where water quality and/or quantity is limited and where there are restrictions on drainage, the hazardous effects of salinity on crop growth and the dangers of either insufficient or excessive leaching are serious concerns. However, crops can be grown with saline waters provided that suitable irrigation and cropping strategies are used.

Management needs to be more intensive and more precise methods should be used for water application and distribution. Water requirements needed for crop use and leaching should be accurately assessed and provided in a timely manner.

Most crop water use coefficients have been developed for non-saline situations. With saline water, growth and consumptive water use are reduced. However, preliminary evidence indicates that some crop water use coefficients may apply over a range of salinities because the water unused by the crop is needed to offset the increase in the leaching fraction requirement.

The greater the salinity of the irrigation water, the greater the need for adequate irrigation and drainage. Rates of salt accumulation in the soil are dependent upon the amount and concentration of the saline water applied and the amount remaining after plant water needs have been met. In a properly managed sustainable system, there may be a high salt content but no continuing accumulation.

Soil salinity is spatially and temporally non-uniform. Salinity often rises during the summer and then decreases with winter rains. This is a desirable condition which helps reduce permanent salt accumulation. However, under such circumstances, correlating yield responses to such variable salinity is difficult. Best management practices include land grading as a method to provide uniform surface irrigation, or the use of sprinkler or drip irrigation.

Crops irrigated with sprinklers are subject to injury not only from salts in the soil but also from salts absorbed directly through wetted leaf surfaces. In general, plants with waxy leaves are less susceptible than others. When saline sprays come into direct contact with leaf surfaces, salts can accumulate to toxic levels in leaf tissue and cause decreased yields. In tree and vine crops, the extent to which leaves are wetted can be minimized by sprinkling under the canopy.

However, even with under-canopy sprinklers, severe damage to the lower leaves can occur. The extent of foliar injury depends on the concentration of salt in the leaves, weather conditions and water stress. For example, salt concentrations that cause severe leaf injury and necrosis after a day or two of hot, dry weather may not cause any symptoms when the weather remains cool and humid.

As foliar injury is related more to frequency of sprinkling than to duration, infrequent heavy irrigations should be applied rather than frequent light irrigations. Slowly rotating sprinklers that allow drying between cycles should be avoided, as this approach increases the wetting-drying frequency. Sprinkling should be done at night or in the early morning when evaporation is less. In general, poorer quality water can be used for surface-applied irrigation than for sprinkler irrigation.

Drip irrigation gives the greatest advantages when saline water is used. Drip irrigation avoids wetting of the leaves with saline water and can be managed to maintain relatively high soil water potentials. As drip irrigation is normally applied frequently, there is a continuous leaching of the soil volume from which the plant extracts water. General leaching can be provided intermittently between growing seasons and it is supplemented by seasonal rainfall.

Leaching Requirement

In order to calculate the leaching requirement (LR), root zone salinity estimates are typically weighted to account for water uptake at different depths. The root zone may be conceptually divided by depth into four quarters, with a typical water uptake distribution pattern of 40:30:20:10 starting with the most shallow profile.

This assumes a 'normal' rooting distribution but modifications should be made according to the frequency or type of irrigation (e.g., drip, sprinkler, alternate furrow). Of the various methods, for calculating LR, the simplest is the equation proposed by Rhoades (1974) used in conjunction with salt-tolerance yield parameters:

$$LR = EC_i/(5EC-EC_i)$$

where ECi is the electrical conductivity of the irrigation water, and EC is either EC_e at t or at the acceptable yield level below t, and LR is the fraction of the irrigation water that must be passed through the root zone to control salinity.

Other Management Techniques

There are a number of cultivation and management methods which may offset yield loss when saline water is used for crop production. Some simple methods include: using more vigorous cultivars; using screens to select seed of larger size and higher seed weight; increasing population densities to offset smaller plant size and reductions in tiller number; and placing seed on sloped or modified seed-beds so that salts drawn to the surface by evaporation accumulate away from the seed line. Another way to move salts away from the seed or plant base is to irrigate in alternate furrows.

An additional method of ameliorating the effects of moderately saline drainage water is to match fertilization requirements with the chemical composition of the water and soils. As drainage waters often contain some of the essential fertilization requirements of plants, applied fertilizers can be reduced.

On the other hand, as ion interaction and competition reactions affect plant uptake, additions of calcium, potassium or some other element may be required for better crop growth. An important consideration is that high sodium concentrations in soils and waters may decrease soil permeability and prevent effective leaching of salts. The suitability of soils and waters is measured using a parameter called the sodium adsorption ratio (SAR). Soil amendments are sometimes a necessary part of salinity management schemes to reduce SAR. On the other hand, high EC (salt concentrations) of the water increase the soil permeability.

DRIP IRRIGATION

Drip irrigation, also known as trickle irrigation or microirrigation, is an irrigation method which saves water and fertilizer by allowing water to drip slowly to the roots of plants, either onto the soil surface or directly onto the root zone, through a network of valves, pipes, tubing, and emitters. It is done with the help of narrow tubes which delivers water directly to the base of the plant.

Drip irrigation has been used since ancient times when buried clay pots were filled with water, which would gradually seep into the grass. Modern drip irrigation began its development in Afghanistan in 1866 when researchers began experimenting with irrigation using clay pipe to create combination irrigation and drainage systems.

In 1913, E.B. House at Colorado State University succeeded in applying water to the root zone of plants without raising the water table. Perforated pipe was introduced in Germany in the 1920s and in 1934, O.E. Nobey experimented with irrigating through porous canvas hose at Michigan State University.

With the advent of modern plastics during and after World War II, major improvements in drip irrigation became possible. Plastic microtubing and various types of emitters began to be used in the greenhouses of Europe and the United States.

Usage of plastic emitter in drip irrigation was developed in Israel by Simcha Blass and his son Yeshayahu. Instead of releasing water through tiny holes, blocked easily by tiny particles, water was released through larger and longer passageways by using velocity to slow water inside a plastic emitter.

The first experimental system of this type was established in 1959 when Blass partnered with Kibbutz Hatzerim to create an irrigation company called Netafim. Together they developed and patented the first practical surface drip irrigation emitter. This method was very successful and subsequently spread to Australia, North America and South America by the late 1960s.

In the United States, in the early 1960s, the first drip tape, called Dew Hose, was developed by Richard Chapin of Chapin Watermatics which was established during 1964. Beginning in 1989, Jain irrigation helped pioneer effective water-management through drip irrigation in India.

Jain irrigation also introduced the 'Integrated System Approach', One-Stop-Shop for Farmers, 'Infrastructure Status to Drip Irrigation and Farm as Industry.' The latest developments in the field involve even further reduction in drip rates being delivered and less tendency to clog. In Pakistan it has been promoted by the Pakistan Atomic Energy Commission, the Agriculture Development Bank (ADB) as well as successive governments.

Modern drip irrigation has arguably become the world's most valued innovation in agriculture since the invention of the impact sprinkler in the 1930s, which offered the first practical alternative to surface irrigation. Drip irrigation may also use devices called micro-spray heads, which spray water in a small area, instead of dripping emitters. These are generally used on tree and vine crops with wider root zones.

Subsurface drip irrigation (SDI) uses permanently or temporarily buried dripperline or drip tape located at or below the plant roots. It is becoming popular for row crop irrigation, especially in areas where water supplies are limited or recycled water is used for irrigation.

Careful study of all the relevant factors like land topography, soil, water, crop and agro-climatic conditions are needed to determine the most suitable drip irrigation system and components to be used in a specific installation.

Components and Operation

Components (listed in order from water source).

- Pump or pressurized water source.
- Water Filter(s) - Filtration Systems: Sand Separator like Hydro-Cyclone, Screen filters, Media Filters.
- Fertigation Systems (Venturi injector) and Chemigation Equipment (optional).
- Backwash Controller (Backflow Preventer).
- Pressure Control Valve (Pressure Regulator).
- Main Line (larger diameter Pipe and Pipe Fittings).
- Hand-operated, electronic, or hydraulic Control Valves and Safety Valves.
- Smaller diameter polytube (often referred to as "laterals").
- Poly fittings and Accessories (to make connections).
- Emitting Devices at plants (ex. Emitter or Drippers, micro spray heads, inline drippers, trickle rings).
- Note that in Drip irrigation systems Pump and valves may be manually or automatically operated by a controller.

Most large drip irrigation systems employ some type of filter to prevent clogging of the small emitter flow path by small waterborne particles. New technologies are now being offered that minimize clogging. Some residential systems are installed without additional filters since potable water is already filtered at the water treatment plant.

Virtually, all drip irrigation equipment manufacturers recommend that filters be employed and generally will not honor warranties unless this is done. Last line filters just before the final delivery pipe are strongly recommended in addition to any other filtration system due to fine particle settlement and accidental insertion of particles in the intermediate lines.

Drip and subsurface drip irrigation is used almost exclusively when using recycled municipal waste water. Regulations typically do not permit spraying water through the air that has not been fully treated to potable water standards.

Fertigation

Because of the way the water is applied in a drip system, traditional surface applications of timed-release fertilizer are sometimes ineffective, so drip systems often mix liquid fertilizer with the irrigation water. This is called fertigation; fertigation and chemigation (application of pesticides and other chemicals to periodically clean out the system, such as chlorine or sulfuric acid) use chemical injectors such as diaphragm pumps, piston pumps, or venturi pumps.

The chemicals may be added constantly whenever the system is irrigating or at intervals. Fertilizer savings of up to 95 per cent are being reported from recent university field tests using drip fertigation and slow water delivery as compared to timed-release and irrigation by micro spray heads.

If properly designed, installed, and managed, drip irrigation may help achieve water conservation by reducing evaporation and deep drainage when compared to other types of irrigation such as flood or overhead sprinklers since water can be more precisely applied to the plant roots. In addition, drip can eliminate many diseases that are spread through water contact with the foliage.

Finally, in regions where water supplies are severely limited, there may be no actual water savings, but rather simply an increase in production while using the same amount of water as before. In very arid regions or on sandy soils, the preferred method is to apply the irrigation water as slowly as possible.

Pulsed irrigation is sometimes used to decrease the amount of water delivered to the plant at any one time, thus reducing runoff or deep percolation. Pulsed systems are typically expensive and require extensive maintenance. Therefore, the latest efforts by emitter manufacturers are focused toward developing new technologies that deliver irrigation water at ultra-low flow rates, i.e. less than 1.0 liter per hour. Slow and even delivery further improves water use efficiency without incurring the expense and complexity of pulsed delivery equipment.

Drip irrigation is used by farms, commercial greenhouses, and residential gardeners. Drip irrigation is adopted extensively in areas of acute water scarcity and especially for crops such as coconuts, containerized landscape trees, grapes, bananas, ber, brinjal, citrus, strawberries, sugarcane, cotton, maize, and tomatoes.

Drip Irrigation for Garden

Drip irrigation for garden available in drip kits are increasingly popular for the homeowner and consist of a timer, hose and emitter. Hoses that are 4 mm in diameter are used to irrigate flower pots.

The advantages of drip irrigation are:

- Minimized fertilizer/nutrient loss due to localized application and reduced leaching.
- High water application efficiency.
- Levelling of the field not necessary.
- Ability to irrigate irregular shaped fields.
- Allows safe use of recycled water.
- Moisture within the root zone can be maintained at field capacity.
- Soil type plays less important role in frequency of irrigation.
- Minimized soil erosion.
- Highly uniform distribution of water i.e., controlled by output of each nozzle.
- Lower labour cost.
- Variation in supply can be regulated by regulating the valves and drippers.
- Fertigation can easily be included with minimal waste of fertilizers.
- Foliage remains dry thus reducing the risk of disease.
- Usually operated at lower pressure than other types of pressurised irrigation, reducing energy costs.

The disadvantages of drip irrigation are:

- *Expense:* Initial cost can be more than overhead systems.
- *Waste:* The sun can affect the tubes used for drip irrigation, shortening their usable life. Longevity is variable.
- *Clogging:* If the water is not properly filtered and the equipment not properly maintained, it can result in clogging.
- *Drip* irrigation might be unsatisfactory if herbicides or top dressed fertilizers need sprinkler irrigation for activation.

- *Drip tape causes extra cleanup costs after harvest*: You'll need to plan for drip tape winding, disposal, recycling or reuse.
- *Waste of water, time and harvest:* If not installed properly. These systems require careful study of all the relevant factors like land topography, soil, water, crop and agro-climatic conditions, and suitability of drip irrigation system and its components.
- *Germination Problems:* In lighter soils subsurface drip may be unable to wet the soil surface for germination. Requires careful consideration of the installation depth.
- *Salinity:* Most drip systems are designed for high efficiency, meaning little or no leaching fraction. Without sufficient leaching, salts applied with the irrigation water may build up in the root zone, usually at the edge of the wetting pattern. On the other hand, drip irrigation avoids the high capillary potential of traditional surface-applied irrigation, which can draw salt deposit up from deposits below.

EMITTING PIPE AND EMITTER

A emitting pipe is a type of drip irrigation tubing with emitters pre-installed at the factory with specific distance & flow per hour as per crop distance.

An emitter is also called a dripper and is used to transfer water from a pipe or tube to the area that is to be irrigated. Typical emitter flow rates are from 0.16 to 4.0 US gallons per hour (0.6 to 16 L/h). In many emitters, flow will vary with pressure, while some emitters are pressure compensating.

These emitters employ silicone diaphragms or other means to allow them to maintain a near-constant flow over a range of pressures, for example from 10 to 50 psi (70 to 350 kPa).

Managing Cycling and Blending Strategies

Cyclic strategies for using waters of different salinities have been proposed and it has been demonstrated that cyclic irrigations can be successfully applied to crops during different growth stages or can be used with crop rotations between tolerant and sensitive crops. The feasibility of cyclic and blended applications of high quality water with drainage water depends on both supply and the availability of storage, mixing and delivery systems. Where non-saline waters are available for critical irrigations, growers can take advantage of the fact that many crops are most salt sensitive during the germination and seedling stages and are much more tolerant during later growth stages.

Plant salt tolerance varies with phenological growth stage, and beneficial effects can be obtained by managing irrigations to take advantage of this fact. For example, at salt-sensitive growth stages, salinity effects can be reduced by providing higher quality water or by minimizing salt accumulation through increasing the number of irrigation cycles. In some crops, higher salinities applied during the later stages of development will improve yield quality by increasing the content of sugars or soluble salts in the fruit. The timely application of saline water during fruit development has been used as a strategy to improve both sugar content in melons and soluble solid content in tomatoes.

In response to some moderate levels of salt and drought stress, fruit trees sometimes exhibit significant increases in fruit set and yield, but usually at a cost in subsequent years due to reduced biomass production. Another disadvantage may be decreases in shipping quality. The increasing salt stress delayed fruit maturation in 'Valencia' oranges but did not effect fruit quality. Their results also indicated that salinity had no effect on total soluble salts (TSS), but slight increases in TSS and sugar contents of 'Shamouti' oranges when the chloride concentration in the irrigation water was 450 mg/litre (m g/g).

For cyclic use strategies, factors that should be considered include the effects of changes in salinity during the growing season, the average salinity distribution in the root zone, the interactions with climatic variables, and the effects of different soil types. After crop establishment, the salinity in the root zone averaged over time may be considered as the effective salinity exposure.

This means that in most cases, once crops are established, there will probably be little measurable difference in a field situation as a result of applying 4 and 10 dS/m water in alternate irrigations applied over a crop cycle as opposed to using a water of 7 dS/m in each irrigation. This is the result of compensating factors in both soils and plants. Models are being developed to predict the effects of different irrigation water salinities during the growing season on crop yield.

Blending is the mixing of poor quality drainage water with good quality irrigation water. Provided that the blended water is sufficiently low in total salinity and toxic ions, this is the most economic and environmentally acceptable means of disposing of drainage water. This strategy can potentially increase the salinity of the groundwater over time. Often, separation of waters of different qualities is the best strategy.

Egypt has an extensive drainage water re-use programme. Over 4000 million m^3 of agricultural drainage water, produced in the upper Nile Delta, are re-used to supplement irrigation water requirements in the lower delta. Pumping stations lift the better quality drainage water into irrigation canals, where mixing occurs. The Ministry of Public Works and Water Resources has an extensive re-use quantity and quality monitoring programme.

Accessible and unpolluted freshwater is a necessity for every nation's stability and well-being. Yet, while the demand for freshwater continues to rise, its sources face increasing threats from salinization, a process whereby the salt content of fresh water rises until the water becomes undrinkable and unusable in agriculture: the more salt in the soil, the lower the crop yield.

Salinization is occurring globally for a number of reasons. Perhaps surprisingly, irrigation is a major cause of salinity. High rates of continuous evaporation and transpiration, caused by irrigation, bring salts up from deep in the soil, contaminating arable land. In dry regions, the change from forest to agriculture moves salt from groundwater into the soil. Finally, rises in sea-level are inundating agricultural lands along the coasts with seawater. Over fifteen years ago, a study found that of the 230 million hectares of land under irrigation, 45 million had seen an increase in salt: nearly 20 per cent of the world's irrigated land.

To confront this problem an article in Science recommends that researchers and governments invest energy and funds on saline agriculture, which proposes growing salt-water crops to feed the world. Approximately one per cent of terrestrial plans are able to grow in water with high salt content. Such salt-friendly species are called halophytes. The authors of the article, Jelte Rozema and Timothy Flowers, believe that many of these halophytes could become important crops, especially in areas where the salt content of the water is about half that of ocean water.

Halophytes grow as quickly as today's agricultural crops, but actually produce higher biomasses. Rozema and Flowers cite the example of Salicomia bigelovii, a species of halophyte that they believe could become an important oilseed crop. Yields of the species are 18 tons per hectare—fifteen times the yield of sunflowers. Such crops could not only be grown in brackish waters, they could also feed the world's growing population.

While the authors admit that "the use of saline water for irrigation is in its infancy", they see enough promise in saline agriculture that they believe it to be "worth serious consideration and development."

Removing the Salt from Iraq

Iraq is taking a different approach to its salinity problems. Historically, Iraq possessed rich agricultural land: the region between the Tigris and

Euphrates rivers was fertile enough to support the world's first major civilization, the Sumerians.

However, after centuries of irrigation, large areas of agricultural land in Iraq have become so inundated with salt as to be useless. To make these fields fertile again, Iraq is pumping out the salt-infused groundwater from six million acres. The process is time-consuming, laborious, and expensive, but has worked in places like Australia.

"It's a huge project: we are seeking to collect and drain all the salty water and remove groundwater from the center and the south (of Iraq)," Water Resources Minister Abdul Latif Rasheed said at the project's launch as reported by Reuters.

Once rich in food production, years of war, continued instability, and little environmental oversight has forced Iraq to import nearly all of its food. Drought has only worsened the problem. Last year Iraq received only a third of its usual rainfall, straining agriculture and water resources. Currently, the Iraqi government is forced to spend a large portion of its budget on food rations for the public.

Salinization particularly affects less-developed nations in arid regions, such as Pakistan, India, Egypt, Tunisia, Peru, Bolivia, and, of course, Iraq. Furthermore, the researchers warn that removing salt from agricultural lands as Iraq is doing may prove problematic, because the saltwater must be evaporated to ensure that it will not return.

Only one per cent of the world's water is fresh and humans already consume half of the readily amount available to us. Another one per cent of the world's water is brackish with salt content measuring somewhere between fresh water and sea water. The rest is seawater.

Solutions like Iraq's could be a temporary fix, but the problem may prove too large for such a laborious and long process. New ideas, like saline agriculture, may prove necessary to ensure ample water resources for the present and the future.

Re-use for Saline Agriculture and Forestry

Today, India ranks second worldwide in farm output. Agriculture and allied sectors like forestry and logging accounted for 16.6 per cent of the GDP in 2007, employed 52 per cent of the total workforce and despite a steady decline of its share in the GDP, is still the largest economic sector and plays a significant role in the overall social-economic development of India.

India is the largest producer in the world of fresh fruit, anise, fennel, badian, coriander, tropical fresh fruit, jute, pigeon peas, pulses, spices, millets, castor oil seed, sesame seeds, safflower seeds, lemons, limes, cow's milk, dry chillies and peppers, chick peas, cashew nuts, okra, ginger, turmeric guavas, mangoes, goat milk and buffalo milk and meat. India is also the largest producer of millets like Jowar Bajra and Ragi. It is second only to China in the production of rice. India is the 6th largest coffee producer in the world It also has the world's largest cattle population (281 million).

It is the second largest producer of cashews, cabbages, cotton seed and lint, fresh vegetables, garlic, egg plant, goat meat, silk, nutmeg. mace, cardamom, onions, wheat, rice, sugarcane, lentil, dry beans, groundnut, tea, green peas, cauliflowers, potatoes, pumpkins, squashes, gourds and inland fish. It is the third largest producer of tobacco, sorghum, rapeseed, coconuts, hen's eggs and tomatoes. India accounts for 10 per cent of the world fruit production with first rank in the production of mangoes, papaya, banana and sapota.

India's population is growing faster than its ability to produce rice and wheat. The agriculture-forestry system and solar evaporator are still at the development stage. The concept compares favourably with other intermediate disposal technologies. It manages drainage water as a resource instead of directly disposing of it into evaporation ponds, rivers or the ocean. Agriculture-forestry systems produce energy (biomass) while some other technologies for the treatment of drainage water have high energy demands.

By significantly reducing the final volume of non-re-usable drainage water, agriculture-forestry systems provide an opportunity for seasonal discharging of drainage water into rivers during high water flows. Solar evaporators are preferable from the standpoint of wildlife safety as they provide for better bird control than do evaporation ponds. The trees create wildlife habitats, reduce air pollution, and enhance the overall environmental quality of fanning regions.

The agriculture-forestry method has been developed and tested in California for salt management on irrigated farmland. It has two objectives:

1. To utilize the drainage water as a resource to produce marketable crops;
2. To reduce the volume of discharged drainage water directly on the farm.

The agriculture-forestry system for the productive use of drainage water and its disposal into a solar evaporator has been developed in semi-arid conditions in California and other regions. The main function of the trees is to use and evaporate large volumes of drainage water. This can be achieved not only through sequential re-use but also by uptake of the drainage water from shallow water tables, or by intercepting the flow of drainage water from upslope.

The trees can be viewed as biological pumps. The tree biomass offers a number of marketing options ranging from electricity generation to the production of biofuels or biochemicals. Drainage water is further concentrated through the irrigation of halophytes that also have marketing potential as food or industrial crops. The salt concentration in the drainage water in each succeeding stage is increased, but the volume of water is reduced.

About eighty per cent of the initial volume of drainage water produced while growing salt-sensitive crops is sequentially re-used to produce salt-tolerant crops. The remaining 15-20 per cent of drainage water, with increased concentration of salt, evaporates in solar evaporators. The design of the solar evaporator consists of a levelled area lined with a plastic liner on which the crystallized salt is collected. The daily amount of drainage water discharged into the solar evaporator is correlated with daily evaporation rates to prevent water ponding.

This makes the facility unattractive to wildlife. This is important as the concentration of Se has proven to be a hazard to wildlife. The agriculture-forestry system for the sequential re-use and reduction of drainage water volume can be viewed as the flow of water from salt-sensitive crops to salt-tolerant trees to more salt-tolerant halophytes and to a solar evaporator. The water flow is programmed and automated using a system of sensor-controlled equipment.

The agriculture-forestry system operating in California for sequential re-use of water and salt removal utilizes drainage water with an initial salt concentration of about 7000 mg/litre, following the irrigation of salt-tolerant crops. This concentration of drainage water has been conventionally disposed of into evaporation ponds, rivers and/or the ocean. The agriculture-forestry system concentrates salt in a significantly reduced volume of drainage water.

This technology offers management options of salt crystallization in a relatively small area on farms (solar evaporators) or the discharge of a reduced volume of drainage water (brine) into solar ponds or natural sinks (e.g., the ocean). The crystallization of salt in solar evaporators provides management options for salt marketing or its (short/long-term) storage on farms or designated landfills for storage in perpetuity.

The system for sequential re-use of drainage water is also effectively reducing the level of Se. A typical Se concentration is 0.5 mg/litre in drainage water applied to trees, and 0.9 mg/litre in the reduced volume of drainage water applied to halophytes. Consequently, the estimated quantity of Se is about 50 kg per 100 000 m^3 of drainage water applied to trees, and it is reduced to about 27 kg per 30 dam^3 of drainage water sequentially re-used to irrigate halophytes.

Selenium is reduced through volatilization and is also taken up by trees and halophytes. Selenium removal by trees is mainly concentrated in leaves, and the measured values (in terms of mg/kg) were 0.5-0.9 for eucalyptus, 0.6-1.0 for casuarina, 2.6-3.6 for athel, and 0.6-1.8 for halophytes. Successful experiments were conducted on the transfer of Se through harvesting halophytes and safely using this forage for cattle feeding.

The required level of investment for the development of marketing, storage and cold storage infrastructure is estimated to be huge. The government has not been able to implement various schemes to raise investment in marketing infrastructure. Among these schemes are construction of rural godowns, market research and information network, and development/strengthening of agricultural marketing infrastructure, grading and standardization.

The Indian Agricultural Research Institute (IARI), established in 1905, was responsible for the research leading to the "Indian Green Revolution" of the 1970s. The Indian Council of Agricultural Research (ICAR) is the apex body in agriculture and related allied fields, including research and education.

The Union Minister of Agriculture is the President of the ICAR. The Indian Agricultural Statistics Research Institute develops new techniques for the design of agricultural experiments, analyses data in agriculture, and specializes in statistical techniques for animal and plant breeding. Recently, Government of India has set-up Farmers Commission to completely evaluate the agriculture programme. However, the recommendations have had a mixed reception.

INDIAN AGRICULTURE POLICY

Indian agriculture policy is aimed essentially at improving food self sufficiency and alleviating hunger through food distribution. Aside from investing in agricultural infrastructure, the government supports agriculture through measures including minimum support prices (MSP) for the major agricultural crops, farm input subsidies and preferential credit schemes. Under the price support policy, MSPs are set annually for basic staples to protect producers from sharp price falls, to stabilise prices and to ensure adequate food stocks for public distribution.

In the past guaranteed prices have been below the prevailing market prices, according to the International Food Policy Research Institute (IFPRI) in 2007.At the same time subsidies on farm inputs including fertilisers, electrical power and irrigation water have led to inefficient use of inputs and indirectly subsidise income. IFPRI concluded that "support for agriculture from 1985-2002 has been largely counter cyclical to world prices".

Slow agricultural growth is a concern for policymakers as some two-thirds of India's people depend on rural employment for a living. Current agricultural practices are neither economically nor environmentally sustainable and India's yields for many agricultural commodities are low.

Poorly maintained irrigation systems and almost universal lack of good extension services are among the factors responsible. Farmers' access to markets is hampered by poor roads, rudimentary market infrastructure, and excessive regulation.

Analysis Low Productivity in India

The low productivity in India is a result of the following factors:

According to World Bank, Indian Branch: Priorities for Agriculture and Rural Development", India's large agricultural subsidies are hampering productivity-enhancing investment. Overregulation of agriculture has increased costs, price risks and uncertainty. Government intervenes in labour, land, and credit markets. India has inadequate infrastructure and services. World Bank also says that the allocation of water is inefficient, unsustainable and inequitable.

The irrigation infrastructure is deteriorating. The overuse of water is currently being covered by over pumping aquifers, but as these are falling by foot of groundwater each year, this is a limited resource.

Illiteracy, general socio-economic backwardness, slow progress in implementing land reforms and inadequate or inefficient finance and marketing services for farm produce.

Inconsistent government policy. Agricultural subsidies and taxes often changed without notice for short term political ends.

The average size of land holdings is very small (less than 20,000 m^2) and is subject to fragmentation due to land ceiling acts, and in some cases, family disputes. Such small holdings are often over-manned, resulting in disguised unemployment and low productivity of labour.

Adoption of modern agricultural practices and use of technology is inadequate, hampered by ignorance of such practices, high costs and impracticality in the case of small land holdings.

Irrigation facilities are inadequate, as revealed by the fact that only 52.6 per cent of the land was irrigated in 2003–04, which result in farmers still being dependent on rainfall, specifically the monsoon season. A good monsoon results in a robust growth for the economy as a whole, while a poor monsoon leads to a sluggish growth. Farm credit is regulated by NABARD, which is the statutory apex agent for rural development in the subcontinent. At the same time overpumping made possible by subsidized electric power is leading to an alarming drop in aquifer levels.

Indian agriculture began by 9000 BC as a result of early cultivation of plants, and domestication of crops and animals. Settled life soon followed with implements and techniques being developed for agriculture.

Double monsoons led to two harvests being reaped in one year. Indian products soon reached the world via existing trading networks and foreign crops were introduced to India. Plants and animals—considered essential to their survival by the Indians—came to be worshiped and venerated.

The middle ages saw irrigation channels reach a new level of sophistication in India and Indian crops affecting the economies of other regions of the world under Islamic patronage. Land and water management systems were developed with an aim of providing uniform growth.

Despite some stagnation during the later modern era the independent Republic of India was able to develop a comprehensive agricultural programme.

System Design and Planning

The design of a solar evaporator is fundamental to the development of an integrated agriculture-forestry system. The size of the solar evaporator is a function of evaporation rates typical for the farming region. The area of the solar evaporator is calculated by:

$$Ae = \frac{1000\ DW_h}{EV \times C_e}$$

where:

Ae area of the solar evaporator (m^2)

DW_h drainage water discharged from halophytes into the solar evaporator (thousand m^3)

EV annual evaporation rate (m)

C_e coefficient of evaporation, for reduced evaporation of saline water.

Further research data are needed to estimate the coefficient of evaporation (Ce). Experimental data indicate that the salt concentration in the drainage water discharged from halophytes into a solar evaporator ranges from 32,000 to 41,000 mg/litre. The final concentration of the crystallized salt exceeds 180 000 mg/litre. The major components of crystallized salt are SO_4^{2-} (56.70 %), Na (23.50%), and Cl^- (8.40%). The Se content ranges from 2 to 8 mg/kg.

The area of halophytes that can be grown is a function of the quantity and quality of drainage water recovered from the trees. Experimental data collected during a period of six years indicate that the increase of salt concentration in water drained from trees is about 2.8 times higher than of the drainage water (from conventional farm crops) applied to trees. This indicates that approximately 65 per cent of the re-used drainage water is consumed by trees. The applied 'tree' water (drained from farm crops) is typically EC 8-10 dS/m and the applied 'halophyte' water (drained from trees) is about 28-30 dS/m.

To maintain adequate control of soil quality, the leaching fraction (the percentage of the infiltrated irrigation water that percolates below the root zone) must be sufficiently high to prevent a build-up of salts, Se and B in the soil profile. The SAR should also be monitored.

An agriculture-forestry area of 16 ha has the capacity to process about 110 000 m^3 of drainage water per year. The size of a farm that can be serviced by the agriculture-forestry system (including solar evaporator) is a function of several factors, such as cropping system, quality of irrigation water, irrigation water management, soil salinity, and the use of trees for controlling groundwater conditions (water uptake from high water-tables or subsurface flows).

It is estimated that 30 ha of trees, halophytes and solar evaporator can utilize and process drainage water from about 1 000 ha of conventional farm crops. The 30 ha area would consist of 18.75 ha of trees, 7.5 ha of halophytes, and 3.75 ha of solar evaporator. The relative size of areas is as follows: irrigated area, 1 000 ha; trees, 10 ha; halophytes, 4 ha; and solar evaporator, 2 ha.

The management of biomass from the trees and halophytes is essential for the performance of agriculture-forestry systems and salt removal. The trees and halophytes need to be selected for their salt tolerance, which should range from about 9 000 to 18 000 mg/litre for trees and 18 000 to 41 000 mg/l for halophytes. The halophytes should preferably be perennial plants. The other required characteristics of trees and halophytes include: high water demands, tolerance to frequent flooding, frost tolerance, and marketability of harvested biomass.

Eucalyptus camaldulensis is the species of choice for this particular salt management system because of its salt tolerance and high water requirements. To improve the quality of eucalyptus trees for agriculture-forestry sites in the San Joaquin Valley, a selective breeding programme was initiated in 1987.

Selected trees have been systematically evaluated each year, and twenty two trees have been chosen for tissue culture propagation. The programme is seeking to achieve a higher diversification of salt-tolerant trees. Additional experimental trees planted include casuarina, athel, acacia, mesquite and poplar.

The selection of halophytes has been based on literature review, field evaluation trials, and a survey of salt-tolerant plants in California. These plants are being selected not only for salt management purposes, but also with a consideration for their biological interaction with conventional farm crops. This is to avoid introducing species that could be potential weeds or host plants for insect vectors or plant viruses.

Halophytes have been selected for salt tolerances ranging from an EC of 20 to 45 dS/m. Based on current field evaluations, the most promising plants include salicornia, iodine bush (*Allenrolfea occidentalis*), salt grass (*Dichtilis spicata*), and cordgrass (*Spartina gracilis*). Other promising halophytes include fivehook bassia (*Bassia hyssopifolia*), Jose tall wheatgrass (*Agropyron elongatum*), fathen (*Atriplex patula*), red sage (*Kochia americana*), Atriplex nummularia and Atriplex lentiformis.

Drainage, Water Management and Health

Proper surface and subsurface drainage to remove excess water in a safe and timely manner plays an important role in controlling water related diseases. Careful control and appropriate reuse of drainage water can help protect the environment and optimize the use of water resources.

The health issues related to drainage water management can be grouped in three categories:

1. water related vector-borne diseases;
2. faecal/orally transmitted diseases; and
3. chronic health issues related to exposure to residues of agrochemicals.

In tropical and subtropical regions there is a close link between the presence of excess water (due to lack of adequate drainage) and the transmission of water related vector-borne diseases. Malaria, schistosomiasis (bilharziasis) and lymphatic filariasis are important water related vector-borne diseases. Despite control programmes, health services and available treatments, these diseases today represent a growing health problem.

Water related vector-borne diseases are caused by bacteria, viruses and parasites (protozoa and helminths) transmitted by water related disease transmitting agents, also called vectors or intermediate hosts. A vector is an animal, often an insect, that transmits an infection from one person to another person or from infected animals to humans.

Most infections can only be transmitted by a particular, disease-specific vector, e.g., malaria by Anopheles mosquitoes. An intermediate host has a similar role to a vector. However, such an organism does not actively transmit a pathogen, like freshwater snails in the case of schistosomiasis. Vectors and intermediate hosts represent critical elements in various disease transmission cycles of parasitic water related diseases. In general, they live in or near aquatic environments.

Direct pathogen transfer and the transmission by vectors and intermediate hosts require specific environmental and socio-economic conditions. The conditions are defined by:

1. quality and quantity of water;
2. type and frequency of human-water contacts;
3. number and distribution of vector or intermediate host breeding sites; and
4. exposure of humans to vector and intermediate host populations.

Consequently, the above-mentioned diseases can also be associated either directly or indirectly with the design and management of treatment and disposal plants for the re-use, treatment or disposal of drainage water. The key criteria for such a health risk are:

1. introduction of temporary or permanent open water surfaces bodies, e.g., constructed wetland, stabilization ponds, or evaporation ponds;
2. suitability of such water for vector breeding;
3. accessibility for the local population;
4. location in relation to human settlements and transport links (e.g., roads); and
5. pollution by organic or inorganic substances.

Misuse and lack of maintenance are the two main reasons why drainage structures (road drainage ditches, culverts, dam site drainage or drainage canals in irrigation schemes, and also drainage water treatment and disposal facilities) are often associated with environmental health problems. Farmers, associations or national agencies generally conduct regular maintenance on irrigation canals. Water quality and flow velocity are relatively high. However, in drainage facilities the opposite conditions are frequent.

Silting, uncontrolled aquatic weed growth, slow water flow or stagnant pools associated with the resulting wetlands offer ideal breeding conditions for mosquitoes and aquatic snails. Farmers seem to concentrate on irrigation water management rather than on drainage management.

Moreover, there is often a lack of adequate domestic water supplies and sanitation facilities. Thus, drainage canals or drainage water treatment and disposal facilities are often misused for washing, drinking and uncontrolled disposal of human excreta or other waste by the poorest and, thus, most vulnerable social groups. In this way, drainage water contributes to disease transmission.

Although the eradication of diseases such as malaria has long been an objective, the problem is far from being solved. According to the most recent information. The malaria situation is serious and deteriorating. Global malaria mortality is estimated at 1.5-2.7 million and global malaria cases at 300-500 million. Malaria is one of the most serious health problems facing African countries and a major limitation on their socio-economic progress. Children under the age of five and pregnant women are most at risk. W.H.O. reports that 90 per cent of the global burden of this disease can be attributed to environmental factors, including land and water management.

Schistosomiasis is almost as widespread as malaria but rarely causes immediate death. An estimated 200 million people are infected and transmission occurs in about 74 countries. The infection is primarily common in children who play in water inhabited by the snail intermediate host. Water development projects, especially those associated with the irrigation of large areas, have often been associated with an increased incidence of schistosomiasis. Intestinal schistosomiasis was unknown or infrequent in the Nile, Senegal and Volta deltas before the construction of the Aswan, Diama and Alosombo dams.

Worldwide parasitic and infectious communicable diseases (including all water related diseases) caused 32 per cent of all deaths in 1993, resulting in the loss of 16.5 million lives; 99 per cent of reported cases occurred in developing countries. In these countries, parasitic and infectious communicable diseases cause 41.5% of all deaths.

Vector-borne Diseases: Transmission by Insects

Insect vectors represent the largest group of disease transmitting agents. In most cases and for the most widespread diseases, mosquitoes are the main vectors. Among a wide range of vector-borne diseases, two diseases, namely, malaria and lymphatic filariasis stand out as serious health hazards in the context of poor drainage.

Malaria

Malaria is caused by a protozoan parasite of the genus Plasmodium. Malaria is a complex disease causing fever, anaemia and an enlargement of the spleen. This causes additional cerebral complications, especially for children. Correspondingly, child mortality rates for P. falciparum, one of the four types of malaria affecting humans, are very high with approximately one million children below the age of five dying in 1993.

Malaria is transmitted by the bite of a mosquito of the genus Anopheles. The transmission cycle is only between man and mosquitoes. Man acts as the intermediate host or reservoir and the mosquitoes as the vector. Protozoan parasites of the genus Plasmodium have to undergo complex development and multiplication processes both in man and mosquito before they can be further transmitted. Only the female mosquitoes are of importance for transmission, as they need a blood meal for oviposition.

Malaria covers not only all developing countries, but is present on almost the entire land surface between the latitudes 40°N and 60°S. However, the distribution is not uniform and depends mainly on climate, altitude, population density and the specific environmental requirements of the mosquitoes species.

Highly endemic areas are sub-Saharan Africa, Central America and the northern part of South America, the Indian subcontinent and Southeast Asia.

In the last two decades, a growing number of malaria cases have been observed. However, this cannot only be explained by the increasing population. To a large extent, this is also due to the increasing number of WRDPs such as irrigation and drainage schemes or hydro-electric dams. With the introduction of new open water surfaces in the form of canals, ponds and artificial lakes, new mosquito breeding sites have been created.

However, the persistence of the disease is also due to the absence of effective long-lasting vaccines, and the growing resistance of malaria pathogens and mosquitoes to treatment and insecticides, respectively. By the end of 1985, 50 of the 150 potential malaria transmitting Anopheles species were already recorded to be resistant to one or more pesticides (including DDT). At least 11 of those 50 species are known to be important and dangerous malaria transmitters.

Furthermore, malaria transmission is not only related to WRDPs. Deforestation, mining, road construction and all the negative consequences of rapid and uncontrolled urbanization are also contributing to the creation of mosquito breeding sites. In this context, urban drainage plays two key roles. On the one hand, it is an essential and effective tool for reducing and eliminating mosquito breeding sites by controlling surface water and waterlogging and by eliminating unnecessary open water surfaces. However, on the other hand poorly maintained drainage canals can represent potential breeding sites for various mosquito species if they are permanently flooded and aquatic weeds are not cleared.

Finally, a fresh risk might result from climatic change. First reports suggest that global warming can change the geographical distribution of mosquito breeding and shift the malaria transmission border line to the north.

Lymphatic Filariasis

Mosquito-borne filariasis includes a group of diseases which lead to inflammations and obstructive lesions of the lymphatic system. Filarial parasites are nematode worms, which also need an insect to complete their life cycle. The main disease is Wuchereria bancrofti or elephantiasis and is transmitted by mosquitoes of the genera Culex. During a bite, a mosquito might take up a number of microfilariae which then undergo a development cycle in the mosquito. When the infected mosquito bites again, the infectious larvae enter first the skin and then the lymph vessels and lymph glands.

Unlike malaria, filarial infection requires repeated and lengthy exposure to the vector due to the low pathogen load per bite. For *W. bancrofti,* long exposure to repeated infection will finally lead to severe and disfiguring deformities of the legs, arms and genitals. Lymphatic filariasis affected about 120 million people in 1994; 80 % of cases were reported either from tropical Africa or India.

Although filariasis is more of a serious urban health problem, it can cause significant health hazard in rural settlements and farming communities where poor surface drainage, lack of sanitation facilities and environmental pollution through uncontrolled waste and excreta disposal are prevalent. The principal vector, *Culex quinquefasciatus* (fatigans), breeds in polluted water in ditches, drains, tanks, barrels, tins and any kind of water accumulation container.

Mosquito Bionomics

There are more than 3 000 known mosquito species. However, of the 150 species that are potential vectors, only 30 are considered dangerous. The three genera Anopheles, Aedes and Culex, from three sub-families, are disease relevant.

The epidemiology and the life cycle stages demonstrate the importance of climatic factors and that water is the essential environmental component for mosquitoes. The immature stages such as eggs, larvae and pupae require an aquatic environment, whereas adult mosquitoes live in terrestrial ecosystems. The quality and quantity of water, whether it is running or standing, shallow or deep, clean or polluted, sweet or brackish, shaded or sunlit, permanent or seasonal, and finally the climate will determine which particular species can breed. A summary of the physical and biological factors is given below.

Physical Factors

In general mosquitoes prefer higher air humidity and average water temperatures between 23°C and 33°C in order to complete their aquatic stages within two weeks. Rainfall can be a limiting as well as a positive factor. Rain will fill ditches, rivers, ponds, etc., but heavy rain can have a flooding effect and flush out breeding places. Mosquitoes do not normally reproduce where excess water is quickly removed. Sunlight or shade can also be positive or negative depending on the species. All these factors also determine the resting and biting habits. Some species rest and feed indoors and/or outdoors. Peak biting activity is usually about one hour before dawn. However, Aedes is a daytime biter, and many Anopheles bite throughout the night.

Biological Factors

The presence of vegetation and floating plants are important for optimal breeding conditions. First, the plants are larval food and, more importantly, they provide shelter from predators and protection against wave movement. Therefore, mosquito larvae are not found on the open surfaces of large water bodies. The abundance of a number of species is linked to the presence of specific plants.

As a group, mosquitoes breed in an almost infinite variety of sizes, types and qualities of water bodies and each species requires specific environmental breeding and living conditions. However, most of the mosquito vectors breed in a rather restricted and narrow range of habitats.

It is the number of potential transmitting species and their population dynamics which makes control efforts difficult. A comprehensive classification by species, country and habitat, including potential environmental management measures, is presented in the Manual on Environmental Management for Mosquito Control.

Natural biological control of mosquitoes can be accomplished with larvivorous fish. Over 250 different species of such fish are known to consume mosquito larvae.

The most common mosquito fish is Gambusia affinis which is found in about 60 countries. Mosquito fish can be propagated commercially and introduced into drainage water. The fish are most effective during the warmer months of the year.

Water-based Diseases: Transmission by Aquatic and Semi-aquatic Snails

Schistosomiasis

There are three major types of schistosomiasis that affect man: *S. haematobium, S. mansoni* and *S. japonicum*. The disease is caused by female and male trematode worms inhabiting the blood vessels of the urinary bladder (*S. haematobium, S. japonicum*) or the portal and mesenteric veins (*S. mansoni*). Typical visible symptoms of schistosomiasis infection are blood in the urine in the case of *S. haematobium*, and intermittent diarrhoea and faeces containing blood in the case of *S. mansoni*. Although effective chemotherapy is available, the costs per treatment and per caput make it too expensive for many developing countries.

The transmission of all three species is based on a complex four-phase cycle which includes the presence of freshwater snails. Eggs expelled in the urine or faeces of an infected person may reach water, where they hatch rapidly into miracidia, a free-swimming brief larval stage. Depending on the species, the miracidia have to find a specific aquatic or semi-aquatic freshwater snail as intermediate host within one day.

S. haematobium, S. mansoni and S. japonicum require snails of the genera Bulinus, Biomphalaria and Oncomelania, respectively. Oncomelania are semi-aquatic snails that live part of the time outside water in moist soil or mud. In the snails, the parasites develop within four two six weeks into cercariae, a second free-swimming larval stage. It is at this stage that they are infectious for man. Snails shed numerous cercariae into the water. These have to find human beings in contact with water in order to penetrate their skin. Having penetrated the skin of the host, the parasites find their way through the veins, heart and lungs to the final organ, there recommencing the cycle with egg production.

Bionomics of Snail Intermediate Hosts

Although individual snail species require a specific physical environment, the variety of aquatic habitats is almost infinite. Marshes and swamps, permanent or temporary ponds and pools, natural or man-made freshwater lakes or reservoirs, seasonal or permanent or slow flowing river streams, irrigation or drainage canals, rice fields and all other types of standing, slow flowing or impounded water are potential snail breeding sites. Generally, the water needs to be shallow, clean or brackish, with little turbidity. The duration of the life cycle depends on water temperatures. The ideal water temperature ranges from 26° C to 28 °C.

Snail intermediate hosts of both S. haematobium and S. mansoni show great tolerance regarding pH values (5.3-9), mean water temperatures (18°-30°C) and salinity. Snails are found in shaded water bodies but are also known to be active when exposed to direct sunlight. The shedding of cercariae correlates with day-time and thus the intensity of sunlight.

Furthermore, snails have a remarkable capability to survive long periods (5-8 months) in moist sand or mud (aestivation). Their main source of food is organic matter originating from decaying submerged or emerged vegetation, different species of algae, bacteria and fungi.

However, both of these aquatic snail species are sensitive to water velocity and water table fluctuations. Tolerable average current speed ranges between 0.0-0.3 m/s. In natural rivers, snails are generally dislodged due to turbulence and fleeting shear stresses along the transition zone between the embankment vegetation and the river bed sediments, which are their actual habitat zone.

WATER-BORNE EXCRETA RELATED INFECTIONS

Most of the aquatic vector or intermediate host habitats correspond to sites where humans access water for washing, bathing, swimming (mainly children) or fishing.

A classification of water-borne diseases in order to more fully understand the effects of excreta disposal:

1. *Faecal-oral diseases (non-bacterial)*: Infections transmitted from person to person due to domestic contamination and lack of personal hygiene. Examples: hepatitis A, giardiasis.
2. *Faecal-oral (bacterial)*: Person-to-person transmission with longer transmission cycles either through contaminated food, crops or water contaminated with faecal material. Examples: Various diarrhoeas and dysenteries like cholera, E. coli diarrhoea or salmonellosis, enteric fevers such as typhoid.
3. *Soil transmitted helminths*: Eggs of parasitic worms are expelled in faeces and require a development stage in moist soils. They reach the human host either by being ingested on vegetables or by penetrating the soles of the feet. Transmission takes place in communal defecation areas or around dirty latrines without clean concrete floors. Examples: ascariasis, trichuriasis, hookworm.
4. *Beef and pork tapeworms*: Transmission cycle includes an intermediate development stage in an animal and infection of man occurs when the meat is eaten without sufficient cooking. Transmission can be

triggered through the application of sewage sludge as fertilizer on grazing land. Examples: taeniasis.

5. *Water-based helminths*: The most typical example is that presented above in the section on schistosomiasis. As indicated, eggs in faeces must reach water in order to undergo the next development stage in an aquatic snail. The guinea worm (fasciolopsiasis) follows a similar cycle.

6. *Excreta related insect vectors*: Filariasis transmitting Culex mosquitoes prefer to breed in highly polluted water. Badly maintained, unventilated latrines or uncovered septic tanks offer the best breeding conditions, mainly in urban areas. However, filariasis may also reach man simply by being carried by flies or cockroaches.

An important characteristic is the persistence of a specific pathogen, i.e., its ability to survive in the environment and whether animals, either in series or parallel, are part of the transmission cycle in view of the above classification, water quality and the environmental conditions around water bodies can be seen to play an essential role in the transmission.

Thus, unlined open drains, stabilization and evaporation ponds or wetlands might become particularly dangerous transmission sites. It is at such sites that excreta disposal, animal feeding and human water contacts might occur in a concentrated and uncontrolled form, so leading to the necessary pathogen-man/animal contacts.

Health Risks and Chemical Pollution

Health risks related to water quality, primarily due to agrochemicals, represent a growing problem. This is mainly due to the intensified production and the expansion of irrigated agriculture, often in association with food processing industries. In this context, both subsurface and open drains can have an impact on human health on four levels:

1. Drainage water re-use. Leaching or surface runoff from fields treated with pesticides, e.g., herbicides, fungicides, insecticides or molluscicides, represents a non-point source of toxic organic substances. If re-used as irrigation water, toxic substances can be ingested by individuals directly or indirectly in the case of drainage water being mixed with drinking water resources.

Another source of direct water contamination with agrochemicals is the washing of spraying equipment in open drains or irrigation canals or the spraying of irrigation canals and reservoirs against aquatic weeds. Leaching also includes the transport of inorganic substances like salts, nitrate, phosphorus or heavy metals. Such substances can lead to health problems if consumed in high enough doses. However, salt will be less of a health problem as a salty taste will prohibit individuals from drinking too much salt polluted water. Trace elements are more of a concern in the case of subsurface drainage water.

2. Drainage water treatment and disposal. As outlined in earlier chapter, both lead to an accumulation, a transfer or a transition of pollutants. In addition, treatment facilities such as constructed wetlands or stabilization ponds introduce new and permanent open water surfaces, and aquatic weed growth. Here, the question is whether this will change the human-water contact patterns and create new vector breeding sites. Furthermore, the quality of inadequately treated drainage water might also represent a potential health risk.
3. The application of insecticides or molluscicides during chemical vector control campaigns. This can lead to short-term high concentrations of toxic chemicals in irrigation or drainage canals. Unprotected workers are exposed to health risks and local populations might consume polluted water without being aware of the risks. Indirect contamination might occur through the ingestion of fish.
4. Uncontrolled disposal of industrial liquid waste in drainage canals or treatment and disposal systems. Due to the lack of environmental regulations and proper treatment plants, especially in urban areas, drains often serve as liquid waste disposal sites for local industries, thus representing dangerous point sources of toxic substances.

Although, health risks arising from chemical pollution are accepted as a major environmental concern, data on medical implications are difficult to obtain and often unavailable for developing countries. Due to the lack of environmental protection and regulation standards as well as the lack of environmental monitoring data, governmental services often neglect the issue of pollution control.

Components of Integrated Control Approaches

Control of water related diseases always requires the interruption of transmission cycles, which include a number of quite different actors: man, animals, or vectors. These all have different functions, react differently to environmental changes and have different capacities in either transmitting a disease or in resisting infection. There are basically three ways to disrupt transmission:

1. By eliminating or reducing vector densities;

2. By protecting the susceptible host through immunization, prophylactic drugs, reduced man-vector contacts using repellents, window screening, bed nets, or by installing adequate water supplies and sanitation facilities; and
3. By reducing the reservoir of infection, by treating infected people or animals and by eliminating the pathogen in the host body.

Therefore, an effective and integrated disease and vector control strategy has to integrate four basic elements chemical vector control, biological vector control, environmental management, and medical treatment. Figure 10 presents an example of an integrated approach to controlling schistosomiasis.

Medical treatment is still considered as most important. In fact most research and financial resources are focused on medical or bio-medical issues. However, it is clear from the magnitude of the present health problems, the increasing number and spread of diseases and the close environmental interactions set forth above, that any intervention can only be successful when all four elements are integrated.

This requires all parties involved to have a sound understanding of all environmental, social, economic and bio-medical implications of the epidemiological dynamics of water related disease transmission.

The core of such an approach can be reduced to the formula: transmission and morbidity control. Transmission control combines chemical, biological and environmental management control of vectors, intermediate hosts, or any activity in the field of water supply, sanitation facilities and water treatment. Morbidity control includes chemotherapy or any medical control of the pathogen and the treatment of the disease. The environmental management component as a vehicle having hygiene education and community participation as wheels rolling on the road of basic infrastructure.

Environmental Management for Vector Control

In 1979, WHO, FAO and UNEP established the Panel of Experts for Environmental Management (PEEM). The aim was to better introduce and develop the environmental management component in the context of vector and disease control. Attached to the panel are thirteen collaborating centres. These are research institutes working in the field of either bio-medical or engineering related topics of tropical disease control. PEEM defines environmental management as all technical and managerial interventions which modify and/or manipulate environmental factors and their interaction with man and vectors.

The overall objectives are to prevent or minimize vector propagation and to reduce man-vector-pathogen contacts in order to achieve an optimal health status for a target population. In 1979, the WHO Expert Committee on Vector Biology and Control defined three categories of environmental management for vector control as shown in Table given below.

Chemical vector control would include the application of repellents, attractants, insecticides, molluscicides and chemosterilants. Biological vector control can be achieved by the release of predators and microbial insecticides and by genetic manipulation. Finally, the medical interventions would focus on morbidity control, such as chemotherapy, vaccines, general treatment, improved nutrition, preventive health safeguards, prophylaxis and health education.

Environmental Management Measures

In the context of drainage water re-use, treatment and disposal, the potential health risks can be analysed within a simplified system of drainage water flow in combination with the transfer of pathogens, toxic substances and the occurrence of potential vector breeding sites. This allows one to differentiate whether a health risk is related to water quality, vector breeding or both.

For each of the three drainage water management options, a number of questions are formulated to identify potential health risks. These are followed by a range of recommendations for possible control and preventive measures.

Drainage Water Treatment, Re-use and Disposal

Direct re-use

At first glance, re-use may appear to be a water quality problem mainly regarding high salt concentrations which can affect plant growth. However, pesticides in different forms can be washed into surface drains and trace elements can be leached out by subsurface drains.

Where drainage water with high loads of pesticides and trace elements is re-used for irrigation, a health risk can occur for irrigation workers or for persons using this water for domestic purposes.

Questions:

1. What is the quality of the drainage water? Is the drainage water used directly or blended with high quality water? What are the maximum loads of toxic substances after the blending? Are there seasonal changes in concentration according to agricultural management schedules?
2. How do individuals or social groups come into contact with irrigation water blended with re-used drainage water? Do people

use this irrigation water for any other purposes such as drinking, washing or cooking? Are children in frequent contact with the water?

3. Are there any other risks? Can polluted water enter other hydrological cycles with high quality freshwater (e.g., groundwater), which will then be used for drinking?

Control and Prevention

In the case of direct re-use, there are few opportunities for the application of environmental management measures. Once drainage water has entered an irrigation system, it is probable that individuals will come into contact with this water. Therefore, effective monitoring of the quality standards of drainage effluents is most important. It is necessary to develop safeguard strategies in case of unacceptable or dangerous contamination levels.

Agriculture-forestry System and Solar Evaporators

This system of drainage water management, which aims at a continuous concentration of salt in progressively smaller volumes of water, is less of a health risk, as saline water is unsuitable for drinking. Here, the question is whether this series of irrigation systems will create new open water surfaces for vector breeding.

CHAPTER – 6

Water-Logging and Salinity

Waterlogging refers to the saturation of soil with water. Soil may be regarded as waterlogged when the water table of the groundwater is too high to conveniently permit an anticipated activity, like agriculture.

WATERLOGGING IN AGRICULTURE

In agriculture, various crops need air (specifically, oxygen) to a greater or lesser depth in the soil. Waterlogging of the soil stops air getting in. How near the water table must be to the surface for the ground to be classed as waterlogged, varies with the purpose in view. A crop's demand for freedom from waterlogging may vary between seasons of the year, as with the growing of rice.

Waterlogging is too much water in the root zone of a plant. The roots cannot absorb enough oxygen to breathe, so the plant stops growing within a few days and may die. Other gases, such as carbon dioxide and ethylene, may also accumulate around and affect the plants.

Inundation is water ponding on the ground surface. Those parts of the plant that are submerged cannot breathe or photosynthesise. Short plants, such as young crops or heavily grazed pastures, may be completely covered and usually die. Inundation is often associated with waterlogging.

Many farmers do not realise that a site is waterlogged until water appears on the soil surface. However, by this stage, plant roots may already be damaged and the yield potential severely affected.

Most data on the cost of waterlogging and inundation are from the Upper Great Southern, although the problems are widespread. Cereal crop yields decrease by about 150 kg/ha for every 10mm of rainfall during August in the Upper Great Southern. In eight Shires from the region, excess rainfall costs farmers an average of $13 million in lost production each year.

Only the most obvious losses are attributed to waterlogging. Remote sensing methods show that symptoms of waterlogging are easiest to detect in the infrared part of the electromagnetic spectrum, which is invisible to the human eye. In 1988, a year with slightly above average rainfall, waterlogging affected about 32 per cent of cereal crops in part of the Cuballing Shire. Cereal losses in four Shires in 1988 were about $23 million.

Waterlogging and inundation slow pasture growth in winter and delay the spring flush. Pasture growth in winter is at least five times more valuable than extra production in late spring. Waterlogged legumes grow more slowly than waterlogged grasses, so waterlogged pastures become grassy and weedy.

In wet years, waterlogging reduced the area that can be cropped. When paddocks are waterlogged shortly after seeding, germination and emergence of crops are often reduced; crops may have to be resown when the soil is form enough to support machinery.

Waterlogged and inundated areas contribute recharge to saline aquifers, are very susceptible to water erosion and are prone to soil structure decline if cultivated or stocked when too wet.

IDENTIFYING PROBLEM AREAS

The best way to identify problem areas is to dig holes about 40 cm deep in winter and see if water flows into them. If it does, the soil is waterlogged. Digging holes for fence posts often reveals waterlogging.

Some farmers put slotted PVC pipe into augered holes. They can then monitor the water levels in their paddocks.

Symptoms of waterlogging include:

- Yellowing of crops and pastures;
- The presence of weeds such as toad rush, cotula, dock and Yorkshire fog grass;
- Grey or greenish coloured soil; and
- The presence of orange mottles in soil profiles (although some mottles may have been caused by waterlogging in previous climates).

SUSCEPTIBLE AREAS

Areas that are most susceptible to waterlogging and inundation are those where:

- The soil has a shallow clay subsoil (particularly on flat land or in water-gaining areas such as rock outcrops, roads, lower slopes and areas where water converges); and
- The soil allows water to infiltrate only slowly, such as clays, loams, soils that set hard and soils with a surface seal.

EFFECTS ON PLANT GROWTH

Low levels of oxygen in the root zone trigger the adverse effects of waterlogging on plant growth. Waterlogging of the seedbed and inundation most affect germinating seeds and young seedings. Established plants are most affected when they are growing rapidly.

Therefore, if a soil becomes waterlogged in July, final yields may not be greatly reduced; soils are cold, the demand for oxygen is low and plant growth is slow at this time of year.

When plants are growing actively, root tips begin to die within a few days of waterlogging. The shallow root systems that then develop limit the uptake of nutrients (particularly nitrogen) and water, particularly when the soil profile starts to dry in spring. As a result plants may ripen early and grains may not fill properly in areas that do not receive seepage water late in the season. Shallow roots also result in more recharge, and this increases salinity.

Nitrogen is lost from waterlogged soils by leaching and denitrification (degassing). These losses, together with the lowered ability of plants to absorb nutrients from water-logged soil, cause the older leaves to yellow. Waterlogging also directly reduces nitrogen fixation by the nodules of legume crops and pastures.

Waterlogging is most obvious on salt-affected land. Unless salt levels are very high, most plants growing in well-drained soils can keep salt out of their roots. Since waterlogging prevents the roots making enough energy to keep the salt out, the salt enters the roots and the plants die.

In irrigated agricultural land, waterlogging is often accompanied by soil salinity as waterlogged soils prevent leaching of the salts imported by the irrigation water. From a gardening point of view, waterlogging is the process whereby the soil blocks off all water and is so hard it stops air getting in and it stops oxygen from getting in.

Environmental Impacts of Irrigation

Environmental impacts of irrigation are the changes in quantity and quality of soil and water as a result of irrigation and the ensuing effects on natural and social conditions at the tail-end and downstream of the irrigation scheme.

The impacts stem from the changed hydrological conditions owing to the installation and operation of the scheme.

An irrigation scheme often draws water from the river and distributes it over the irrigated area. As a hydrological result it is found that:

- The downstream river discharge is reduced.
- The evaporation in the scheme is increased.
- The groundwater recharge in the scheme is increased.
- The level of the water table rises.
- The drainage flow is increased.

These may be called direct effects.

The effects thereof on soil and water quality are indirect and complex, Water logging and soil salination are part of these, whereas the subsequent impacts on natural, ecological and socio-enonomic conditions is very intricate.

Irrigation can also be done extracting groundwater by (tube)wells. As a hydrological result it is found that the level of the water descends. The effects may be water mining, land/soil subsidence, and, along the coast, saltwater intrusion.

The reduced downstream river discharge may cause:

- Reduced downstream flooding.
- Disappearance of ecologically and economically important wetlands or flood forests.
- Rduced availability of industrial, municipal, household, and drinking water.
- Reduced shipping routes. Water withdrawal poses a serious threat to the Ganges. In India, barrages control all of the tributaries to the Ganges and divert roughly 60 per cent of river flow to irrigation.
- Reduced fishing opportunities. The Indus River in Pakistan faces scarcity due to over-extraction of water for agriculture. The Indus is inhabited by 25 amphibian species and 147 fish species of which 22 are found nowhere else in the world. It harbors the endangered

Indus River dolphin, one of the world's rarest mammals. Fish populations, the main source of protein and overall life support systems for many communities, are also being threatened

- Reduced discharge into the sea, which may have various consequences like coastal erosion (e.g. in Ghana) and salt water intrusion in delta's and estuaries (e.g. in Egypt, see Aswan dam). Current water withdrawal from the river Nile for irrigation is so high that, despite its size, in dry periods the river does not reach the sea. The Aral sea has suffered an "environmental catastrophe" due to the interception of river water for irrigation purposes.

Increased Groundwater Recharge, Waterlogging, Soil Salinity

Looking over the shoulder of a Peruvian farmer in Huarmey delta at waterlogged and salinised irrigated land with poor crop stand. This illustrates an environmental impact of upstream irrigation developments causing an increased flow of groundwater to this lower lying area leading to the adverse conditions.

The increased groundwater recharge stems from the unavoidable deep percolation losses occurring in the irrigation scheme. The lower the irrigation efficiency, the higher the losses.

Although, fairly high irrigation efficiencies of 70 per cent or more (i.e. losses of 30% or less) can be obtained with sophisticated techniques like sprinkler irrigation and drip irrigation, or by precision land levelling for surface irrigation, in practice the losses are commonly in the order of 40 to 60 per cent. This may cause:

- Rising water-tables.
- Increased storage of groundwater that may be used for irrigation, municipal, household and drinking water by pumping from wells.
- Waterlogging and drainage problems in villages, agricultural lands, and along roads with mostly negative consequences. The increased level of the water table can lead to reduced agricultural production.
- Shallow water tables are a sign that the aquifer is unable to cope with the groundwater recharge stemming from the deep percolation losses.
- Where water tables are shallow, the irrigation applications are reduced. As a result, the soil is no longer leached and soil salinity problems develop.
- Stagnant water tables at the soil surface are known to increase the incidence of water borne diseases like malaria, filariasis, yellow

fever, dengue, and schistosomiasis (Bilharzia) in many areas. Health costs, appraisals of health impacts and mitigation measures are rarely part of irrigation projects, if at all.

- To mitigate the adverse effects of shallow water tables and soil salinization, some form of watertable control, soil salinity control, drainage and drainage system is needed.
- As drainage water moves through the soil profile it may dissolve nutrients (either fertilizer based or naturally occurring) such as nitrates, leading to a built up of those nutrients in the ground water aquifer. High nitrate levels in drinking water can be harmful to humans particularly for infants under six months where it is linked to 'blue-baby syndrome'.

Case studies:

1. In India, 2,189,400 ha have been reported to suffer from waterlogging in irrigation canal commands. Also 3,469,100 ha were reported to be seriously salt-affected here.
2. In the Indus Plains in Pakistan, more than 2 million hectares of land is waterlogged. The soil of 13.6 million hectares within the Gross Command Area was surveyed, which revealed that 3.1 million hectares (23%) was saline. 23 per cent of this was in Sindh and 13 per cent in the Punjab. More than 3 million ha of water-logged lands have been provided with tube-wells and drains at the cost of billions of rupees, but the reclamation objectives were only partially achieved. The Asian Development Bank (ADB) states that 38 per cent of the irrigated area is now waterlogged and 14 per cent of the surface is too saline for use.
3. In the Nile delta of Egypt, drainage is being installed in millions of hectares to combat the water-logging resulting from the introduction of massive perennial irrigation after completion of the High Dam at Assuan.
4. In Mexico, 15 per cent of the 3.000.000 ha if irrigable land is salinized and 10 per cent is waterlogged.
5. In Peru some 300,000 ha of the 1,050,000 ha of irrigable land suffers from this problem.
6. Estimates indicate that roughly one-third of the irrigated land in the major irrigation countries is already badly affected by salinity or is expected to become so in the near future. Present estimates for Israel are 13 per cent of the irrigated land, Australia

20 per cent, China 15 per cent, Irak 50 per cent, Egypt 30 per cent. Irrigation-induced salinity occurs in large and small irrigation systems alike.

7. Food Agricultural Organization (FAO) has estimated that by 1990 about 52×10^6 ha of irrigated land will need to have improved drainage systems installed, much of it subsurface drainage to control salinity.

Reduced Downstream Drainage and Groundwater Quality

- The downstream drainage water quality may deteriorate owing to leaching of salts, nutrients, herbicides and pesticides. This may negatively affect the health of the population at the tail-end and downstream of the irrigation scheme, as well as the ecological balance. The Aral sea, for example, is seriously polluted by drainage water.
- The downstream quality of the groundwater may deteriorate in a similar way as the downstream drainage water and have similar consequences.

Reduced Downstream River Water Quality

Owing to drainage of surface and groundwater in the project area, which waters may be salinized and polluted by agricultural chemicals like biocides and fertilizers, the quality of the river water below the project area can deteriorate, which makes it less fit for industrial, municipal and household use. It may lead to reduced public health.

Polluted river water entering the sea may adversely affect the ecology along the sea shore.

Affected Downstream Water Users

Downstream water users often have no legal water rights and may fall victim of the development of irrigation. Pastoralists and nomadic tribes may find their land and water resources blocked by new irrigation developments without having a legal recourse.

Flood-recession cropping may be seriously affected by the upstream interception of river water for irrigation purposes.

- In Baluchistan, Pakistan, the development of new small-scale irrigation projects depleted the water resources of nomadic tribes traveling annually between Baluchistan and Gujarat or Rajastan, India

- After the closure of the Kainji dam, Nigeria, 50 to 70 per cent of the downstream area of flood-recession cropping was lost.

Lost Land Use Opportunities

Irrigation projects may reduce the fishing opportunities of the original population and the grazing opportunities for cattle. The livestock pressure on the remaining lands may increase considerably, because the ousted traditional pastoralist tribes will have to find their subsistence and existence elsewhere, overgrazing may increase, followed by serious soil erosion and the loss of natural resources.

The Manatali reservoir formed by the Manantali dam in Mali intersects the migration routes of nomadic pastoralists and destroyed 43,000 ha of savannah, probably leading to overgrazing and erosion elsewhere. Further, the reservoir destroyed 120 km² of forest. The depletion of groundwater aquifers, which is caused by the suppression of the seasonal flood cycle, is damaging the forests downstream of the dam.

When more groundwater is pumped from wells than replenished, storage of water in the aquifer is being mined. Irrigation from groundwater is no longer sustainable then. The result can be abandoning of irrigated agriculture.

The hundreds of tubewells installed in the state of Uttar Pradesh, India, with World Bank funding have operating periods of 1.4 to 4.7 hours/day, whereas the were designed to operate 16 hours/day. In Baluchistan, Pakistan, the development of tubewell irrigation projects was at the expense of the traditional qanat or karez users.

Groundwater-related subsidence of the land due to mining of groundwater occurred in the U.S.A. at a rate of 1m for each 13m that the watertable was lowered.

Homes at Greens Bayou near Houston, Texas, where 5 to 7 feet of subsidence has occurred, were flooded during a storm in June 1989 as shown in the picture.

Simulation and Prediction

The effects of irrigation on watertable, soil salinity and salinity of drainage and groundwater, and the effects of mitigative measures can be simulated and predicted using agro-hydro-salinity models like SaltMod and SahysMod.

SOIL SALINITY

Soil salinity is the salt content in the soil. Salt-affected soils are caused by excess accumulation of salts, typically most pronounced at the soil surface.

Salts can be transported to the soil surface by capillary transport from a salt laden water table and then accumulate due to evaporation. They can also be concentrated in soils due to human activity, for example the use of potassium as fertilizer, which can form sylvite, a naturally occurring salt. As soil salinity increases, salt effects can result in degradation of soils and vegetation.

Salinization is a process that results from:

- High levels of salt in the soils.
- Landscape features that allow salts to become mobile. (movement of water table)
- Climatic trends that favor accumulation.
- Human activities such as land clearing, aquaculture activities and the salting of icy roads

NATURAL OCCURRENCE

Salt is a natural element of soils and water. The ions responsible for salinization are: Na^+, K^+, Ca^{2+}, Mg^{2+} and Cl^-.

As the Na^+ (sodium) predominates, soils can become sodic. Sodic soils present particular challenges because they tend to have very poor structure which limits or prevents water infiltration and drainage.

Over long periods of time, as soil minerals weather and release salts, these salts are flushed or leached out of the soil by drainage water in areas with sufficient precipitation. In addition to mineral weathering, salts are also deposited via dust and precipitation. In dry regions salts may accumulate, leading to naturally saline soils.

This is the case, for example, in large parts of Australia. Human practices can increase the salinity of soils by the addition of salts in irrigation water. Proper irrigation management can prevent salt accumulation by providing adequate drainage water to leach added salts from the soil. Disrupting drainage patterns that provide leaching can also result in salt accumulations.

An example of this occurred in Egypt in 1970 when the Aswan High Dam was built. The change in the level of ground water before the construction had enabled soil erosion, which led to high concentration of salts in the water table. After the construction, the continuous high level of the water table led to the salination of the arable land.

DRY LAND SALINITY

Salinity in drylands can occur when the water table is between two to three metres from the surface of the soil. The salts from the groundwater are raised by capillary action to the surface of the soil. This occurs when groundwater is saline (which is true in many areas), and is favored by land use practices allowing more rainwater to enter the aquifer than it could accommodate. For example, the clearing of trees for agriculture is a major reason for dryland salinity in some areas, since deep rooting of trees has been replaced by shallow rooting of annual crops.

Salinity from irrigation can occur over time wherever irrigation occurs, since almost all water (even natural rainfall) contains some dissolved salts. When the plants use the water, the salts are left behind in the soil and eventually begin to accumulate. Since soil salinity makes it more difficult for plants to absorb soil moisture, these salts must be leached out of the plant root zone by applying additional water.

This water in excess of plant needs is called the leaching fraction. Salination from irrigation water is also greatly increased by poor drainage and use of saline water for irrigating agricultural crops.

Salinity in urban areas often results from the combination of irrigation and groundwater processes. Irrigation is also now common in cities (gardens and recreation areas).

The consequences of salinity are :

- Detrimental effects on plant growth and yield.
- Damage to infrastructure (roads, bricks, corrosion of pipes and cables).
- Reduction of water quality for users, sedimentation problems.
- Soil erosion ultimately, when crops are too strongly affected by the amounts of salts.

Salinity is an important land degradation problem. Soil salinity can be reduced by leaching soluble salts out of soil with excess irrigation water. Soil salinity control involves watertable control and flushing in combination with tile drainage or another form of subsurface drainage.

A comprehensive treatment of soil salinity is available from the FAO. High levels of soil salinity can be tolerated if salt-tolerant plants are grown. Sensitive crops lose their vigor already in slightly saline soils, most crops are negatively affected by (moderately) saline soils, and only salinity resistant crops thrive in severely saline soils. The University of Wyoming and the Government of Alberta report data on the salt tolerance of plants.

Regions Affected

From the FAO/UNESCO Soil Map of the World the following salinised areas can be derived.

Region	Area (10^6ha)
Africa	69.5
Near and Middle East	53.1
Asia and Far East	19.5
Latin America	59.4
Australia	84.7
North America	16.0
Europe	20.7

Soil Salinity Control

Soil salinity control relates to controlling the problem of soil salinity and reclaiming salinized agricultural land. The aim of soil salinity control is to prevent soil degradation by salinization and reclaim already salty (saline) soils. Soil reclamation is also called soil improvement, rehabilitation, remediation, recuperation, or amelioration.

The primary man-made cause of salinization is irrigation. River water or groundwater used in irrigation contains salts, which remain behind in the soil after the water has evaporated.

The primary method of controlling soil salinity is to permit 10-20 per cent of the irrigation water to leach the soil, be drained and discharged through an appropriate drainage system. The salt concentration of the drainage water is normally 5 to 10 times higher than that of the irrigation water, thus salt export matches salt import and it will not accumulate.

Soil Salinity Problem

Salty (saline) soils are soils that have a high salt content. The predominant salt is normally sodium chloride (NaCl, "table salt"). Saline soils are therefore also sodic soils but there may be sodic soils that are not saline, but alkaline.

Salty soils are a common feature and an environmental problem in irrigated lands in arid and semi-arid regions. They have poor or little crop production. The problems are often associated with high water tables, caused by a lack of natural subsurface drainage to the underground. Poor subsurface drainage may be caused by insufficient transport capacity of the aquifer or because water cannot exit the aquifer for instance, if it is situated in a topographical depression.

Worldwide, the major factor in the development of saline soils is a lack of precipitation. Most naturally saline soils are found in (semi)arid regions and climates of the globe.

Primary Cause

The primary cause of man-made salinization is the salt brought in with irrigation water. All irrigation water derived from rivers or groundwater, however 'sweet', contains salts that remain behind in the soil after the water has evaporated, which may create the environmental issue.

For example, assuming irrigation water with a low salt concentration of 0.3 g/l (equal to 0.3 kg/m^3 corresponding to an electric conductivity of about 0.5 dS/m) and a modest annual supply of irrigation water of 10,000 m^3/ha (almost 3 mm/day) brings 3,000 kg salt/ha each year. In the absence of sufficient natural drainage (as in waterlogged soils) and without a proper leaching and drainage programme to remove salts, this would lead to a high soil salinity and reduced crop yields in the long run.

Much of the water used in irrigation has a higher salt content than in this example, which is compounded by that fact that many irrigation projects use a far greater annual supply of water. Sugar cane, for example, needs about 20000 m^3/ha of water per year. As a result, irrigated areas often receive more than 3,000 kg/ha of salt per year and some receive as much as 10,000 kg/ha/year.

Secondary Cause

The secondary cause of salinization is waterlogging in irrigated land. Irrigation causes changes to the natural water balance of irrigated lands. Large quantities of water in irrigation projects are not consumed by plants and must go somewhere. In irrigation projects it is impossible to achieve 100 per cent irrigation efficiency where all the irrigation water is consumed by the plants.

The maximum attainable irrigation efficiency is about 70 per cent but usually it is less than 60 per cent. This means that minimum 30 per cent, but usually more than 40 per cent of the irrigation water is not evaporated and it must go somewhere.

Most of the water lost this way is stored underground which can change the original hydrology of local aquifers considerably. Many aquifers cannot absorb and transport these quantities of water and, the water table rises leading to water logging.

Waterlogging causes three problems:

- The shallow water table and lack of oxygenation of the root zone reduces the yield of most crops.
- It leads to an accumulation of salts brought in with the irrigation water as their removal through the aquifer is blocked.

- With the upward seepage of groundwater more salts are brought into the soil and the salination is aggravated.

Salt Affected Area

Normally, the salinization of agricultural land affects a considerable area of irrigation projects, on the order of 20 to 30 per cent. When the agriculture in such a fraction of the land is abandoned, a new salt and water balance is attained, a new equilibrium is reached, and the situation becomes stable.

In India alone, thousands of square kilometres have been severely salinized. China and Pakistan do not lag much behind (perhaps China has even more salt affected land than India). A regional distribution of the 3,230,000 km^2 of saline land world wide is shown in the following table derived from the FAO/UNESCO Soil Map of the World.

Region	Area (10^6ha)
Australia	84.7
Africa	69.5
Latin America	59.4
Near and Middle East	53.1
Europe	20.7
Asia and Far East	19.5
North America	16.0

Spatial Variation

Although the principles of the processes of salinization are fairly easy to understand, it is more difficult to explain why certain parts of the land suffer from the problems and other parts do not, or to predict accurately which part of the land will fall victim. The main reason for this is the variation of natural conditions in time and space, the usually uneven distribution of the irrigation water, and the seasonal or yearly changes of agricultural practices.

Only in lands with undulating topography the explanation and prediction is pretty simple: the depressional areas will degrade the most.

The preparation of salt and water balances for distinguishable sub-areas in the irrigation project, or the use of agro-hydro-salinity models , can be helpful in explaining or predicting the extent and severity of the problems.

Diagnosis

Measurement

Soil salinity is measured as the salt concentration of the soil solution in tems of g/l or electric conductivity (EC) in dS/m. The relation between these two units is about 5/3 : y g/l => 5y/3 dS/m. Sea water may have a salt concentration of 30 g/l (3%) and an EC of 50 dS/m.

The standard for the determination of soil salinity is from an extract of a saturated paste of the soil, and the EC is then written as ECe. The extract is obtained by centrifugation. The salinity can more easily be measured, without centrifugation, in a 2:1 or 5:1 water:soil mixture (in terms of g water per g dry soil) than from a saturated paste. The relation between ECe and $EC_{2:1}$ is about 4, hence : ECe = 4 $EC_{1:2}$.

Classification

Soils are considered saline when the ECe > 4. When 4 < ECe < 8, the soil is called slightly saline, when 8 < ECe < 16 it is called (moderately) saline, and when ECe > 16 severely saline.

Crop Tolerance

Sensitive crops loose their vigor already in slightly saline soils, most crops are negatively affected by (moderately) saline soils, and only salinity resistant crops thrive in severely saline soils. The University of Wyoming and the Government of Alberta report data on the salt tolerance of plants.

Principles of Salinity Control

Drainage is the primary method of controlling soil salinity. The system should permit a small fraction of the irrigation water (about 10 to 20% the drainage or leaching fraction) to be drained and discharged out of the irrigation project.

In irrigated areas where salinity is stable, the salt concentration of the drainage water is normally five to ten times higher than that of the irrigation water. Salt export matches salt import and salt will not accumulate.

When reclaiming already salinized soils, the salt concentration of the drainage water will initially be much higher than that of the irrigation water (for example fifty times higher). Salt export will greatly exceed salt import, so that with the same drainage fraction a rapid desalinization occurs.

After one or two years, the soil salinity is decreased so much, that the salinity of the drainage water has come down to a normal value and a new, favourable, equilibrium is reached.

In regions with pronounced dry and wet seasons, the drainage system may be operated in the wet season only, and closed during the dry season. This practice of checked or controlled drainage saves irrigation water.

The discharge of salty drainage water may pose environmental problems to downstream areas. The environmental hazards must be considered very carefully and, if necessary mitigating measures must be taken. If possible, the drainage must be limited to wet seasons only, when the salty effluent inflicts the least harm.

Drainage Systems

Land drainage for soil salinty control is usually by horizontal drainage system (figure left), but vertical systems (figure right) are also employed. The drainage system designed to evacuate salty water also lowers the water table.

To reduce the cost of the system, the lowering must be reduced to a minimum. The highest permissible level of the water table (or the shallowest permissible depth) depends on the irrigation and agricultural practices and kind of crops.

In many cases a seasonal average water table depth of 0.6 to 0.8 m is deep enough. This means that the water table may occasionally be less than 0.6 m (say 0.2 m just after an irrigation or a rain storm). This automatically implies that, in other occasions, the water table will be deeper than 0.8 m (say 1.2 m). The fluctuation of the water table helps in the breathing function of the soil while the expulsion of carbon dioxide (CO_2) produced by the plant roots and the inhalation of fresh oxygen (O_2) is promoted.

The establishing of a not too deep water table offers the additional advantage that excessive field irrigation is discouraged, as the crop yield would be negatively affected by the resulting elevated water-table, and irrigation water may be saved.

The statements made above on the optimum depth of the watertable are very general, because in some instances the required water table may be still shallower than indicated (for example in rice paddies), while in other instances it must be considerably deeper (for example in some orchards). The establishment of the optimum depth of the water table is in the realm of agricultural drainage criteria.

Soil Leaching

The unsaturated zone or vadose zone of the soil below the soil surface and the watertable is subject to four main hydrological inflow and outflow factors:

- Infiltration of rain and irrigation water (Irr) into the soil through the soil surface (Inf) :
- Inf = Rain + Irr
- Evaporation of soil water through plants and directly into the air through the soil surface (Evap)
- Percolation of water from the unsaturated zone soil into the groundwater through the watertable (Perc)
- Capillary rise of groundwater moving by capillary suction forces into the unsaturated zone(Cap)

In steady state (i.e. the amount of water stored in the unsaturated zone does not change in the long run) the water balance of the unsaturated zone reads: Inflow = Outflow, thus:

- Inf + Cap = Evap + Perc or :
- Irr + Rain + Cap = Evap + Perc

  and the salt balance is

- Irr.Ci + Cap.Cc = Evap.Fc.Ce + Perc.Cp + Ss

where Ci is the salt concentration of the irrigation water, Cc is the salt concentration of the capillary rise, equal to the salt concentration of the upper part of the groundwater body, Fc is the fraction of the total evaporation transpired by plants, Ce is the salt concentration of the water taken up by the plant roots, Cp is the salt concentration of the percolation water, and Ss is the increase of salt storage in the unsaturated soil.

This assumes that the rainfall contains no salts. Only along the coast this may not be true. Further it is assumed that no runoff or surface drainage occurs.

The amount of salts removed by plants (Evap.Fc.Ce) is usually negligibly small: Evap.Fc.Ce = 0

Leaching Curves, Calibrating Leaching Efficiency

The salt concentration Cp can be taken as a part of the salt concentration of the soil in the unsaturated zone (Cu) giving: Cp=Le.Cu, where Le is the leaching efficiency. The leaching efficiency is often in the order of 0.7 to 0.8, but in poorly structured, heavy clay soils it may be less. In the Leziria Grande polder in the delta of the Tagus river in Portugal it was found that the leaching efficiency was only 0.15.

Assuming that one wishes to avoid the soil salinity to increase and maintain the soil salinity Cu at a desired level Cd we have:

Ss = 0, Cu = Cd and Cp = Le.Cd. Hence the salt balance can be simplified to:

- Perc.Le.Cd = Irr.Ci + Cap.Cc

Setting the amount percolation water required to fulfill this salt balance equal to Lr (the leaching requirement) it is found that:

- Lr = (Irr.Ci + Cap.Cc) / Le.Cd .

Substituting herein Irr = Evap + Perc " Rain " Cap and re-arranging gives:

- Lr = [(Evap"Rain).Ci + Cap(Cc"Ci)]/(Le.Cd " Ci)

With this the irrigation and drainage requirements for salinity control can can be computed too.

In irrigation projects in (semi)arid zones and climates it is important to check the leaching requirement, whereby the field irrigation efficiency (indicating the fraction of irrigation water percolating to the underground) is to be taken into account.

The desired soil salinity level Cd depends on the crop tolerance to salt. The University of Wyoming, U.S.A., and the Government of Alberta, Canada, report crop tolerance data.

Drainage means the process of removing water from the soil that is in excess of the needs of crop plants. Drainage is the removal of excess gravitational water from the soil by artificial means to enhance crop production.

A soil may need artificial drainage for one or two reasons.

1. When there is a high water table that should be lowered or

2. When excess surface water cannot move downward through the soil or ever the surface of the soil fast enough to prevent the plant roots from suffocating.

Advantages of drainage:

1. The field will net get waterlogged and crop can get sufficient water and air
2. After the rains are received, the soil comes in tilth earlier and it is possible to carryout agriculture operations properly and in time.
3. The structure of soil improves
4. There is good aeration and warmth in the root zone which are essential for proper growth.

5. Bacteria that change organic matter into plant foods get necessary air and warm temperature in the soil.
6. Desirable chemical reactions take place and nutrient become available to the plants easily.
7. There is proper root development and absorption of nutrients is accelerated.
8. Seeds germinate faster and better stand of crop is obtained.
9. Due to healthy growth of plants they can resist the attack of pest and diseases better.
10. Weed growth can be checked by timely weeding and inter culturing operations.
11. Roots go down deep and can draw up on moisture at greater depth and with stand periods of through better.
12. Good drainage permits the removal of many toxic salts and thus, reduces damage to crops.

Drainage Problems

Drainage problem occur on lands, which we consider as an arid. The causes of drainage problems are as follows. This is also termed as causes of bad drainage or why soils become water logged or ill-drained.

1. *Excessive use of water:* Water that is plentiful and cheap often is used in excess. The result is general water logged condition. Wild flooding continuous irrigation or excessively long irrigation turns to promote water logging.
2. *Seepage of canals laterals or ditches:* The seepage enters underground strata at elevations higher than those of irrigated lands enter and often becomes a direct source of water logging at low lying areas.
3. *Internal stratification or irrigated soils:* The internal natural drainage of soils is often poor. The slowly permeable soils, which when irrigation water is applied, impede the percolation of the excess water. The water cannot move down wards fast enough and accumulate on the surface forming a thin layer and obstruct aeration.
4. *Low lying area:* The area is low lying and excess rain cannot be carried away as a surface runoff rapidly into the drain causing water logged condition.

5. The water table may be high and the additional gravitational water just accumulates and checks the air spaces and saturates the surface and sub soil.

6. There may be a hard pan that affects seepage of water to lower strata.

7. There may be salts affecting water absorption by roots.

Purpose of Artificial Draining

The main purpose of artificial draining is to remove the water that is harmful for plant growth. In areas with rolling topography, the excess water is carried away as a surface run off seepage water through natural depressions into the nalas and rivers. But in flat areas and in soils having an imperious substratum, the natural drainage system is not well developed and therefore water saturates and accumulates in low lying areas until evaporated or drained out slowly. The soils that remains saturated for long time needs artificial drainage.

The artificial of soil water consists of providing man made channels through which the free water is carried away to natural drains such as nalas, rivers. This can done either by digging open channels to the required depth or by laying underground tile pipelines of suitable dimensions at the proper intervals and at required depth.

When such artificial openings are provided in saturated soil, the water in the underground water table is lowered until it reaches the bottom level of the drainage line. The surface line of the water table does not remain horizontal but it depress over the drains. This happens, because water over the drains has the shortest distance to travel and it has the least resistance to flow through the pore spaces of the soil.

The horizontal distance over which water will flow in the drains depends upon the type of soil. If the soil porous the distance is grater. Therefore, drainage must be at short intervals and at shallower depth if the soil is sandy and porous. Thus, it can be seen that the factors, which determine the depth and spacing of the drainage system, are the soil type and the desired of the water table.

STRIP CROPPING: AN ALTERNATIVE

In irrigated lands with scarce water resources suffering from drainage (high water-table) and soil salinity problems, strip cropping is sometimes practiced with strips of land where every other strip is irrigated while the strips in between are left permanently fallow.

Owing to the water application in the irrigated strips they have a higher watertable which induces flow of groundwater to the unirrigated strips. This flow functions as subsurface drainage for the irrigated strips, whereby the water table is maintained at a not-too-shallow depth, leaching of the soil is possible, and the soil salinity can be controlled at an acceptably low level.

In the unirrigated (sacrificial) strips the soil is dry and the groundwater comes up by capillary rise and evaporates leaving the salts behind, so that here the soil salinizes. Nevertheless, they can have some use for livestock, sowing salinity resistant grasses or weeds.

Moreover, useful salt resistant trees can be planted like Casuarina, Eucalyptus or Atriplex, keeping in mind that the trees have deep rooting systems and the salinity of the wet subsoil is less than of the topsoil. In these ways wind erosion can be controlled. The unirrigated strips can also be used for salt harvesting.

SOIL SALINITY MODELS

The majority of the computer models available for water and solute transport in the soil (e.g. SWAP, DrainMod-S, UnSatChem), are based on Richard's differential equation for the movement of water in unsaturated soil in combination with a differential salinity dispersion equation.

The models require input of soil characteristics like the relation between unsaturated soil moisture content, water tension, hydraulic conductivity and dispersivity. These relations vary to a great extent from place to place and are not easy to measure. The models use short time steps and need at least a daily data base of hydrological phenomena.

Altogether this makes model application to a fairly large project the job of a team of specialists with ample facilities.

Simpler models, like SaltMod, based on seasonal water and soil balances and an empirical capillary rise function, are also available. They are useful for long-term salinity predictions in relation to irrigation and drainage practices. Spatial variations owing to variations in topography can be simulated and predicted using salinity cum groundwater models, like SahysMod.

CHAPTER – 7

Canal Irrigation and Quality of Water

Canal usually draws their supplies from rivers. They are not provided with any headwork for diversion of river water to the canal. They are however provide with a canal head-regulators and finally water from the canal is directly supplied to main ditch and then to the secondary ditch.

Method of Canal Irrigation

Canal irrigation is a permanent irrigation conduit constructed to convey water from the source of supply to one or more farms. In India, canal irrigation is one of the principal methods used for improving the growth of the crops. After wells and tube wells, canal irrigation is the second most important irrigation source.

However, this method is only extended to those areas that are large level plains of deep fertile soil and are drained by well distributed perennial rivers. That is why it is quite natural that canal irrigation procedure is only limited to the plain areas of northern India, valleys of Indian peninsular plateau, coastal lowlands etc.

Much more challenging than that of groundwater is the improvement of performance of canal systems, which will remain the dominant water transfer technique in developing countries in the future. The standards used for design of irrigation canals in many countries have not kept up with the development of new technologies. Most traditional delivery systems have no or little flexibility built into them. Their control strategies and control structures are inadequate for good water management practices. Water deliveries at farm level are not compatible with the key requirements of modern agriculture. Thoughts on how to assess the performance of canal projects are evolving.

The engineering concept of efficiency at different levels of a canal system is important for planning, designing and even operating a canal irrigation system. However, water resources experts have criticised this concept which could be misleading. These experts argue that seepage losses contribute to the recharge of aquifers and losses from a project can be recovered downstream if the water quality has not deteriorated beyond certain limits. These arguments are valid when considering the development of water resources at basin level or even at broader levels when aquifers extend beyond basin boundaries.

Water Conservation Measures

Advocates of water conservation measures, such as canal lining, then respond that water quality may decline in the recycling process, lands adjacent to canals may be affected by waterlogging and salinization, and an important volume of water can be lost from wasteland. Furthermore, farmers have to support the cost of groundwater pumping to which opponents can argue that farmers use groundwater more efficiently than canal water which is too often unreliable. The application of water conservation measures in irrigation can have negative or positive impact on third parties. The theoretical debate is endless.

Efficiency alone is not a sufficient indicator to define the performance of an irrigation system. Indicators of water productivity expressed in terms of production or value of production per unit of water are very important in increasingly water-scarce situation. A canal irrigation system may have high conveyance efficiency with a minimum of seepage and operational losses. However, if water delivery is too rigid or unreliable, there will be considerable waste further down at the farm level. A water productivity indicator provides a global indication of the effectiveness of water conservation measures and of the quality of service provided to the users, as well as the farm use of water and other inputs.

Digging of canals is quite expensive in uneven rocky areas. Moreover, it is of limited use. Thus, huge lands in the Indian plateau are irrigated through other methods other than canals. Canals can be both perennial as well as non-perennial.

Apart from these canals, there are several stream canals that are taken off from the rivers without the construction of the barrages. But, in such cases the beds of the inundation canals are generally at a higher level comparatively than those of the rivers, the canals get enough water supplies only when the river is in flood. As a result, the stream canals are of limited use.

Constant attempts have been made to replace the inundated canals by the perennial ones. In mitigating the miseries and sufferings of the farmers, canal irrigation works have gone a long way. Every village in India has a pond or tank for preserving the rain water.

Monsoons have been really uncertain in the country. In those areas where potable ground water is not sufficient like for instance, the zones of Indian plateau, water is supplied from reserved dams. In the past, irrigation works were small sized but with the passage of time, larger canal irrigation projects have been made possible.

Water soaks into the ground under the bed of unlined canal. That is why with the irregular supplies of water, level of sub-soil water in the canal irrigated areas also rises. In some areas, where the perennial unlined canals flow at the ground level and between raised high banks, it is quite possible that the water might reach the surface and render the cultivable soil entirely waterlogged.

In India, canal irrigation is important in various states like Assam, Jammu and Kashmir, Andhra Pradesh, West Bengal and Haryana. Interestingly, more than half of the total irrigated area particularly of these states is irrigated with the usage of canals. Apart from these states, there are several other states where canal irrigation holds significance.

These are Bihar, Madhya Pradesh, Tamil Nadu, Karnataka, Punjab, Bihar and Uttar Pradesh. However, every year more and more cultivated land is being made useless in the canal irrigated areas.

Canals are man-made channels for water. There are two types of canal:

1. *Waterways:* Navigable transportation canals used for carrying ships and boats shipping goods and conveying people, further subdivided into two kinds:
   - *(a)* Those connected to existing lakes, rivers, or oceans. Included are inter-basin canals, such as the Suez Canal, Erie Canal, and the Panama Canal.
   - *(b)* Those connected in a city network: such as the Canal Grande and others of Venice Italy; the gracht of Amsterdam, and the waterways of Bangkok.
2. *Aqueducts:* Water supply canals that are used for the conveyance and delivery of potable water for human consumption, municipal uses, and agriculture irrigation. Rills and acequias are small versions.

Canals are created in one of three ways, or a combination of the three, depending on available water and available path:

A canal can be created where no stream presently exists. Either the body of the canal is dug or the sides of the canal are created by piling dirt, stone, concrete, or other building materials. The water for the canal must be provided from an external source like other streams or reservoirs. Examples include canals that connect valleys over a higher body of land, like Canal du Midi and Canal de Briare.

A stream can be canalized to make its navigable path more predictable and easier to maneuver. Canalization modifies the stream to more safely carry traffic by controlling the flow of the stream with dredging, damming, and modifying its path. Examples include Basse Saône, Canal de Mines de Fer de la Moselle, and Aisne River. Riparian zone restoration may be required.

When a stream is too difficult to modify with canalization, a second stream can be created next to the existing stream. This is called a lateral canal. The existing stream usually acts as the water source and its banks provide a path for the new body. Examples include the Chesapeake and Ohio Canal, Canal latéral à la Loire, Garonne Lateral Canal, and Canal latéral à l'Aisne.

Smaller transportation canals can carry barges or narrowboats, while ship canals allow seagoing ships to travel to an inland port (e.g., Manchester Ship Canal), or from one sea or ocean to another (e.g., Caledonian Canal, Panama Canal).

At their simplest, canals consist of a trench filled with water. Depending on the stratum the canal passes through, it may be necessary to line the cut with some form of watertight material such as clay or concrete. When this is done with clay it is known as puddling.

Canals need to be level, and, while small irregularities in the lie of the land can be dealt with through cuttings and embankments, for larger deviations, other approaches have been adopted. The most common is the pound lock, which consists of a chamber within which the water level can be raised or lowered connecting either two pieces of canal at a different level or the canal with a river or the sea. When there is a hill to be climbed, flights of many locks in short succession may be used.

Prior to the development of the pound lock in 984AD in China by Chhaio Wei-Yo and later in Europe in the 15th century, either flash locks consisting of a single gate were used or ramps, sometimes equipped with rollers, were used to change level. Flash locks were only practical where there was plenty of water available.

Locks use a lot of water, so builders have adopted other approaches. These include boat lifts, such as the Falkirk wheel, which use a caisson of water in which boats float while being moved between two levels; and inclined planes where a caisson is hauled up a steep railway.

To cross a stream or road, the solution is usually to bridge with an aqueduct. To cross a wide valley (where the journey delay caused by a flight of locks at either side would be unacceptable) the centre of the valley can be spanned by an aqueduct-a famous example in Wales is the Pontcysyllte aqueduct across the valley of the River Dee.

Another option for dealing with hills is to tunnel through them. An example of this approach is the Harecastle Tunnel on the Trent and Mersey Canal. Tunnels are only practical for smaller canals.

Some canals attempted to keep changes in level down to a minimum. These canals known as contour canals would take longer winding routes, along which the land was a uniform altitude. Other generally later canals took more direct routes requiring the use of various methods to deal with the change in level.

Tackling Problem of Water Supply

Canals have various features to tackle the problem of water supply. In some cases such as the Suez Canal the canal is simply open to the sea. Where the canal is not at sea level a number of approaches have been adopted. Taking water from existing rivers or springs was an option in some cases, sometimes supplemented by other methods to deal with seasonal variations in flow.

Where such sources were unavailable, reservoirs - either separate from the canal or built into its course - and back pumping were used to provide the required water. In other cases, water pumped from mines was used to feed the canal. In certain cases, extensive "feeder canals" were built to bring water from sources located far from the canal.

Where large amounts of goods are loaded or unloaded such as at the end of a canal a canal basin may be built. This would normally be a section of water wider than the general canal. In some cases, the canal basins contain wharfs and cranes to assist with movement of goods.

When a section of the canal needs to be sealed off so it can be drained for maintenance stop planks are frequently used. These consist of planks of wood placed across the canal to form a dam. They are generally placed in pre existing grooves in the canal bank. On more modern canals, "guard locks" or gates were sometimes placed to allow a section of canal to be quickly closed off, either for maintenance, or to prevent a major loss of water due to a canal breach.

The opinions differ among experts on the causes of poor performance of canal systems. The following statement epitomises the thinking of many irrigation professionals:

> "Irrigation schemes in many parts of the world are known to be performing well below their full potential... There is now wide recognition that deficiencies in management and related institutional problems, rather than technology of irrigation, were the chief constraints of poor performance of irrigation systems".

There is no question that management of irrigation systems has been haunted by a multitude of problems. Admittedly, there are some important management-related and institutional deficiencies, such as conflicts between farmers and irrigation agencies, farmer interference and lack of discipline, poor coordination between government agencies and poor recovery of investments and recovery costs and poor farmer incentives.

Few irrigation experts have challenged the widespread wisdom that these are the main causes of poor performance of irrigation systems. A noticeable exception is a recent publication by IWMI.

According to the author, Prof. Horst, the underlying reason for the writing of that book was a combination of the denial of the importance of technology vis-à-vis management, the increasing indifference to system design and the lack of transparency of technology and operational procedures. The preface of that book challenges the well-accepted wisdom on irrigation issues with rather provocative questions:

Is management really the crux of irrigation problems? ... Do we not apply cosmetic surgery by only trying to improve the management environment without considering the technology? Is it not time to examine the root of the problems: the design of irrigation systems?

Why is there so little recognition of the importance of irrigation technology as a principal cause of poor project performance? What are the causes of deficiencies in designing irrigation systems?

Most civil engineers are well trained in structural engineering and construction techniques but not in the practical and theoretical aspects of unsteady flow hydraulics that are the norm in most irrigation systems. They are also unfamiliar with the constraints of the end user - i.e. on-farm irrigation management requirements. Appropriate irrigation design and management is much more complicated than most engineers, administrators and donors assume.

Second, designers are rarely confronted with the consequences of how their designs function once they are installed.

Third, many irrigation agencies cling to outdated design standards and often resist changes by external experts. Most consulting firms have no contractual motivation and no financial incentives to introduce new concepts.

Operational failures of irrigation systems are not dramatic and are not widely publicized. Operation staff can operate canal for a while by infringing on freeboard and farmers are adjusting to the poor delivery by sinking wells or building reservoirs.

Many failures and problems are caused by a design approach that pays insufficient attention to operational aspects. The point is that if hydraulic systems were simple to operate to attain good water delivery service, safety and efficiency, then management and institutional problems may disappear. Many management and institutional problems are self-inflicted wounds that could be minimized or eliminated with proper designs and operational instructions.

A frequently heard argument is that modernization is too costly and too sophisticated. In modern schemes, irrigation is provided as a service to users that should be as efficient and convenient as possible. Modernization is a thought process that starts with the definition of a proper operational plan. The selection of water control equipment is then done in the light of the operational objectives and the requirements of the farming systems.

In most cases, proper hydraulic design and simple automation techniques can make significant improvements. A good design, even with sophisticated devices, results in simple rules of operation at all levels in canal systems.

The case of the National Irrigation Authority (NIA) in the Philippines illustrates that point. Created in 1964 as a public corporation, NIA has been experimenting with agency restructuring since then. However, NIA has been unable to accomplish its goal of financing itself despite transferring the operational and management responsibilities to user organizations, reducing NIA staff and increasing collection rates of irrigation service fees. In response to rice shortages and financial problems, the government of the Philippines recently reinstated public subsidies to NIA and reduced service fees. The reasons for this suggested by donors are the lack of political will and weak leadership allowing NIA to avoid making the difficult political decisions needed to become financially self-sufficient. These are not the only causes of the failure of the restructuring experiment in the Philippines.

Lending for irrigation in that country during the last two decades has mostly supported rehabilitation and deferred maintenance. No diagnosis was made to identify the causes of rapid deterioration of the water control infrastructure. The water allocation and delivery was basically unchanged.

The conclusion is that the focus was on the financial sustainability of NIA, not on the profitability of farming as has been the case in the State of Victoria and in Mali.

A much better approach was adopted in Vietnam for the preparation of a water resources development project with a major irrigation modernisation component. Intensive capacity building programme through workshops on irrigation performance and modernisation and study tours is part of the efforts of preparation to broaden government commitment to modernisation and to build up capacity in planning, designing, building and operating modern systems.

The importance of technology in combination with management and policy to improve performance of large irrigation systems is progressively recognized at national and regional levels. However, this should be more forcefully promoted by donors and international irrigation and water resources organizations.

OLDEST IRRIGATION CANALS

The oldest known canals were irrigation canals, built in Mesopotamia circa 4000 BC, in what is now modern day Iraq and Syria. The Indus Valley Civilization, in Pakistan and North India, (circa 2600 BC) had sophisticated irrigation and storage systems developed, including the reservoirs built at Girnar in 3000 BC. In Egypt, canals date back at least to the time of Pepi I Meryre (reigned 2332–2283 BC), who ordered a canal built to bypass the cataract on the Nile near Aswan.

In ancient China, large canals for river transport were established as far back as the Warring States (481–221 BC), the longest one of that period being the Hong Gou (Canal of the Wild Geese), which according to the ancient historian Sima Qian connected the old states of Song, Zhang, Chen, Cai, Cao, and Wei.

By far the longest canal was the Grand Canal of China, still the longest canal in the world today. It is 1,794 kilometres (1,115 mi) long and was built to carry the Emperor Yang Guang between Beijing and Hangzhou. The project began in 605 and was completed in 609, although much of the work combined older canals, the oldest section of the canal existing since at least 486 BC. Even in its narrowest urban sections it is rarely less than 30 metres (98 ft) wide.

Greek engineers were the first to use canal locks, by which they regulated the water flow in the Ancient Suez Canal as early as the third century BC.

In the Middle Ages, water transport was cheaper and faster than transport overland. This was because roads were unpaved and in poor condition and greater amounts could be transported by ship. The first artificial canal in Christian Europe was the Fossa Carolina built at the end of the 8th Century under personal supervision of Charlemagne. More lasting and of more economic impact were canals like the Naviglio Grande built between 1127 and 1257, the most important of the lombard "navigli", Later, canals were built in the Netherlands and Flanders to drain the polders and assist the transportation of goods.

Canal building was revived in this age because of commercial expansion from the 12th century AD. River navigations were improved progressively by the use of single, or flash locks. Taking boats through these used large amounts of water leading to conflicts with watermill owners and to correct this, the pound or chamber lock first appeared, in 10th century AD in China and in Europe in 1373 in Vreeswijk, Netherlands. Another important development was the mitre gate, which was, it is presumed, introduced in Italy by Bertola da Novate in the 16th century. This allowed wider gates and also removed the height restriction of guillotine locks.

To break out of the limitations caused by river valleys, the first summit level canals were developed with the Grand Canal of China in 581–617 AD whilst in Europe the first, also using single locks, was the Stecknitz Canal in Germany in 1398. The first to use pound locks was the Briare Canal connecting the Loire and Seine (1642), followed by the more ambitious Canal du Midi (1683) connecting the Atlantic to the Mediterranean. This included a staircase of 8 locks at Béziers, a 157 metres (515 ft) tunnel and three major aqueducts.

Canal building progressed steadily in Germany in the 17th and 18th centuries with three great rivers, the Elbe, Oder and Weser being linked by canals. In post-Roman Britain, the first canal built appears to have been the Exeter Canal, which opened in 1563. The oldest canal built for industrial purposes in North America is Mother Brook in Dedham, MA. It was constructed in 1639 to provide water power for mills. In Russia, the Volga-Baltic Waterway, a nationwide canal system connecting the Baltic and Caspian seas via the Neva and Volga rivers, was opened in 1718.

Canals were important for industrial development. The greatest stimulus to canal system building came from the Industrial Revolution with its need for cheap transport of unprecedented quantities of raw materials and manufactured items.

In Europe, particularly Britain and Ireland, and then in the young United States and the Canadian colonies, inland canals preceded the development of railroads during the earliest phase of the Industrial Revolution. The opening of the Sankey Canal in 1757, followed by the Bridgewater Canal in 1761, which halved the price of coal in Liverpool and Manchester, respectively, triggered a period of "canal mania" in Britain so that between 1760 and 1820 over one hundred canals were built.

As well as industrial uses, the Royal Military Canal on the Romney Marsh was built so as create a barrier against invading troops, and hiding places for British troops during the Napoleonic Wars.

The Blackstone Canal in Massachusetts and Rhode Island fulfilled a similar role in the early industrial revolution between 1828–48. The Blackstone Valley was a major contributor of the American Industrial Revolution where Samuel Slater built his first mill.

In addition to their transportation purposes, parts of the United States, particularly in the Northeast, had enough fast-flowing rivers that water power was the primary means of powering factories (usually textile mills) until after the American Civil War. For example, Lowell, Massachusetts, considered to be "The Cradle of the American Industrial Revolution," has 6 miles (9.7 km) of canals, built from around 1790 to 1850, that provided water power and a means of transportation for the city. The output of the system is estimated at 10,000 horsepower. Other cities with extensive power canal systems include Lawrence, Massachusetts, Holyoke, Massachusetts, Manchester, New Hampshire, and Augusta, Georgia.

Competition from the railway network from the 1830s, and in the 20th century the roads, made the smaller canals obsolete for most commercial transportation, and many of the British canals fell into decay. Only the Manchester Ship Canal and the Aire and Calder Canal bucked this trend. Yet in other countries canals grew in size as construction techniques improved. During the 19th century in the US, the length of canals grew from 100 miles (161 km) to over 4,000, with a complex network making the Great Lakes navigable, in conjunction with Canada, although some canals were later drained and used as railroad rights-of-way.

In the United States, navigable canals reached into isolated areas and brought them in touch with the world beyond. By 1825, the Erie Canal, 363 miles (584 km) long with 82 locks, opened up a connection from the populated Northeast to the Great Lakes. Settlers flooded into regions serviced by such canals, since access to markets was available. The Erie Canal (as well as other canals) was instrumental in lowering the differences in commodity prices between these various markets across America.

The canals caused price convergence between different regions because of their reduction in transportation costs, which allowed Americans to ship and buy goods from farther distances for much lower prices compared to before. Ohio built many miles of canal, Indiana had working canals for a few decades, and the Illinois and Michigan Canal connected the Great Lakes to the Mississippi River system until replaced by a channelized river waterway.

Three major canals with very different purposes were built in what is now Canada. The first Welland Canal, which opened in 1829 between Lake Ontario and Lake Erie, bypassing Niagara Falls and the Lachine Canal (1825), which allowed ships to skirt the nearly impassable rapids on the St. Lawrence River at Montreal were built for commerce.

The Rideau Canal, completed in 1832, connects Ottawa, on the Ottawa River to Kingston, Ontario on Lake Ontario. The Rideau Canal was built as a result of the War of 1812 to provide military transportation between the British colonies of Upper Canada and Lower Canada as an alternative to part of the St. Lawrence River, which was susceptible to blockade by the United States.

In France, a steady linking of all the river systems—Rhine, Rhône, Saône, and Seine—and the North Sea was boosted in 1879 by the establishment of the Freycinet gauge, which specified the minimum size of locks so that canal traffic doubled in the first decades of the 20th century.

Many notable sea canals were completed in this period, starting with the Suez Canal (1869), and the Kiel Canal (1897), which carries tonnage many times that of most other canals, though the Panama Canal was not opened until 1914.

In the 19th century, a number of canals were built in Japan including the Biwako canal and the Tone canal. These canals were partially built with the help of engineers from the Netherlands and other countries.

GANGA ACTION PLAN

There are fourteen major river basins in India with natural waters that are being used for human and developmental activities. These activities contribute significantly to the pollution loads of these river basins. Of these river basins the Ganga sustains the largest population.

The Central Pollution Control Board (CPCB), which is India's national body for monitoring environmental pollution, undertook a comprehensive scientific survey in 1981-82 in order to classify river waters according to their designated best uses.

This report was the first systematic document that formed the basis of the Ganga Action Plan (GAP). It detailed land-use patterns, domestic and industrial pollution loads, fertiliser and pesticide use, hydrological aspects and river classifications. This inventory of pollution was used by the Department of Environment in 1984 when formulating a policy document.

Realising the need for urgent intervention the Central Ganga Authority (CGA) was set up in 1985 under the chairmanship of the Prime Minister. The

Ganga Project Directorate (GPD) was established in June 1985 as a national body operating within the National Ministry of Environment and Forest. The GPD was intended to serve as the secretariat to the CGA and also as the Apex Nodal Agency for implementation. It was set up to coordinate the different ministries involved and to administer funds for this 100 per cent centrally-sponsored plan.

The programme was perceived as a once-off investment providing demonstrable effects on river water quality. The execution of the works and the subsequent operation and management (O&M) were the responsibility of the state governments, under the supervision of the GPD. The GPD was to remain in place until the GAP was completed.

The plan was formally launched on 14 June 1986. The main thrust was to intercept and divert the wastes from urban settlements away from the river. Treatment and economical use of waste, as a means of assisting resource recovery, were made an integral part of the plan.

It was realised that comprehensive coordinated research would have to be conducted on the following aspects of Ganga:

- The sources and nature of the pollution.
- A more rational plan for the use of the resources of the Ganga for agriculture, animal husbandry, fisheries, forests, etc.
- The demographic, cultural and human settlements on the banks of the river.
- The possible revival of the inland water transport facilities of the Ganga, together with the tributaries and distributaries.

One outcome of this initiative was a multi-disciplinary study of the river in which the fourteen universities located in the basin participated in a well co-ordinated, integrated research programme. This was one of largest endeavours, involving several hundred scientists, ever undertaken in the country and was funded under the GAP. The resultant report is a unique, integrated profile of the river.

The GAP was only the first step in river water quality management. Its mandate was limited to quick and effective, but sustainable, interventions to contain the damage. The studies carried out by the CPCB in 1981-82 revealed that pollution of the Ganga was increasing but had not assumed serious proportions, except at certain main towns on the river such as industrial Kanpur and Calcutta on the Hoogly, together with a few other towns.

These locations were identified and designated as the "hot-spots" where urgent interventions were warranted. The causative factors responsible for these situations were targeted for swift and effective control measures.

This strategy was adopted for urgent implementation during the first phase of the plan under which only twenty five towns identified on the main river were to be included. The studies had revealed that:

- Seventy Five per cent of the pollution load was from untreated municipal sewage.
- Eighty Eight per cent of the municipal sewage was from the Twenty Five Class I towns on the main river.
- Only a few of these cities had sewage treatment facilities (these were very inadequate and were often not functional).
- All the industries accounted for only Twenty Five per cent of the total pollution (in some areas, such as Calcutta and Kanpur, the industrial waste was very toxic and hard to treat).

Attainable Objectives

The broad aim of the GAP was to reduce pollution and to clean the river and to restore water quality at least to Class B (i.e. bathing quality: 3 mg l^{-1} BOD and 5 mg l^{-1} dissolved oxygen). This was considered as a feasible objective and because a unique and distinguishing feature of the Ganga river was its widespread use for ritualistic mass bathing.

The other environmental benefits envisaged were improvements in, for example, fisheries, aquatic flora and fauna, aesthetic quality, health issues and levels of contamination.

The multi-pronged objectives were to improve the water quality, as an immediate short-term measure, by controlling municipal and industrial wastes. The long-term objectives were to improve the environmental conditions along the river by suitably reducing all the polluting influences at source.

These included not only the creation of waste treatment facilities but also invoking remedial legislation to control such non-point sources as agricultural run-off containing residues of fertilisers and pesticides, which are harmful for the aquatic flora and fauna. Prior to the creation of the GAP, the responsibilities for pollution of the river were not clearly demarcated between the various government agencies.

The pollutants reaching the Ganga from most point sources did not mix well in the river, due to the sluggish water currents, and as a result such pollution often lingered along the embankments where people bathed and took water for domestic use.

Multi-prolonged Strategy

The GAP had a multi-pronged strategy to improve the river water quality. It was fully financed by the central Government, with the assets created by the central Government to be used and maintained by the state governments. The main thrust of the plan was targeted to control all municipal and industrial wastes. All possible point and non-point sources of pollution were identified. The control of point sources of urban municipal wastes for the 25 Class I towns on the main river was initiated from the 100 per cent centrally-invested project funds. The control of urban non-point sources was also tackled by direct interventions from project funds.

The control of non-point source agricultural run-off was undertaken in a phased manner by the Ministry of Agriculture, principally by reducing use of fertiliser and pesticides. The control of point sources of industrial wastes was done by applying the polluter-pays-principle.

A total of 261 sub-projects were sought for implem-entation in 25 Class I (population above 100,000) river front towns. This would eventually involve a financial outlay of Rs 4,680 million (equivalent to about US$ 156 million). More than 95 per cent of the programme has been completed and the remaining sub-projects are in various stages of completion. The resultant improvement in the river water quality, although noticeable, is hotly debated in the media by certain non-governmental organisations (NGOs). The success of the programme can be gauged by the fact that

Phase II of the plan, covering some of the tributaries, has already been launched by the Government. In addition, the earlier action plan has now evolved further to cover all the other major national river-basins in India, including a few lakes, and is known as the "National Rivers Conservation Plan".

Domestic Waste

The major problem of pollution from domestic municipal sewage (1.34 $\times$ 106 m^3 d^{-1}) arising from the 25 selected towns was handled directly by financing the creation of facilities for interception, diversion and treatment of the wastewater, and also by preventing the other city wastes from entering the river. Out of the 1.34×10^6 m^3 d^{-1} of sewage assessed to be generated, 0.873×10^6 m^3 d^{-1} was intercepted by laying 370 km of trunk sewers with 129 pumping stations as part of 88 sub-projects. The laying of sewers and the renovation of old sewerage was restricted only to that required to trap the existing surface drains flowing into the river.

Facilities for solid waste collection using mechanised equipment and sanitary landfill, low-cost toilet complexes (2,760 complexes), partly-subsidised individual pour flush toilets (48,000), 28 electric crematoriums for human corpses, and 35 schemes of river front development for safer ritualistic bathing, were also included. A total of 261 such projects were carried out in the 25 towns. The programme also included thirty five modern sewage treatment plants. The activities of the various sub-projects can be summarised as follows:

Industrial Waste

About 100 industries were identified on the main river itself. Sixty-eight of these were considered grossly polluting and were discharging 260×10^3 m^3 d^{-1} of wastewater into the river. Under the Water Prevention and Control of Pollution Act 1974 and Environment.

(Protection) Act 1986, 55 industrial units (generating 232×10^3 m^3 d^{-1}) out of the total of 68 (identified) grossly polluting industrial units complied and installed effluent treatment plants. In addition, two others have treatment plants under construction and currently one unit does not have a treatment plant. Legal proceedings have been taken against the remaining 12 industrial units which were closed down for non-compliance.

Modern Uses

Large-scale ship canals such as the Panama Canal and Suez Canal continue to operate for cargo transportation, as do European barge canals. Due to globalization, they are becoming increasingly important, resulting in expansion projects such as the Panama Canal expansion project.

The narrow early industrial canals, however, have ceased to carry significant amounts of trade and many have been abandoned to navigation, but may still be used as a system for transportation of untreated water. In some cases, railways have been built along the canal route, an example being the Croydon Canal.

A movement that began in Britain and France to use the early industrial canals for pleasure boats, such as hotel barges, has spurred rehabilitation of stretches of historic canals. In some cases, abandoned canals such as the Kennet and Avon Canal have been restored and are now used by pleasure boaters. In Britain, canalside housing has also proven popular in recent years.

The Seine-Nord Europe Canal is being developed into a major transportation waterway, linking France with Belgium, Germany, and the Netherlands.

Canals have found another use in the present century, as easements for the installation of fibre optic tele-communications network cabling, avoiding having them buried in roadways while facilitating access and reducing the hazard of being damaged from digging equipment.

Canals are still used to provide water for agriculture. An extensive canal system exists within the Imperial Valley in the Southern California desert to provide irrigation to agriculture within the area.

Canals are so deeply identified with Venice that many canal cities have been nicknamed "the Venice of...." The city is built on marshy islands, with wooden piles supporting the buildings, so that the land is man-made rather than the waterways. The islands have a long history of settlement; by the 12th century, Venice was a powerful city state.

Liverpool Maritime Mercantile City is a UNESCO World Heritage Site near the centre of Liverpool, England, where a system of intertwining waterways and docks is now being developed for mainly residential and leisure use.

Canal Estates (commonly known as bayous) are a form of subdivision popular in cities like Miami, Florida, Texas City, Texas and the Gold Coast, Queensland; the Gold Coast has over 700 km of residential canals. Wetlands are difficult areas upon which to build housing estates, so dredging part of the wetland down to a navigable channel provides fill to build up another part of the wetland above the flood level for houses. Land is built up in a finger pattern that provides a suburban street layout of waterfront housing blocks.

Inland canals have often had boats specifically built for them. An example of this is the British narrowboat, which is up to 72 feet (21.95 m) long and 7 feet (2.13 m) wide and was primarily built for British Midland canals. In this case the limiting factor was the size of the locks. This is also the limiting factor on the Panama canal where Panamax ships are limited to a length of 294.1 m (965 ft) and a width of 32.3 m (106 ft).

For the lockless Suez Canal the limiting factor for Suezmax ships is generally draft, which is limited to 16 m (52.5 ft). At the other end of the scale, tub-boat canals such as the Bude Canal were limited to boats of under 10 tons for much of their length due to the capacity of their inclined planes or boat lifts. Most canals have a limit on height imposed either by bridges or by tunnels.

TUBE WELL

A tube well is a type of water well in which a long 100–200 mm (5 to 8 inch) wide stainless steel tube or pipe is bored into the underground aquifer. The lower end is fitted with a strainer, and a pump at the top lifts water for irrigation. The required depth of the well depends on the depth of the water-table.

In the villages of India (especially Punjab) and Pakistan, a small reservoir of water is made at the outlet of the tube well. This reservoir is used for bathing and recreational purposes, especially by children. In most South Asian countries including India, Pakistan, Bangladesh, etc., taking a bath in the tube well is popular as it allows people to avoid paying for their own electricity and water for a bath. Bathing in tube well reservoirs can lead to illness.

Because children often urinate in the reservoir, the irrigation water may contain urine. In the past, the pump was driven by large diesel engines. However, now electric motors are being used, as they are a much cheaper source of power.

The tube well casing houses the inlet, cylinder, piston valves and rising main of a "down-the-hole" type handpump. Casing to support the external surfaces of the borehole against collapse may be needed, either temporarily or permanently, and is often made of PVC pipe, which is both cheap and inert.

Seepage down the tube well bore is prevented by the sanitary seal. Seepage from the ground above the aquifer is excluded by the lengths of plain casing. Water to be pumped is admitted through slots in the lower lengths of casing.

Water abstracted from aquifers in relatively soft ground usually contains sand or silt particles, which are liable to cause rapid wear to pump valves and cylinders (and dissatisfaction among consumers). Methods of preventing these particles from reaching the pump are of two general types, screening and sand/gravel packing.

Screening

The drawing shows slots in the PVC casing which can be cut on site, using a hacksaw. More elaborate, and far more compact, screens are available commercially; some can be bolted on to pump inlets. Materials used include woven wire and man-made fabric; the latter can be wrapped around the pump inlet assembly. Screening is nearly always needed in some form.

Sand/gravel Packing

The drawing shows graded sand and gravel, which is placed from the top of the borehole. More compact, pre-bonded, packs of sand and/or gravel are available commercially; some of these can also form part of the pump inlet assembly. Sand and/or gravel packing is meant to eliminate particles from the water before they reach the screen and would otherwise have passed through the screen. The introduction of tube wells has led to major arsenic poisoning in Bangladesh.

WATER-TABLE

The water-table is the level at which the submarine pressure is far from atmospheric pressure. It may be conveniently visualized as the 'surface' of the subsurface materials that are saturated with groundwater in a given vicinity. However, saturated conditions may extend above the water table as surface tension holds water in some pores below atmospheric pressure. Individual points on the water table are typically measured as the elevation that the water rises to in a well screened in the shallow groundwater.

The groundwater may be from infiltrating precipitation or from groundwater flowing into the aquifer. In areas with sufficient precipitation, water infiltrates through pore spaces in the soil, passing through the unsaturated zone. At increasing depths water fills in more of the pore spaces in the soils, until the zone of saturation is reached.

In permeable or porous materials, such as sands and well fractured bedrock, the water table forms a relatively horizontal plane. Below the water-table, in the phreatic zone, permeable units that yield groundwater are called aquifers.

The ability of the aquifer to store groundwater is dependent on the primary and secondary porosity and permeability of the rock or soil. In soil that are less permeable, such as tight bedrock formations and historic lakebed deposits, the water table may be more difficult to define.

The water-table should not be confused with the water level in a deeper well. If a deeper aquifer has a lower permeable unit that confines the upward flow, then the water level in a well screened in this aquifer may rise to a level that is greater or less than the elevation of the actual water table. The elevation of the water in this deeper well is dependent upon the pressure in the deeper aquifer and is referred to as the potentiometric surface, not the water table.

The water-table may vary due to seasonal changes in precipitation, evapotranspiration, topography and structural geology. In undeveloped regions with permeable soils that receive sufficient amounts of precipitation, the water table typically slopes toward rivers that act to drain the groundwater away and release the pressure in the aquifer.

Springs, rivers, lakes and oases occur when the water table reaches the surface. Springs commonly form on hillsides, where the Earth's slanting surface may "intersect" with the water table. Groundwater entering rivers and lakes accounts for the base-flow water levels in water bodies.

Surface Topography

Within an aquifer, the water table is rarely horizontal, but reflects the surface relief due to the capillary effect in soils, sediments and other porous media. In the aquifer, groundwater flows from points of higher pressure to points of lower pressure, and the direction of groundwater flow typically has both a horizontal and a vertical component.

The slope of the water table is known as the hydraulic gradient, which depends on the rate at which water is added to and removed from the aquifer and the permeability of the material. The water table does not always mimic the topography due to variations in the underlying geological structure (e.g. folded, faulted, fractured bedrock).

Perched Water-tables

A perched water-table (or perched aquifer) is an aquifer that occurs above the regional water table, in the vadose zone. This occurs when there is an impermeable layer of rock or sediment (aquiclude) or relatively impermeable layer (aquitard) above the main water table/aquifer but below the surface of the land. If a perched aquifer's flow intersects the Earth's dry surface, at a valley wall for example, the water is discharged as a spring.

Tidal Fluctuations

On low-lying oceanic islands with porous soil, fresh water tends to collect in lenticular pools on top of the denser seawater intruding from the sides of the islands. Such an island's freshwater lens, and thus the water table, rises and falls with the tides.

Seasonal Fluctuations

In some regions, for example, Great Britain or California, winter precipitation is often higher than summer precipitation and so the groundwater storage is not fully recharged in summer. Consequently, the water table is lower in the summer period yearly. This disparity between the level of the winter and summer water table is known as the zone of intermittent saturation, wherein the water table will fluctuate in response to climatic conditions.

Long-term Fluctuations

Fossil water is groundwater that has remained in an aquifer for millennia, and occurs mainly in deserts. Fossil water is non-renewable by present day rainfall due to its depth below the surface, and any extraction causes a permanent change in the water table in such regions.

Effects on Climate

Aquifer drawdown or overdrafting and the pumping of fossil water increases the total amount of water in the hydrosphere that is subject to transpiration and evaporation thereby causing accretion in water vapour and cloud cover which are the primary absorbers of infrared radiation in the earth's atmosphere. Adding water to the system has a forcing effect on the whole earth system, an accurate estimate of which hydrogeological fact is yet to be quantified.

Salinity

Salinity is the saltiness or dissolved salt content of a body of water. It is a general term used to describe the levels of different salts such as sodium chloride, magnesium and calcium sulfates, and bicarbonates. Salinity in Australian English and North American English may also refer to the salt content of soil.

Salinity in the ocean refers to the water's "saltiness". In oceanography, it has been traditional to express salinity not as per cent, but as parts per thousand (‰), which is approximately grams of salt per kilogram of solution. Other disciplines use chemical analyses of solutions, and thus salinity is frequently reported in mg/L or ppm (parts per million). Prior to 1978, salinity or halinity was expressed as per cent usually based on the electrical conductivity ratio of the sample to "Copenhagen water", an artificial sea water manufactured to serve as a world standard.

In 1978, oceanographers redefined salinity in the Practical Salinity Scale (PSS) as the conductivity ratio of a sea water sample to a standard KCl solution. As PSS is a ratio, it has no units. It is not the case that a salinity of 35 exactly equals 35 grams of salt per litre of solution.

These seemingly esoteric approaches to measuring and reporting salt concentrations may appear to obscure their practical use; but it must be remembered that salinity is the sum weight of many different elements within a given volume of water. It has always been the case that to get a precise salinity as a concentration and convert this to an amount of substance (sodium chloride, for instance) required knowing much more about the sample and the measurement than just the weight of the solids upon evaporation (one method of determining salinity).

For example, volume is influenced by water temperature; and also the composition of the salts is not a constant (although generally very much the same throughout the world ocean). Saline waters from inland seas can have a composition that differs from that of the ocean. For the latter reason, these waters are termed saline as differentiated from ocean waters, where the term haline applies (although is not universally used). Contour lines of constant salinity are called isohales.

SYSTEMS OF CLASSIFICATION OF WATER BODIES BASED SALINITY OF EUHALINE SEAS

Marine waters are those of the ocean, another term for which is euhaline seas. The salinity of euhaline seas is 30 to 35. Brackish seas or waters have salinity in the range of 0.5 to 29 and metahaline seas from 36 to 40. These waters are all regarded as thalassic because their salinity is derived from the ocean and defined as homoiohaline if salinity does not vary much over time (essentially constant).

In contrast to homoiohaline environments are certain poikilohaline environments which may also be thallassic in which the salinity variation is biologically significant. Poikilohaline water salinities may range anywhere from 0.5 to greater than 300.

The important characteristic is that these waters tend to vary in salinity over some biologically meaningful range seasonally or on some other roughly comparable time scale. Put simply, these are bodies of water with quite variable salinity. Highly saline water, from which salts crystallize or are about to, is referred to as brine.

Environmental Considerations

Salinity is an ecological factor of considerable importance, influencing the types of organisms that live in a body of water. As well, salinity influences the kinds of plants that will grow either in a water body, or on land fed by a water (or by a groundwater). A plant adapted to saline conditions is called a halophyte. Organisms (mostly bacteria) that can live in very salty conditions are classified as extremophiles, halophiles specifically. An organism that can withstand a wide range of salinities is euryhaline.

Salt is expensive to remove from water, and salt content is an important factor in water use such as potability. The degree of salinity in oceans is a driver of the world's ocean circulation, where density changes due to both salinity changes and temperature changes at the surface of the ocean produce changes in buoyancy, which cause the sinking and rising of water masses.

Changes in the salinity of the oceans are thought to contribute to global changes in carbon dioxide as more saline waters are less soluble to carbon dioxide. In addition, during glacial periods, the hydrography is such that a possible cause of reduced circulation is the production of stratified oceans. Hence it is difficult in this case to subduct water through the thermohaline circulation.

DESALINATION

It refers to any of several processes that remove some amount of salt and other minerals from water. More generally, desalination may also refer to the removal of salts and minerals, as in soil desalination.

Water is desalinated in order to convert salt water to fresh water so it is suitable for human consumption or irrigation. Sometimes the process produces table salt as a by-product. Desalination is used on many seagoing ships and submarines. Most of the modern interest in desalination is focused on developing cost-effective ways of providing fresh water for human use in regions where the availability of fresh water is, or is becoming, limited.

Large-scale desalination typically uses extremely large amounts of energy as well as specialized, expensive infrastructure, making it very costly compared to the use of fresh water from rivers or groundwater.

However, along with recycled water this is one of the only non-rainfall dependent water sources particularly relevant to countries like Australia which traditionally have relied on rainfall in dams to provide their drinking water supplies.

The world's largest desalination plant is the Jebel Ali Desalination Plant (Phase 2) in the United Arab Emirates. It is a dual-purpose facility that uses multi-stage flash distillation and is capable of producing 300 million cubic metres of water per year. By comparison the largest desalination plant in the United States is located in Tampa Bay, Florida and operated by Tampa Bay Water, which began desalinating 34.7 million cubic meters of water per year in December 2007.

The Tampa Bay plant runs at around 12% the output of the Jebel Ali Desalination Plants. According to International Desalination Association 2009, there are 14,451 desalination plants in operation worldwide, producing 59.9 million cubic meters per day (15.8 billion gallons a day), a year on year increase of 12.3 per cent.

TRADITIONAL PROCESS

The traditional process used in these operations is vacuum distillation—essentially the boiling of water at less than atmospheric pressure and thus a much lower temperature than normal. This is because the boiling of a liquid occurs when the vapour pressure equals the ambient pressure and vapor pressure increases with temperature. Thus, because of the reduced temperature, energy is saved. A leading distillation method is multi-stage flash distillation accounting for 85 per cent of production worldwide in 2004.

The principal competing processes use membranes to desalinate, principally applying reverse osmosis technology. Membrane processes use semi-permeable membranes and pressure to separate salts from water.

Reverse osmosis plant membrane systems typically use less energy than thermal distillation, which has led to a reduction in overall desalination costs over the past decade. Desalination remains energy intensive, however, and future costs will continue to depend on the price of both energy and desalination technology.

Criticism

Cogeneration

Cogeneration is the process of using excess heat from power production to accomplish another task. For desalination, cogeneration is the production of potable water from seawater or brackish groundwater in an integrated, or "dual-purpose", facility in which a power plant is used as the source of energy for the desalination process.

The facility's energy production may be dedicated entirely to the production of potable water (a stand-alone facility), or excess energy may be produced and incorporated into the energy grid (a true cogeneration facility). There are various forms of cogeneration, and theoretically any form of energy production could be used. However, the majority of current and planned cogeneration desalination plants use either fossil fuels or nuclear power as their source of energy.

Most plants are located in the Middle East or North Africa, due to their petroleum resources and subsidies. The advantage of dual-purpose facilities is that they can be more efficient in energy consumption, thus making desalination a more viable option for drinking water in areas of scarce water resources.

In a December 26, 2007, opinion column in the *The Atlanta Journal-Constitution*, Nolan Hertel, a professor of nuclear and radiological engineering at Georgia Tech, wrote:

> ". . . nuclear reactors can be used ... to produce large amounts of potable water. The process is already in use in a number of places around the world, from India to Japan and Russia.
>
> Eight nuclear reactors coupled to desalination plants are operating in Japan alone ... nuclear desalination plants could be a source of large amounts of potable water transported by pipelines hundreds of miles inland. . ."

Additionally, the current trend in dual-purpose facilities is hybrid configurations, in which the permeate from an RO desalination component is mixed with distillate from thermal desalination. Basically, two or more desalination processes are combined along with power production. Such facilities have already been implemented in Saudi Arabia at Jeddah and Yanbu.

A typical aircraft carrier in the U.S. military uses nuclear power to desalinate 400,000 US gallons (1,500,000 l; 330,000 imp gal) of water per day.

Operating Costs for Desalination

A number of factors determine the capital and operating costs for desalination: capacity and type of facility, location, feed water, labor, energy, financing, and concentrate disposal. Desalination stills now control pressure, temperature and brine concentrations to optimize the water extraction efficiency. Nuclear-powered desalination might be economical on a large scale.

While noting that costs are falling, and generally positive about the technology for affluent areas that are proximate to oceans, one study argues that "Desalinated water may be a solution for some water-stress regions, but not for places that are poor, deep in the interior of a continent, or at high elevation.

Unfortunately, that includes some of the places with biggest water problems." and "Indeed, one needs to lift the water by 2,000 metres (6,600 ft), or transport it over more than 1,600 kilometres (990 mi) to get transport costs equal to the desalination costs.

Thus, it may be more economical to transport fresh water from somewhere else than to desalinate it. In places far from the sea, like New Delhi, or in high places, like Mexico City, high transport costs would add to the high desalination costs. Desalinated water is also expensive in places that are both somewhat far from the sea and somewhat high, such as Riyadh and Harare. In many places, the dominant cost is desalination, not transport; the process would therefore be relatively less expensive in places such as Beijing, Bangkok, Zaragoza, Phoenix, and, of course, coastal cities like Tripoli." After being desalinated at Jubail, Saudi Arabia, water is pumped 200 miles (320 km) inland through a pipeline to the capital city of Riyadh. For cities on the coast, desalination is being increasingly viewed as an untapped and unlimited water source.

Desalination makes sense only after less expensive options are exhausted, including recycling water and fixing broken infrastructure. Water is reused in Las Vegas NV, Fountain Valley CA, Fairfax VA, El Paso TX and Scottsdale AZ. Compared to desalinated sea water, recycling requires 50% less energy due to the significantly lower salt content and produces new water at 30% less cost to the consumer, without the damage to marine life and ecosystems common to desalination plants.

Israel is now desalinating water at a cost of US$0.53 per cubic meter. Singapore is desalinating water for US$0.49 per cubic meter. Many large coastal cities in developed countries are considering the feasibility of seawater desalination, due to its cost effectiveness compared with other water supply options, which can include mandatory installation of rainwater tanks or stormwater harvesting infrastructure.

Studies have shown that the desalination option is more cost-effective than large-scale recycled water for drinking, and more cost-effective in

Sydney than the vastly expensive option of mandatory installation of rainwater tanks or stormwater harvesting infrastructure.

The city of Perth has been successfully operating a reverse osmosis seawater desalination plant since 2006, and the Western Australian government have announced that a second plant will be built to serve the city's needs. A desalination plant is now operating in Australia's largest city of Sydney, and the Wonthaggi desalination plant under construction in Wonthaggi, Victoria.

The Perth desalination plant is powered partially by renewable energy from the Emu Downs Wind Farm. A wind farm at Bungendore in NSW has been purpose-built to generate enough renewable energy to offset the energy use of the Sydney plant, mitigating concerns about harmful greenhouse gas emissions, a common argument used against seawater desalination due to the energy requirements of the technology.

The purchase or production of renewable energy to power desalination plants naturally adds to the capital and/or operating costs of desalination. However, recent experience in Perth and Sydney indicates that the additional cost is acceptable to communities, as a city may then augment its water supply without doing environmental harm to the atmosphere.

The Queensland state government also purchased renewable energy certificates on behalf of its Gold Coast plant which will see the plant offset its carbon emissions for the initial 18 to 20 months of operations, bringing its environmental footprint down, in line with the other major plants that will be operating around the same time, in Perth and Sydney.

In December 2007, the South Australian government announced that it would build a seawater desalination plant for the city of Adelaide, Australia, located at Port Stanvac. The desalination plant is to be funded by raising water rates to achieve full cost recovery. An online, unscientific poll showed that nearly 60% of votes cast were in favor of raising water rates to pay for desalination.

Improved technology has cut the cost of desalination in half in the past decade, making it more competitive ... Poseidon plans to sell the water for about US $950 per acre-foot [1,200 cubic metres (42,000 cu ft)]. That compares with an average US$700 an acre-foot that local agencies now pay for water." $1,000 per acre-foot works out to $3.06 for 1,000 gallons, or $.81 for 1 cubic meter, which is the unit of water measurement that residential water users are accustomed to being billed in.

While this regulatory hurdle was met, Poseidon Resources is not able to break ground until the final approval of a mitigation project for the damage done to marine life through the intake pipe, as is required by California law. Poseidon Resources has made progress in Carlsbad, CA, despite its unsuccessful attempt to complete construction of Tampa Bay Desal, a desalination plant in Tampa Bay, FL, in 2001.

The Board of Directors of Tampa Bay Water were forced to buy Tampa Bay Desal from Poseidon Resources in 2001 to prevent a third failure of the project. Tampa Bay Water faced five years of engineering problems and operation at 20% capacity due to marine life and growth captured and stuck to reverse osmosis filters prior to fully utilizing this facility in 2007. A San Leandro, California, company called Energy Recovery Inc. has been desalinating water for US $0.46 per cubic meter.

A new desalination technology has invented that is alleged to be between 600 per cent and 700 per cent more water output per square meter of membrane than current technology.

Environmental Consideration

Intake

One of the main environmental considerations of ocean water desalination plants is the impact of the open ocean water intakes, especially when co-located with power plants. Many proposed ocean desalination plants' initial plans relied on these intakes despite perpetuating ongoing impacts on marine life.

In the United States, due to a recent court ruling under the Clean Water Act, these intakes are no longer viable without reducing mortality, by 90%, of the life in the ocean; the plankton, fish eggs and fish larvae. There are alternatives, including beach wells that eliminate this concern, but require more energy and higher costs while limiting output. Other environmental concerns include air pollution and greenhouse gas emissions from the power plants.

Outflow

To limit the environmental impact of returning the brine to the ocean, it can be diluted with another stream of water entering the ocean, such as the outfall of a waste water treatment plant or power plant. While seawater power plant cooling water outfalls are not freshwater like waste water treatment plant outfalls, the salinity of the brine will still be reduced. If the power plant is medium- to large-sized and the desalinaticn plant is not enormous, the flow of the power plant's cooling water is likely to be at least several times larger than that of the desalination plant.

Another method to reduce the increase in salinity is to spread the brine via a diffuser to mix in a mixing zone so that there is only a slight increase in salinity. For example, once the pipeline containing the brine reaches the sea floor, it can split off into many branches, each one releasing the brine gradually along its length through small holes. This method can be used in combination with the joining of the brine with power plant or waste water plant outfalls.

There are methods of desalination, particularly in combination with open pond evaporation (solar desalination), that do not discharge brine back into the ocean at all.

The concentrated seawater has the potential to harm ecosystems, especially marine environments in regions with low turbidity and high evaporation that already have elevated salinity. Examples of such locations are the Persian Gulf, the Red Sea and, in particular, coral lagoons of atolls and other tropical islands around the world.

The UAE, Qatar, Bahrain, Saudi Arabia, Kuwait and Iran have 120 desalination plants between them. These plants flush nearly 24 tons of chlorine, 65 tons of algae-harming antiscalants used to descale pipes, and around 300 kg of copper into the Persian Gulf every day.

Because the brine is denser than the surrounding sea water due to the higher solute concentration, discharge into water bodies means that the ecosystems on the bed of the water body are most at risk because the brine sinks and remains there long enough to damage the ecosystems. Careful re-introduction can minimize this problem.

For example, for the desalination plant and ocean outlet structures to be built in Sydney from late 2007, the water authority states that the ocean outlets will be placed in locations at the seabed that will maximize the dispersal of the concentrated seawater, such that it will be indistinguishable from normal seawater between 50 and 75 metres (160 and 246 ft) from the outlet points. Sydney is fortunate to have typical oceanographic conditions off the coast that allow for such rapid dilution of the concentrated byproduct, thereby minimizing harm to the environment.

In Perth, Australia, in 2007, the Kwinana Desalination Plant was opened. The water is sucked in from the ocean at only 0.1 metres per second (0.33 ft/s), which is slow enough to let fish escape. The plant provides nearly 140,000 cubic metres (4,900,000 cu ft) of clean water per day. This is the same at Queensland's Gold Coast Desalination Plant and Sydney's Desalination Plant.

Desalination Compared to Other Water Supply Options

Increased water conservation and water use efficiency remain the most cost-effective priorities in areas of the world where there is a large potential to improve the efficiency of water use practices. While comparing ocean water desalination to waste water reclamation for drinking water shows desalination as the first option, using reclamation for irrigation and industrial use provides multiple benefits.

Urban runoff and storm water capture also provide benefits in treating, restoring and recharging groundwater. A proposed alternative to desalinization in the state of California and other areas in the American Southwest is the commercial importation of bulk water either by very large crude carriers converted to water carriers, or via pipelines.

The idea is politically unpopular in Canada, where governments have been scrambling to impose trade barriers to bulk water exports as a result of a claim filed in 1999 under Chapter 11 of the North American Free Trade Agreement (NAFTA) by Sun Belt Water Inc. a company established in 1990 in Santa Barbara, California, to address pressing local needs due to a severe drought in that area. Sun Belt maintains a web site where documents relating to their dispute are posted online.

Experimental Techniques

In the past, many novel desalination techniques have been researched with varying degrees of success. One such process which has recently been commercialised by Modern Water plc is a forward osmosis based process for desalinated water, with a number of plants reported in operation. Other techniques have also attracted research funding. For example, to offset the energy requirements of desalination, the U.S. government is working to develop practical solar desalination.

As an example of newer theoretical approaches for desalination, focusing specifically on maximizing energy efficiency and cost effectiveness, the Passarell Process may be considered.

Other approaches involve the use of geothermal energy. From an environmental and economic point of view, in most locations geothermal desalination can be preferable to using fossil groundwater or surface water for human needs, as in many regions the available surface and groundwater resources already have long been under severe stress.

Recent research in the U.S. indicates that nanotube membranes may prove to be extremely effective for water filtration and may produce a viable water desalination process that would require substantially less energy than reverse osmosis.

Use of Biomimetic Membranes

Another method being looked into for water desalination is the use of biomimetic membranes.

On June 23, 2008, it was reported that Siemens Water Technologies had developed a new technology, based on applying electric field on seawater, that desalinates one cubic meter of water while using only 1.5 kWh of energy, which, according to the report, is one half the energy that other processes use. Fresh water can also be produced by freezing seawater, as happens naturally in the polar regions, and is known as freeze-thaw desalination. According to MSNBC, a report by Lux Research estimated that the worldwide desalinated water supply will triple between 2008 and 2020.

Low-temperature Thermal Desalination

Low-temperature thermal desalination (LTTD) takes advantage of the fact that water boils at low pressures, even as low as ambient temperature. The system uses vacuum pumps to create a low pressure, low-temperature environment in which water boils at a temperature gradient of 8 to 10 °C between two volumes of water. Cooling water is supplied from sea depths of as much as 600 metres (2,000 ft). This cold water is pumped through coils to condense the evaporated water vapor. The resulting condensate is purified water.

The LTTD process may also take advantage of the temperature gradient available at power plants, where large quantities of warm waste water are discharged from the plant, reducing the energy input needed to create a temperature gradient. The principle of LTTD is known for a long time, originally stemming from ocean thermal energy conversion research. Some experiments were conducted in U.S. and Japan to test the low-temperature driven desalination technology. In Japan, a spray flash evaporation system was tested by Saga University. In US, at Hawaii Islands, the National Energy Laboratory tested an open-cycle OTEC plant with fresh water and power production using a temperature of 20 °C between surface water and water at a depth of around 500 m. LTTD was studied by India's National Institute of Ocean Technology (NIOT) from 2004. Their first LTTD plant was opened in 2005 at Kavaratti in the Lakshadweep islands. The plant's capacity is 100,000 litres 22,000 imp gal; 26,000 US gal/day, at a capital cost of INR 50 million (•922,000). The plant uses deep water at a temperature of 7 to 15 °C (45 to 59 °F). In 2007, NIOT opened an experimental floating LTTD plant off the coast of Chennai with a capacity of 1,000,000 litres 220,000 imp gal; 260,000 US gal/day. A smaller plant was established in 2009 at the North Chennai Thermal Power Station to prove the LTTD application where power plant cooling water is available.

Thermo-ionic Process

In October 2009, Saltworks Technologies, a Canadian firm, announced a process that uses solar or other thermal heat to drive an ionic current that empties all the sodium and chlorine ions from the water.

Existing Facilities and Facilities Under Construction

Aruba

The island of Aruba has a large (world's largest at the time of its inauguration) desalination plant with the total installed capacity of 42,000 metric tons (11.1 million gallons or 42×10^3 m^3) per day.

Australia

A combination of increased water usage and lower rainfall/drought in Australia has caused State governments to build a number of desalination plants, including the recently commissioned Kurnell Desalination Plant serving the Sydney area. While desalination has been adopted by state governments to secure water supply, it is highly energy intensive (nearly 140 energy demand/ML) and has a high carbon footprint due to continued reliance on Australia's coal-based energy generation.

Bahrain

The Al Hidd Desalination Plant on Muharraq island treats seawater through a multistage flash process, and produces 30 million gallons per day. This project was completed in 2000. The Al Hidd distillate forwarding station, comprises a 410 million litres distillate water storage in 45 million litres steel tanks. A 135 million litres/day forwarding pumping station sends flows to the Hidd blending station, Muharraq blending station, Hoora blending station, Sanabis blending station and Seef blending station and which has an option for gravity supply for low flows to blending pumps and pumps which forward to Janusan, Budiya and Saar.

When completed in three phases, the Durrat Al Bahrain sea water reverse osmosis (SWRO) desalination plant will have a capacity of 36,000 cubic meters of potable water per day which will serve the irrigation needs of the entire Durrat Al Bahrain development. The Bahrain-based utility company, Energy Central Co (ECC) will provide the plant a 25-year design, build and operate contract.

China

China operates the Beijiang Desalination Plant in Tianjin, a combination desalination and coal-fired power plant designed to alleviate Tianjin's critical water shortage. Though the facility has the capacity to produce 200,000 cubic metres of potable water per day, it has never operated at more than one quarter capacity due to difficulties with local utility companies and an inadequate local infrastructure.

Cyprus

There are also desalination plants in Cyprus, like the one near the town of Larnaca. This is called the Dhekelia Desalination Plant, which utilises the reverse osmosis system.

Gibraltar

The fresh water supply in Gibraltar is supplied by a number of reverse osmosis and multi-stage flash desalination plants. There is also a demonstration forward osmosis desalination plant operational.

Maldives

Maldives is a small island nation and most of the islands depend on desalination as a source of water.

Saudi Arabia

The Saline Water Conversion Corporation of Saudi Arabia provides fifty per cent of the municipal water in the Kingdom, operates a number of desalination plants, and has contracted $1892 million to a Japanese-South Korean consortium to build one capable of producing a billion litres a day, opening at the end of 2013.

They currently operate approximately fourteen plants in the Kingdom; one example at Shoaiba cost $1060 million and produces 450 million litres a day.

Spain

Lanzarote, Canary Islands

Lanzarote is the easternmost of the autonomous Canary Islands. It is of volcanic origin and has only very limited natural water supplies. A commercial desalination plant was installed in 1964 as a private initiative. This served the whole island and started off the tourism industry.

In 1974, the venture was injected with investments from local and municipal governments and a larger infrastructure was put in place. In 1989, INALSA was formed as the Lanzarote Island Waters Consortium. The plant has been inspected by foreign visitors from places with interest in desalination.

El Prat del Llobregat, Catalonia

El Prat, near Barcelona, has a desalination plant completed in 2009 and meant to provide water to the Barcelona metropolitan area, specially during the periodic severe droughs that put the drinking water provision under serious stress.

United Arab Emirates (Abu Dhabi)

- Taweelah A1 Power and Desalination Plant has an output 385,000,000 litres 85,000,000 imp gal; 102,000,000 US gal per day of clean water.
- Umm Al Nar Desalination Plant has an output of 394,000,000 litres 87,000,000 imp gal; 104,000,000 US gal per day of clean water.
- Fujairah F2 is to be completed by July 2010 will have a water production capacity of 492,000,000 litres 108,000,000 imp gal; 130,000,000 US gal per day.

United Kingdom

Beckton Desalination Plant

The first large scale water desalination plant in the United Kingdom, the Thames Water Desalination Plant, has been built in Beckton, east London for Thames Water by Acciona Agua

United States

El Paso (Texas) Desalination Plant

Brackish groundwater has been treated at the El Paso plant since around 2004. Producing 27,500,000 US gallons (104,000,000 litres; 22,900,000 imp gal) of fresh water daily (about 25% of total freshwater deliveries) by reverse osmosis, it is a crucial contribution to water supplies in this water-stressed city.

Tampa Bay Water Desalination Project

The Tampa Bay Water Desalination project was originally a private venture led by Poseidon Resources. This project was delayed by the bankruptcy of Poseidon Resources' successive partners in the venture, Stone & Webster, then Covanta (formerly Ogden) and its principal subcontractor Hydranautics.

Poseidon's relationship with Stone & Webster through S & W Water LLC ended in June 2000 when Stone & Webster declared bankruptcy and Poseidon Resources purchased Stone & Webster's stake in S & W Water LLC.

Poseidon Resources partnered with Covanta and Hydranautics in 2001, changing the consortium name to Tampa Bay Desal. Through the inability of Covanta to complete construction bonding of the project, the Tampa Bay Water agency was forced to purchase the project from Poseidon on May 15, 2002, and underwrite the project financing under its own credit rating.

Tampa Bay Water then contracted with Covanta Tampa Construction, which produced a project that did not meet required performance tests. Covanta Tampa Construction's parent company filed bankruptcy in October 2003 to prevent losing the contract with Tampa Bay Water. Then, Covanta Tampa Construction filed bankruptcy prior to performing renovations that would have satisfied contractual agreements. This resulted in nearly six months of litigation between Covanta Tampa Construction and Tampa Bay Water.

In 2004, Tampa Bay Water hired a renovation team, American Water/ Acciona Aqua, to bring the plant to its original, anticipated design. The plant was deemed fully operational in 2007 and is designed to run at a maximum capacity of 25 million gallons per day. Nevertheless, the plant continues to be set with problems limiting it to producing only about half that amount (14 million gallons per day or 42 af/day in 2009.

Yuma Desalting Plant (Arizona)

The Yuma Desalting Plant was constructed under authority of the Colorado River Basin Salinity Control Act of 1974 to treat saline agricultural return flows from the Wellton-Mohawk Irrigation and Drainage District. The treated water is intended for inclusion in water deliveries to Mexico thereby preserving the like amount of water in Lake Mead.

Construction of the plant was completed in 1992 and it has operated on two occasions since then. The plant has been maintained, but largely not operated due to surplus and then normal water supply conditions on the Colorado River.

An agreement was reached in April 2010 between the Southern Nevada Water Authority, the Metropolitan Water District of Southern California, the Central Arizona Project and the U.S. Bureau of Reclamation to underwrite the cost of running the plant in a year long pilot project.

The Republic of Trinidad and Tobago is using desalination to free up more of the island's water supply for drinking purposes. The desalination facility, opened in March 2003, is considered to be the first of its kind. It is the largest desalination facility in the Americas and will process 28,800,000 US gallons (109,000,000 litres; 24,000,000 imp gal) of water a day and sell water at the price of $2.67 per 1,000 US gallons (3,800 litres; 830 imp gal).

This facility will be located at Trinidad's Point Lisas Industrial Estate, a park of more than twelve companies in various manufacturing and processing functions and will allow for easy access to water for both factories and residents in the country.

Seabirds distill sea water, by using Countercurrent exchange in a gland with a Rete mirabile. The gland secretes highly concentrated brine stored near the nostrils above the beak. The bird then "sneezes" the brine out to the sea. As freshwater is not available in their environment, seabirds like pelicans, petrels, albatrosses, gulls and terns possess this gland which allows the birds to drink the salty water from their environment while they are hundreds miles away from land.

Mangroves are trees which grow in sea water. Mangroves are able to secrete the salt by trapping it into parts of the root, which are then eaten by animals (usually crabs). Additional salt removal is done by storing it in leaves which then fall off. Some types of mangrove have glands on the leaf, which work in a similar way to the seabird desalination gland. Salt is extracted to the leaf exterior as small crystals, which then fall off the leaf.

Willow trees and Reeds are known to uptake salt and other contaminants, effectively desalinating the water. This is used in artificial constructed wetlands, for treating sewage. Rain and dew are the outcome of large scale desalination through evaporation, in what is known as the water cycle.

Fresh water floats above sea water, so during storms or in lakes where there is undersea volcanic activity causing the water to boil and then condensate, large bodies of freshwater can be found at the sea or lake surface, covering the more salty seawater below. Freshwater on the surface of seawater is common at estuaries.

CHAPTER – 8

Waste Water Treatment and Use in Agriculture

The field of agricultural water management covers irrigation and drainage as well as water management in rainfed agriculture. Worldwide, irrigated agriculture covers 18 per cent of all cropland (about 277 million hectare), and is estimated to produce 40 per cent of all crops. Rainfed agriculture covers 82 per cent of the cropland, and produces 60 per cent of the crops.

AGRICULTURAL WATER MANAGEMENT

The World Bank support for agricultural water management reached a high of $1.1 billion in financial year 2010. This amounts to about a fifth of all lending commitments to the water sector, and to more than a quarter of the commitments to the agriculture, fishing and forestry sector rural development.

Recent concerns about, on the one hand, rising food prices and food security and, on the other hand, increasing water scarcity, climate change, and the high proportion of water used in agriculture are drawing attention to the urgent need to improve water management in both irrigated and rainfed agriculture.

The quality of irrigation water is of particular importance in arid zones where extremes of temperature and low relative humidity result in high rates of evaporation, with consequent deposition of salt which tends to accumulate in the soil profile. The physical and mechanical properties of the soil, such as dispersion of particles, stability of aggregates, soil structure and permeability, are very sensitive to the type of exchangeable ions present in irrigation water.

Thus, when effluent use is being planned, several factors related to soil properties must be taken into consideration. Another aspect of agricultural concern is the effect of dissolved solids (TDS) in the irrigation water on the growth of plants. Dissolved salts increase the osmotic potential of soil water and an increase in osmotic pressure of the soil solution increases the amount of energy which plants must expend to take up water from the soil.

As a result, respiration is increased and the growth and yield of most plants decline progressively as osmotic pressure increases. Although, most plants respond to salinity as a function of the total osmotic potential of soil water, some plants are susceptible to specific ion toxicity.

Organized society has made managing our wastewater fairly easy, compared with the founders of our country who had little technology to rid themselves of polluted water. Without monitoring and management of our water wastes, disease and sickness would be much more rampant. Household waste water can cause just as many problems as industrial wastewater, so take a few tips from the EPA for reducing wastewater and improving your septic tank performance.

EFFECTIVE IRRIGATION WATER MANAGEMENT

It begins with accurate water measurement. Water measurement is required to determine both total volumes of water and flow rates pumped. Measurement of volumes will verify that the proper amount of water is applied at each irrigation and that amounts permitted by water management districts are not exceeded. Flow rate measurements help to ensure that the irrigation system is operating properly. For example, lower than normal flow rates may indicate the need for pump repair or adjustment, partially closed or obstructed valves or pipelines, or clogged drip emitters. Higher than normal flow rates may indicate broken pipelines, defective flush valves, too many zones operating simultaneously, or eroded sprinkler nozzles.

Pumping rate, application rate, or tree water use rate is measured in units of volume (or depth) per unit of time. Volume can be calculated from the depth applied if the area to which the water is applied is known. The volume can also be calculated by multiplying the flow rate (gallons per minute = gpm) by the duration of flow (min). The depth of application is calculated by multiplying the application rate (inches/hr) by the duration of application (hr).

Velocity refers to the speed at which water flows (distance per unit time) as opposed to flow rate (volume per unit time). Thus, the terms flow rate and velocity cannot be used interchangeably. Both the velocity and cross-sectional area of flow must be known in order to calculate flow rates.

Volume (V) is commonly expressed as gallons, acre-inches (ac-in), and acre-feet (ac-ft). An acre-inch is the volume of water that would be required to cover an area of one acre to a depth of 1 inch. The relationships among these units are:

1 acre-inch = 27,154 gallons = 102,642 liters = 102.8 cubic meters (m^3)

1 acre-foot = 12 acre-inches = 12.34 ha-cm

1 acre-foot = 325,848 gallons = 1233.5 cubic meters

Depth (D) units are used to express soil moisture (e.g., water-holding capacity expressed as inches of water per foot of soil depth) and irrigations are scheduled after a fraction of the soil water in the tree or plant root zone has been depleted.

Example: Calculate the amount of water to be applied per irrigation for the following conditions:

Fine sand soil with 0.75 in/ft available water-holding capacity (AWHC). AWHC is calculated as water available at field capacity minus the water available at wilting point. The root zone depth is 2.0 ft and irrigations are scheduled at 50 per cent depletion of AWHC.

Total soil water storage is calculated as:

Dstored = 0.75 in/ft × 2 ft soil depth = 1.5 in

Amount to be applied per irrigation is:

Dirrigation = 50% × 1.5 in = 0.75 in

Note that the amount of water to be pumped will need to be greater than the 0.75 inches needed to be stored in the plant's root zone since some water will be lost during application. Application efficiencies are always less than 100 per cent because of water losses due to factors such as evaporation, wind drift, and non-uniform water application.

Depth units are also convenient for comparison with rainfall depths. For example, a 1-inch rainfall would supply the same volume of water as a 1-inch irrigation. Evapotranspiration (ET) rates are also usually expressed in inches per day.

Example: For a tree with an ET rate of 0.20 in/day and the root zone that holds 1.2 inches, calculate the irrigation interval for an allowable soil water depletion of 50 per cent.

1.2 inch × 50% / 0.20 inch/day = 3 days

The irrigation would be required early on the fourth day to avoid depleting more than 50 per cent of the available soil water in the root zone.

When irrigation amounts are expressed as depths, it means that the depth is to be applied over the entire area to be irrigated.

Example: For an irrigated area that is 1.0 acre and an applied depth of 1.0 inch, calculate the volume applied.

V = depth × area

= 1.0 inch depth × 1.0 acre = 1.0 ac-in or 27,154 gallons

If the irrigated area was 20 acres, the volume of water applied would be:

V = 20 ac × 1.0 inch = 20 ac-in

20 ac-in × 27,154 gal/ac-in = 543,080 gal

Thus, depth units are used interchangeably with volume units because it is convenient to use depth units when referring to soil water depletion, rainfall, and plant ET rates. However, when referring to amounts of water permitted or pumped, volume units are preferred.

Flow rate (Q) is defined as the volume of water per unit of time flowing past a point in the system. Commonly used units for flow rate are gallons per minute (gal/min or gpm) and acre-inches per hour (ac-in/hr). Equivalent units in metric systems will be cubic meter per hr (1 cubic meter/hr = 4.40 gpm) and hectare–cm/hr (1 hectare-cm/hr = 9728 ac-in/hr). Water management district consumptive use permits are often expressed in units of million gallons per day (mgd). For estimating storm water runoff, cubic feet per second (cfs) is used.

The relationships between these units are:

1 gal/min (gpm) = 0.00221 ac-in/hr

1 gpm = 0.00144 mgd

1 ac-in/hr = 453 gpm = 0.652 mgd

1 mgd = 694.4 gpm = 1.53 ac-in/hr

1 cfs = 448 gpm

Since flow rate is volume per unit time, the volume of water applied during irrigation can be calculated if the flow rate and irrigation duration (time) are known.

Example: Find the volume of water applied and depth of application for a pump that discharges 800 gpm for a duration of 4 hours.

The volume of water applied is:

V = 800 gpm × 60 min/hr × 4 hr = 192,000 gal

or V = 192,000 gal / 27,154 gal/ac-in = 7.1 ac-in

The depth of water applied can be calculated by multiplying the application rate by the duration of irrigation. An application rate of 0. 10 in/hr with a 6 hr irrigation duration results in a gross depth of water applied of 0.6 inches (D = 0. 10 in/hr × 6 hr = 0.6 inches).

Note that the actual depth of water stored in the tree's root zone and available for plant use would be less than 0.6 inches because of water losses during application. A typical application efficiency for microsprinkler irrigation systems is 85 per cent for Florida conditions. Thus, only 0.51 inches (0.6 inches × 85% = 0.51 inches) of the 0.6 inches pumped would be expected to be stored in the root zone and available for plant use. To supply 0.6 in of water in the root zone, 0.71 in (100/85 x 0.6 in) of pumped water will be needed.

MEASURING FLOW TECHNIQUES AND MEASURES

Accuracy

Measurement accuracy is the difference between the true flow and the flow measured with a meter. The measured flow should be as close as possible to the actual amount of water flowing in the pipe. Most irrigation meters should have an accuracy of + 2.0 per cent of the actual amount. The accuracy for a meter may be specified as a percentage of actual rate or as a per cent of full scale. In most instances, flowmeters with rate accuracy should be selected. If a flowmeter is operated above or below its recommended range, the accuracy may be reduced.

Inserting a propeller into the water flow will cause friction, resulting in pressure or head losses in the pipeline. The pressure loss depends on the velocity and pipe diameter (flow rate). The higher the flow rate, the more pressure will be lost due to the flowmeter. Pressure losses from the propeller meters are generally small. For example, with a ten-inch diameter flowmeter, the pressure loss is typically less than 1 psi when flow rates are less then 2,000 gpm.

Since propeller meters are mechanical devices and have moving parts, a scheduled maintenance programme is recommended. Most installations have no power or communication ability; therefore, a user must visually inspect his/her meters on site. Often the inaccuracies of a propeller flowmeter arise from mechanical problems that are easily discovered. If a propeller meter is inaccurate, it is often a mechanical problem.

Often times, inaccurate flow measurements in propeller meters result from debris lodged inside the meter. If electronic registers are used with the meter, signal and all connections should be checked carefully. Small problems in electrical parts can make the measurement system inaccurate.

When checking an unfamiliar meter, the manufacturer's recommendations should be followed to ensure that the meter is properly installed. The instruction, operation, and maintenance manual should be reviewed for details regarding the requirement for straight pipe lengths before and after the meter. Recommended maintenance should be undertaken according to the manual's suggestions. For propeller meters, the pipeline must remain full of water. If the pipe is sloped, errors will be introduced due to the lack of a completely full pipe under certain flow conditions.

If field checks fail to identify the cause of measurements inaccuracies, a full calibration of the meter is required. This normally necessitates removing the meter from the line and sending it to a calibration laboratory. The propeller meters should be calibrated on a test rig that has been calibrated at the National Institute of Standards and Technology (NIST). The laboratory accuracy should be four times as accurate as the meter tested. For a meter with an accuracy of + 2 per cent, the laboratory should have an accuracy rate of at least + 0.5 per cent.

Flowmeters

Flowmeters are one of the key components of a microirrigation system. Flowmeters are critical for managing irrigation efficiently and for monitoring system performance. Managing irrigation efficiently requires knowing how much water the crop has used since the last irrigation (irrigation scheduling) and operating the irrigation system to apply the required amount of water. Flowmeters provide the information necessary to apply the correct amount of water.

Monitoring the performance of an irrigation system makes it possible to identify changes in flow rate during the season (measured at the same pressure). This change may indicate problems such as clogging of emitters or filters, leaks in the system, or problems with the pump or well. The rate of water flow in an irrigation system depends on a variety of hydraulic factor as well as pump and system constraints. Various types of flowmeters are available in the market. These flowmeters vary in their installation, maintenance, accuracy, cost, and other factors. Major types of the flowmeters commonly used in irrigation and drainage are discussed below.

Propeller Meters

Propeller meters are the most commonly used type of water measurement devices in irrigation systems. Propeller meters need to be installed in straight sections of pipeline according to manufacturer's recommendations. To minimize turbulence and the resulting inaccuracies caused by elbows, valves, and other fittings flowmeters should have at least a distance of ten times the pipe diameter upstream of the meter free of obstructions (straight pipe). In addition, there should also be a distance of 5 pipe diameters of straight pipe downstream of the meter.

If the required upstream and downstream unobstructed distances cannot be met, straightening vanes may be used to minimize the effects of turbulence caused by obstructions. For accurate measurement the pipe must flow full. The readout of the flowmeter is through direct gears, cable connections, or magnetic drives. Models are available with both total and instantaneous flow rate measurements. Propeller meters are typically accurate to within two per cent when new.

Example: Determine the minimum distance downstream from an elbow required for installing a flowmeter in a 12 inch class 160 PVC pipe (inside diameter = 11.77 in.).

Upstream distance = 10 x 11.77 in. = 118 in.

Downstream distance = 5 x 11.77 in. = 59 in.

Note: due to the high upstream distances required for large pipe diameters, most installations in agricultural microirrigation systems utilize straightening vanes.

It is important to be aware that propeller meters have some potential problems. Debris in the water may entangle or damage the propeller and affect its operation. Many times the meter continues to register, however the rates registered are less than the true rate. If the debris is sufficient, the meter may fail to register completely. There is a small amount of pressure lost as water flows through the meter (typically 2 psi or less if the meter is of proper size).

These drawbacks in propeller meters are minor. In fact, debris that might affect the propeller meter would also clog the emitters and is therefore usually filtered out. Pressure losses caused by the meter can be compensated for in the irrigation system design. Propeller meters are the meter of choice for the irrigation market for several reasons.

They are intended to measure water flow rates mechanically and typically indicate instantaneous flow rate and total volume. Because the reading is purely mechanical, it requires no power. The meters can be used in remote areas where power is not available.

Propeller meters can be fitted with different types of electronic readouts and outputs. Propeller meters are relatively low cost and can be used economically even if the service need is short. With a typical accuracy of + 2 per cent of rate, the propeller meter gives irrigation users excellent control and accountability of their water. If needed, the meters can be made of high stainless steels for harsh environments.

The propeller should be lightweight so it can respond to fast changes in the flow rates without inertial problems, and stiff enough to resist bending under fast-changing conditions. Friction in the drive system of the meter should be minimal to allow accurate measurement at low velocity ranges of the meter. The propeller must also measure most of the pipe area (full bore measurement) to ensure accurate readings.

Propeller flowmeters normally have a propeller linked with a cable or shafts and gears to flow indicator. These flowmeters can be installed in several different ways. It can be inserted into a short section of pipe, which is then either welded or bolted into the pipeline. Designs are available which allow the meter to be clamped, strapped, or welded onto the pipeline as a saddle-type meter or to be inserted into the pipe discharge. Propeller meters can also be installed as in-line meters in a short section of portable pipe. Couplings are welded onto each end of the flowmeter pipe section to connect sections of the portable pipe.

Propeller meters must be matched to the correct pipe size since the gear mechanism connecting the propeller to the indicator is based on the pipe diameter and the anticipated flow rate. Most flow rate indicators report in gallons per minute or in cubic feet per second, while total flow indicators (totalizers) report in gallons, acre-feet, or cubic feet. Some indicators report in metric units.

The flowmeter should be installed at a location of minimal water turbulence since too much turbulence will cause the flow rate indicator to oscillate wildly, causing unreliable measurement. A centrifugal sand separator or a series of elbows in the pipeline may cause a swirl or rotation in the flowing water. These swirls may be present even at one hundred pipe diameters downstream.

The remedy is to place straightening vanes in the pipeline just in front of the flowmeter. Reliable measurements can normally be made with even short sections of pipe if straightening vanes are used.

A relatively stable rate indicator reading means that turbulence is minimal. Wide variations in indicator readings are a symptom of turbulence in the pipeline. If the readings are extremely erratic, air or gas may be present in the water. Propeller flowmeters operate properly only if the pipe is flowing full. If the pipe is partially full, the flow rate measurement will not be accurate. In pressurized irrigation systems, flow will usually be full at the pump discharge, but in the pumps with an open discharge, as into an irrigation ditch, pipe flow may not be full.

This problem can be remedied by creating a slight rise in the pipe, installing a gooseneck at the pipe discharge, or by installing an elbow (discharge end pointing upward at the pipe discharge). Recommended upstream distance of straight pipe should be followed to minimize effects of obstructions on flowmeter accuracy.

Magnetic Flowmeters

Magnetic flowmeters have the advantage of not causing obstructions in the pipe. This feature eliminates the problem of possible entanglement from debris in the water as well as any pressure loss across the device. Magnetic flowmeters measure the flow of conductive liquids flowing in filled pipes. The sensor creates a pulsating, alternating magnetic field on the inside of a pipe. The liquid in the pipe will move through this magnetic field and generate a signal current proportional to its velocity.

This information is collected by the electrodes and then processed by a microprocessor to provide the user with the flow information. Magnetic flowmeters also require less maintenance than propeller meters, have long-term accuracy, and can be installed only five pipe diameters of straight pipe upstream from the meter. However, they have the disadvantages of a higher initial cost and the need for an external power supply.

Ultrasonic Flowmeters

It measure flow velocity (and indirectly, flow rate) by directing ultrasonic pulses diagonally across the pipe both upstream and downstream. The difference in time required for the signal to travel through the moving water is measured and converted to flow velocity. The operation of an ultrasonic flowmeter is based on the frequency shift (Doppler Effect) of an ultrasonic signal reflected by suspended particles or gas bubbles in the water stream.

This metering technique utilizes the physical pheno-menon of a sound wave changing frequency when it is reflected by moving bubbles in the flowing water. In operation, ultrasonic sound is transmitted into a pipe with flowing liquids. The bubbles in the water reflect the ultrasonic wave with a slightly different frequency; the frequency difference being directly proportional to the flow of the liquid.

The transducer is mounted on the exterior of the pipe. It receives electronic impulses from the transmitter through an interconnecting cable. The transducer generates an ultrasonic signal which it transmits through the pipe into the flowing liquids. It simultaneously receives an ultrasonic signal reflected from the particles in this flowing liquid.

The transmitter measures the difference between its output and input frequency and converts this different frequency into electronic pulses which are processed for an analog indication, and the pulses are scaled and totalized for flow quantity in gallons.

Ultrasonic flowmeters are as accurate as propeller meters and, since they have no moving parts, require little maintenance. Because all attachments are external, these meters can easily be moved to different locations. Ultrasonic flowmeters generally cost more than other types of meters.

Paddlewheel Meters

It can provide economical flow measurement for pipe diameters ranging from one inch to very large pipe with diameters of 36-48 inches or more. As water moves through the pipe, the paddle wheel rotates. The rotation velocity is proportional to the flow rate in the pipe. As the paddle wheel rotates past the base of the pickup coil, a voltage pulse is induced. An electronic unit converts pulses to units of flow based on the diameter and flow characteristics of the pipe.

Because the paddles contact only a limited cross section of the flow, the insertion depth of the rotor and the proper flow profile are critical to accurate readings. These meters are inserted to a specific depth into the pipe in which flow is measured. With proper calibration, the pulse rate represents an accurate measurement of velocity, and in turn flow rate. Paddle wheel flowmeters have an accuracy comparable to that of propeller flowmeters (within 2%).

Paddle wheel flowmeters normally need to be installed with at least 10 pipe diameters of straight pipeline upstream and 5 pipe diameters downstream from the sensor to ensure correct operation. However, if there are obstructions, longer upstream straight runs are recommended. Some paddle wheel flowmeters can be installed in several sizes of pipe, which provides flexibility in system design. The applicability and cost are comparable to that of propeller meters.

Venturi Meters

It consist of a section of pipe with a restriction of a specific shape, across which pressure change is measured. The magnitude of this pressure change depends on the flow rate through the device. Venturi flowmeters have the advantages of unobstructed water flow, no moving parts in the main pipeline, little pressure loss across the meter, and good accuracy. Venturi flowmeters typically have low maintenance requirements; however, they cost slightly more than propeller meters.

Shunt Meters

It work on the principle that a fraction of the water in the irrigation main pipeline is shunted through a small diameter pipeline. The small diameter pipe is parallel to the mainline for a short distance where it is measured before it is returned to the mainline. The small diameter shunt pipeline is equipped with a totalizing flowmeter which measures only the shunted flow. Flow in the main pipeline is proportional to the amount of flow measured in the shunt pipeline.

A head loss is required in the main pipeline to create the pressure difference that causes water to flow through the shunt pipeline. Because the shunt flow rate depends on the head loss in the main pipeline, the relationship between the head loss and shunted flow must be determined by calibration. Some of the commercially available shunt flow meters use a venturi constriction to create the head loss in the main pipeline to operate the shunt flow meter. The constriction increases velocity and decreases pressure in the throat of the venturi.

The venturi is constructed in tube diameters to be compatible with mainline pipe diameters from 6 to 10.75 inches. The venturi design has the advantage that much of the pressure loss in the throat of the venturi is recovered downstream of the constriction. The venturi is also a simple device whose hydraulic properties are well understood. More importantly, there are no moving parts to wear out.

Flow is registered by a small, low-cost totalizing water meter on the shunt pipeline. The meter gears and register used are sized to indicate the total flow in the main plus shunt pipelines. This design has the advantage that all of the register components are contained on the shunt line where they are readily accessible for calibration, repair, or replacement.

Calibration can be performed without removal of the meter. The meter register is a totalizer which does not directly measure flow rate. Rather, total volume of flow is measured in gallons, and this volume must be divided by the time of operation to determine the flow rate for any period of operation. The register components cost less than $100 if the entire register needs to be replaced.

Measurement accuracy of shunt meters can be as good as + 2 per cent. To improve accuracy, straightening vanes can be inserted in the mainline meter tube. However, as with all in-line flowmeters, certain minimal lengths of straight pipeline are required upstream of the meter. Because the straightening vanes are used, the minimum upstream distance of straight pipeline recommended by the manufacturer is only 2 pipe diameters as compared to the 6 to 10 diameters required for conventional impeller meters without straightening vanes.

ESTIMATING FLOW RATE WITH TRAJECTORY METHOD

With a free-flowing horizontal pipe, the flow can be estimated by measuring the trajectory of the discharge. The distance water flows horizontally past the end of the pipe is dependant on the velocity of the flow. The calculation requires measurements of the vertical drop in the trajectory compared to the horizontal distance the stream travels past the end of the pipe.

ESTIMATING VOLUME/FLOW IN DITCHES OR CANALS

Sometimes it is necessary to estimate the volume or flow rate in an open canal or ditch. Accurate measurement requires the installation of a weir or flume. However, estimates adequate for most purposes can be made from some simple measurements. Volume measurements require determining the cross-sectional area.

Typically, measurements should be taken at several points along the ditch to obtain the average depth profile. In addition, if the width is not uniform, several measurements should be taken and the average width determined. The average cross-sectional area is calculated by the average depth times the average width as:

$$Axc = Da \times Wa \qquad \text{(Eq. 1)}$$

where:

Axc = average cross-sectional area (ft^2)

Da = average depth (ft)

W = average canal/ditch width

The volume of water in the ditch can be calculated by multiplying the cross-sectional area by the length of ditch (typically distance between structures). To convert to gallons, Multiply ft^3 by 7.48, or to calculate ac-ft, multiply ft^3 by 0.00028.

$$Vol = Aac \times L \qquad \text{(Eq. 2)}$$

where:

Vol = Volume of water (ft^3)

L = Length of ditch (ft)

Example: For the following measurements related to locations, determine the cross-sectional area and volume for a ditch that is 1,200 feet long. Assume that the measurements represent the average for entire length of ditch.

Width: w = 10 ft

Depth measurements taken 2 ft apart (equally spaced increments):

a = 2 ft., b = 3 ft., c = 4 ft., d = 4.5 ft., e = 2 ft

$Axc = 10\ ft \times 3.1\ ft = 31\ ft^2$

$Vol = 31\ ft2 \times 1200\ ft = 37{,}200\ ft^3$

In order to calculate the flow rate in the ditch, the average velocity of water flow must be known. The velocity can be determined by measuring the time required for a floating object to travel a known distance. The velocity multiplied by the cross-sectional area will yield flow rate.

$$Q = AXC \times Vavg \quad \text{(Eq. 3)}$$

where:

Axc = average cross-sectional area (ft^2)

Vavg = average velocity (ft/sec)

Q = flow rate (ft^3 /sec)

Water along the banks of a ditch or canal flows slower than it does in the center. This is because the banks tend to resist the water flow. This resistance varies with shape and channel roughness. For most ditches and canals, a factor of 0.8 times the indicated velocity of flow can be used to estimate the average velocity.

Example: Using the previous example cross-sectional area and length, if the time required for a float to travel 100 ft in the center of the ditch is 70 seconds, estimate the flow rate of the ditch. Use a factor of 0.8 to convert measured velocity in the center of ditch (Vc) to average velocity (Vavg)

$Vc = 100\ ft/70\ sec = 1.43\ ft/sec$

$Vavg = V \times 0.8 = 1.43\ ft/sec \times 0.8 = 1.14\ ft/sec$

$Q = A \times V = 31\ ft^2 \times 1.14\ ft/sec = 35.5\ ft^3/sec$

$Q = 35.5\ ft^3/sec \times 7.48\ gal/ft^3 \times 60\ sec/min = 15{,}708\ gal/min$

PRESSURE MEASUREMENTS

Measurement of pressure at key points of a network is of major importance for a system operator. It gives him an effective and simple tool for controlling the performance of the system. A proper gauge type and reasonably chosen measuring points help in discovering leakage and clogging, ascertaining an effective flow distribution, and verifies correct operation of different control devices in a system. Pressure measurements can also give an estimate of the flow rates in various zones of the irrigation system. Therefore, the reliability and accuracy of the pressure measuring equipment is an important feature of the irrigation system.

Pressure gauges should be installed in easily accessible places, so that they are convenient to read and maintain in proper working condition. They should be able to withstand large pressure fluctuations. A pressure gauge must be selected according to the local conditions of installation and to the working pressure range. A properly selected gauge has a scale that will measure up to at least twice the normal working pressure. This allows for pressure surges in the pipeline without damaging the gauge. It also keeps the pointer in the middle of the scale where the accuracy is best under normal operating conditions.

The main type of pressure gauge used in irrigation systems is the Bourdon gauge. This type of gauge uses a C-shaped tube made of copper or stainless alloy. One end of the tube is connected to the inlet of the gauge and the other end is sealed. As the pressure increases, the coiled tube begins to uncoil slightly. This movement of the C-shaped tube is mechanically transferred to the pointer, which moves around a calibrated dial. The dial is typically calibrated in psi. This gauge is available for various pressure ranges.

The accuracy of the pressure gauge depends on the readability of the scale and the precision of the mechanism. Usually, gauge readings can only be made to ½ the span increment between scale measurements. For instance, readings for the gauge would be about 1 psi since the scale is of 2 psi increments. The accuracy of the gauge often changes with the range of the scale. Usually, the most accurate readings are in the range of 25-75 per cent of the full scale reading. Accuracies of 1-2 per cent in this region are normally adequate for irrigation systems.

The proper size of a gauge depends on working conditions. A larger dial permits finer gradation of the scale and easier readout. Larger gauges (4-6 inch) diameter serve as master gauges for testing or as panel instruments in control rooms. Small dials should not be used for stationary control, as they cannot depict the system pressures with sufficient accuracy. Typically 2 ½ -3 inch gauges are satisfactory for most irrigation system applications.

The materials that make up the gauge box, the transparent face pane, and the internal parts are of the utmost importance. For corrosive conditions, the Bourdon tube and mechanism parts should be made of high grade stainless steel or plastic. In working conditions where mechanical vibrations and pressure fluctuations occur frequently, the rackpinion gear should be reinforced to resist rapid wear.

Special attention should be given to the transparent panes of gauges. They should be made of glass plate only. Gauges with plastic transparent panes tend to become cloudy quickly when used outdoors and exposed to the sun. Dials of pressure gauges for indicating water pressure are usually made of sheet steel. They should be painted white with black graduation marks and have large, easy to read digits. Pressure gauges with dials painted red, blue or green are destined for fluids other than water (i.e., air, oxygen, coolants, etc.) and are not usually suitable for irrigation system service.

Pressure units used (typically psi) should be clearly marked on the dial, together with the name or trade mark of the manufacturer. Date of the last calibration and adjustment of the gauge should be recorded in ink on the dial.

Gauges for measuring water pressure usually have an externally threaded inlet at the bottom of the gauge, typically NPT in nominal sizes of 1/8 to 1 inch depending on the size of the gauge. If necessary, the threads can be sealed with Teflon tape. Care should be taken not to cover the orifice.

When installing a gauge, its base should be held firmly with a wrench at the square or hexagonal part of the nipple above the thread. Holding the gauge by the box, and turning it while engaging the connecting threads, is a bad practice. It may impair the calibration and accuracy of the gauge, permanently damaging the gauge mechanism.

While handling and installing a pressure gauge, special care must be given to the small orifice at the end of the nipple. This part, which forms the inlet to the Bourdon tube, is extremely delicate, and careless handling may damage the orifice and plug the gauge inlet. In places where the gauge may be subjected to severe pressure fluctuations or water hammer, it should be protected with a valve that can be used to shut off the pressure. When installing the gauge directly in the outlet of a valve, the length of the threads must be considered. The gauge inlet orifice must never touch the rotating element of the ball valves. In systems where the gauge must constantly indicate the pressure and cannot be shut when not in use, vibration choking devices can minimize the effect of pressure fluctuations and water hammer. In these cases, the gauge may be filled with a high viscosity liquid such as glycerin.

Another way of protecting a gauge from effects of surge is to connect it through a vertical loop of small diameter tubing. The upper part of the loop should contain air, which can compress and so compensate the pressure fluctuations. In such an arrangement the presence of air in the loop should be checked periodically. If the air leaks and the loop fills with water, the device becomes ineffective.

Where mechanical vibration in the piping may be a problem, such as near a pumping plant, a flexible connection of gauges, using small diameter, reinforced tubing may prevent the transfer of vibration to the gauge mechanism, and so decrease wear of the parts of mechanism. Such resilient connections may, in certain instances, even prevent the damaging effects of water hammer. The plastic piping must be appropriately chosen and adapted to the working pressure, and to the possible pressure transients in the system.

Managing wastewater goes back hundreds of years, but wastewater treatment was fairly primitive until the last 100 years. According to a 2000 report on the history of urban wastewater management, the early methods for managing polluted water were very decentralized. Most water was simply dumped into cesspools. Because of the sparse population of early America, this did not cause many hazards or problems, even in urban areas. However, management shifted to centralized systems using familiar public sewage systems as population grew and sanitation became a greater concern.

Wastewater management works essentially like it sounds; monitoring the amount of wastes—whether it be fecal matter or chemicals—that go into our water resources to keep quality at acceptable levels, according to the Environmental Protection Agency.

Management of wastewater also includes ensuring the proper method of disposal of wastewater. Pollution in public water sources are regulated by state and local governments in partnership with the United States EPA's Office of Wastewater Management.

Wastewater management serves a vital role in maintaining the safety of environmental and public health, according to the EPA. Wastes we dump in our waters often come back to hurt ourselves. Toxins leached from wastewater can destroy or contaminate marine life. Because marine are an important source of food, contaminants in fish often make people sick. Even if you do not eat fish, drinking polluted water can still cause sickness and illness.

Industries and businesses that wish to rid themselves of pollutants by putting them in water sources must receive a permit from the National Pollutant Discharge Elimination System, according to the EPA's NPDES website. The NPDES programme is decentralized with states approving permits instead of a federal office. Individual homes that use a septic system or a municipal waste system are not required to obtain a NPDES permit.

One can do his or her part to improve the health of the environment and reduce the spread of disease by improving the efficiency of your septic tank. Septic tank maintenance not only protects your home and raises its value, but it can also prevent spillage that contaminates the water you drink.

The EPA's septic tank owner guide claims that you should have your tank inspected every three years. You should never pour wastes down the drain. Finally, try reducing water usage; consider a low-flow toilet as toilets account for up to 30 per cent of household wastewater.

Many of the ions which are harmless or even beneficial at relatively low concentrations may become toxic to plants at high concentration, either through direct interference with metabolic processes or through indirect effects on other nutrients, which might be rendered inaccessible.

Morishita (1985) has reported that irrigation with nitrogen-enriched polluted water can supply a considerable excess of nutrient nitrogen to growing rice plants and can result in a significant yield loss of rice through lodging, failure to ripen and increased susceptibility to pests and diseases as a result of over-luxuriant growth.

He further reported that non-polluted soil, having around 0.4 and 0.5 ppm cadmium, may produce about 0.08 ppm Cd in brown rice, while only a little increase up to 0.82, 1.25 or 2.1 ppm of soil Cd has the potential to produce heavily polluted brown rice with 1.0 ppm Cd.

Important agricultural water quality parameters include a number of specific properties of water that are relevant in relation to the yield and quality crops, maintenance of soil productivity and protection of the environment. These parameters mainly consist of certain physical and chemical characteristics of the water.

ELECTRICAL CONDUCTIVITY

Electrical conductivity is widely used to indicate the total ionized constituents of water. It is directly related to the sum of the cations (or anions), as determined chemically and is closely correlated, in general, with the total salt concentration. Electrical conductivity is a rapid and reasonably precise determination and values are always expressed at a standard temperature of 25°C to enable comparison of readings taken under varying climatic conditions.

It should be noted that the electrical conductivity of solutions increases approximately 2 per cent per °C increase in temperature. In this publication, the symbol EC_w, is used to represent the electrical conductivity of irrigation water and the symbol EC_e is used to designate the electrical conductivity of the soil saturation extract. The unit of electrical conductivity is deciSiemen per metre (dS/m).

SODIUM ADSORPTION RATIO

Sodium is an unique cation because of its effect on soil. When present in the soil in exchangeable form, it causes adverse physico-chemical changes in the soil, particularly to soil structure. It has the ability to disperse soil, when present above a certain threshold value, relative to the concentration of total dissolved salts.

Dispersion of soils results in reduced infiltration rates of water and air into the soil. When dried, dispersed soil forms crusts which are hard to till and interfere with germination and seedling emergence. Irrigation water could be a source of excess sodium in the soil solution and hence it should be evaluated for this hazard.

An exchangeable sodium percentage (ESP) scale is included in the nomogram to estimate the ESP value of the soil that is at equilibrium with the irrigation water. Using the nomogram, it is possible to estimate the ESP value of a soil that is at equilibrium with irrigation water of a known SAR value.

Under field conditions, the actual ESP may be slightly higher than the estimated equilibrium value because the total salt concentration of the soil solution is increased by evaporation and plant transpiration, which results in a higher SAR and a corres-pondingly higher ESP value.

It should also be noted that the SAR from Eq. 1 does not take into account changes in calcium ion concentration in the soil water due to changes in solubility of calcium resulting from precipitation or dissolution during or following an irrigation. However, the SAR calculated according to Eq 1 is considered an acceptable evaluation procedure for most of the irrigation waters encountered in agriculture.

If significant precipitation or dissolution of calcium due to the effect of carbon dioxide (CO_2), bicarbonate (HCO_3^-) and total salinity (EC_w) is suspected, an alternative procedure for calculating an Adjusted Sodium Adsorption Ratio, SAR_{adj}. can be used. The details of this procedure are reported by Ayers and Westcot.

TOXIC IONS

Irrigation water that contains certain ions at concentrations above threshold values can cause plant toxicity problems. Toxicity normally results in impaired growth, reduced yield, changes in the morphology of the plant and even its death. The degree of damage depends on the crop, its stage of growth, the concentration of the toxic ion, climate and soil conditions.

The most common phytotoxic ions that may be present in municipal sewage and treated effluents in concentrations such as to cause toxicity are: boron (B), chloride (Cl) and sodium (Na). Hence, the concentration of these ions will have to be determined to assess the suitability of waste-water quality for use in agriculture.

A number of elements are normally present in relatively low concentrations, usually less than a few mg/l, in conventional irrigation waters and are called trace elements. They are not normally included in routine analysis of regular irrigation water, but attention should be paid to them when using sewage effluents, particularly if contamination with industrial wastewater discharges is suspected.

These include Aluminium (A1), Beryllium (Be), Cobalt (Co), Fluoride (F), Iron (Fe), Lithium (Li), Manganese (Mn), Molybdenum (Mo), Selenium (Se), Tin (Sn), Titanium (Ti), Tungsten (W) and Vanadium (V).

Heavy metals are a special group of trace elements which have been shown to create definite health hazards when taken up by plants. Under this group are included, Arsenic (As), Cadmium (Cd), Chromium (Cr), Copper (Cu), Lead (Pb), Mercury (Hg) and Zinc (Zn). These are called heavy metals because in their metallic form, their densities are greater than 4g/cc.

The pH is an indicator of the acidity or basicity of water but is seldom a problem by itself. The normal pH range for irrigation water is from 6.5 to 8.4; pH values outside this range are a good warning that the water is abnormal in quality. Normally, pH is a routine measurement in irrigation water quality assessment.

RECLAIMED WASTEWATER USES

Beneficial use of wastewater has been practised in California since the 1890s, when raw sewage was applied on 'sewer farms'. By 1987, more than 0.899 Mm^3/d of municipal wastewater (7-8% of the production) were being used for the various applications.

Historically, agricultural use has dominated, and continues to do so, but over the past decade reclaimed wastewater has been increasingly used for landscape irrigation in urban areas and for groundwater recharge. Most of the reclaimed water (78%) is used in the Central Valley and South Coastal regions of California. Two hundred reclamation plants throughout California produce the volume of treated effluent indicated above and save 0.759 Mm^3/d of fresh water.

The major wastewater reclamation systems are shown in Table. In agricultural use of treated effluent, at least twenty different food crops are being irrigated as well as at least eleven other crops and nursery products.

Wastewater reclamation criteria have been in force in California since 1978, as issued by the California Department of Health Services (1978). For surface irrigation of food crops the requirement is for the effluent to be adequately disinfected and oxidized so that the median number of coliform organisms does not exceed 2.2 per 100 ml over seven days, except that orchards and vineyards may be surface irrigated with effluent having a quality equivalent to that of primary effluent.

Reclaimed wastewater use for spray irrigation of food crops must be at all times adequately disinfected, oxidized, coagulated, clarified, filtered wastewater with a bacteriological quality such that the seven day median number of coliform organisms does not exceed 2.2 per 100 ml and the number of coliform organisms does not exceed 23 per 100 ml in more than one sample within any 30-day period.

Exceptions to these quality requirements may be allowed by the State Department of Health on an individual case basis where the food crop is to undergo extensive commercial physical or chemical processing sufficient to destroy pathogenic agents before human consumption.

For irrigation of fodder, fibre and seed crops the wastewater need only have received primary treatment. However, reclaimed wastewater used to irrigate pasture to which milking cows or goats have access must be at all times adequately disinfected and oxidized to achieve a median number of coliform organisms not exceeding 23 per 100 ml over seven days.

For groundwater recharge of domestic water supply aquifers by surface spreading, the reclaimed wastewater must be at all times of a quality that protects public health. The State Department of Health Services advises Regional Water Quality Control Boards on an individual case basis for proposed groundwater recharge projects and for expansion of existing projects.

Recommendations are based on all relevant aspects of each project, including treatment provided, effluent quality and quantity, spreading area operations, soil characteristics, hydrogeology, residence time and distance to withdrawal. A public hearing is held prior to making the final determination regarding the public health aspects of each groundwater recharge project.

WASTEWATER TREATMENT

The Water Recycling of the California State Water Resources Control Board recognizes four levels of treatment beyond primary treatment, based on the unit processes and on the types of effluent use taking place:

1. Secondary treatment in stabilization ponds, including disinfection if provided
2. Other secondary treatment, for example by the activated sludge process, including disinfection if provided
3. Title 22 tertiary treatment, using filtration and other processes intended to comply with the requirement in the reclamation criteria, published in Title 22 of the California Code of Regulations for adequately disinfected, oxidized, coagulated, clarified, filtered wastewater, or approved equivalent. Usually secondary effluent is treated by the approved equivalent of 'direct filtration', that is, coagulent addition and mixing directly followed by filtration.
4. Other tertiary treatment, consisting of any process following secondary treatment, except tertiary treatment intended to comply with wastewater reclamation criteria in Title 22 of the California Code of Regulations.

In the survey reported in the review of California municipal wastewater reclamation in 1987 all the wastewater treatment plants producing effluents for beneficial uses were found to provide at least secondary treatment.

With one exception, chlorination was believed to have been the sole method of disinfection applied. Tertiary treatment processes falling under category (iv) above were found to include filtration, carbon adsorption, denitrification, air stripping and reverse osmosis. A summary of the treatment levels provided for specific types of effluent use.

Monterey Wastewater Reclamation Study for Agriculture

The Monterey Wastewater Reclamation Study for Agriculture (MWRSA) was a 10-year, US $ 7.2 million field-scale project designed to evaluate the safety and feasibility of irrigating food crops (many eaten raw) with reclaimed municipal wastewater. Demonstration fields at Castroville in the lower Salinas Valley, California were used to study full-scale farm practices using reclaimed municipal wastewater.

Two 5-hectare experimental plots provided large amounts of data on crop response which were subjected to statistical analysis. On one plot artichokes were grown, while on the other a succession of broccoli, cauliflower, lettuce and celery was raised over a 5-year period starting in late 1980.

Secondary effluent from the 1500 m^3/d Castroville wastewater treatment plant of the Monterey Regional Water Pollution Control Agency was upgraded in a pilot tertiary reclamation plant before being used to irrigate the plots. Two parallel tertiary treatment processes were used, complete treatment in a 'Title 22' (T-22) process and a direct filtration process, termed the 'filtered effluent' (FE) process. The T-22 train included coagulation, clarification, filtration and disinfection, the full treatment process required for spray irrigation of food crops in the Wastewater Reclamation Criteria.

Alum dosages of 50 to 200 mg/l and polymer dosage of 0.2 mg/l were applied in this process. In the FE process, low alum dosages between 0 and 15 mg/l and polymer dosages from 0 to 0.18 mg/l were applied with a combination of either static or mechanical rapid mixing and dual-media gravity filtration at 3.4 l/m^2s.

The chlorine contact tank had a 90 minute theoretical retention time. Flocculation chambers were added to the FE process in October 1983 to enhance floe formation prior to filtration, producing a filtered effluent flow stream designated FE-F. Dechlorination of final effluent with sulphur dioxide was practised over the first three years but was discontinued in June 1983 to determine the effects, if any, of a chlorine residual on crops and to prevent microbial regrowth. No adverse effects of chlorine residual on crops was observed and further microbial regrowth in storage tanks and pipelines was prevented.

.ed

CHAPTER – 9

Waste Water Re-use for Irrigation

Water reuse can be defined as the use of reclaimed water for a direct beneficial purpose. The use of reclaimed water for irrigation and other purposes has been employed as a water conservation practice in Florida, California, Texas, Arizona, and other states for many years.

Reclaimed water, also known as recycled water, is water recovered from domestic, municipal, and industrial wastewater treatment plants that has been treated to standards that allow safe reuse. Properly reclaimed water is typically safe for most uses except human consumption.

Wastewater is not reclaimed water. Wastewater is untreated liquid industrial waste and/or domestic sewage from residential dwellings, commercial buildings, and industrial facilities. Gray water, or untreated wastewater from bathing or washing, is one form of wastewater. Wastewater may be land applied, but this is considered to be land treatment rather than water reuse.

WHY RE-USE WATER?

The demand for fresh water in Virginia is growing as the state's population increases. This demand can potentially exceed supply during times of even moderate drought. In recent years, the normal seasonal droughts that have occurred in Virginia have caused local and state government to enact water conservation ordinances. These ordinances limit the use of potable water (water suitable for human consumption) for such things as car washing and landscape irrigation.

The potential for developing new sources of potable water is limited. Conservation measures, such as irrigating with reclaimed water, are one way to help ensure existing water supplies are utilized as efficiently as possible.

The environmental benefits of using reclaimed water includes:

1. Increased water quantity.
2. Decreased diversion of freshwater from wetlands and other ecosystems.
3. Reduced use of potable water by industrial, housing, and recreational development projects that use reclaimed water.
4. Reduction in the amount of groundwater withdrawal, which impacts base flow in many rivers and streams.
5. Reduction in the amount of nutrients entering the Chesapeake Bay, its tributaries, and other water bodies.

WASTE WATER TREATMENT PLANT

Reclaimed water typically comes from municipal wastewater treatment plants, although some industries (e.g., food processors) also generate water that may be suitable for nonpotable uses. During primary treatment at a wastewater treatment plant, inorganic and organic suspended solids are removed from plant influent by screening, and settling.

The decanted effluent from the primary treatment process is then subjected to secondary treatment, which involves biological decomposition of organic material and settling to further separate water from solids. If a wastewater treatment plant is not equipped to perform advanced treatment, water is disinfected and discharged to natural water bodies following secondary treatment.

Advanced or tertiary treatment consists of further removal of suspended and dissolved solids, including nutrients, and disinfection. Advanced treatment can include:

1. Nutrient (nitrogen and/or phosphorus) removal by biological or chemical methods.
2. Removal of organics and metals by carbon adsorption or chemical precipitation.
3. Further removal of suspended and dissolved solids by filtration, coagulation, ion exchange, reverse osmosis, and other techniques.
4. Removal of organic chemicals by oxidation with hydrogen peroxide or ozone.

Water that has undergone advanced treatment is disinfected prior to being released or reused. Reclaimed water often requires greater treatment than effluent that is discharged to local streams or rivers because users will typically have more direct contact with undiluted reclaimed water than undiluted effluent.

OPTIONS FOR WATER RE-USE

Although the primary focus of this publication is on the use of reclaimed water for agricultural, municipal, and residential irrigation, reclaimed water can be used for many other purposes. Non-irrigation uses for reclaimed water include:

1. Urban reus: Ornamental landscape water features and golf course water features such as ponds and fountains, fire protection, dust control and concrete mixing on construction sites, vehicle and window washing, toilet flushing in public, commercial, and industrial buildings.
2. Industrial reuse, Cooling water, Boiler make-up water, Industrial process water.
3. Intentional indirect potable reuse. Intentional indirect potable reuse means that reclaimed water is discharged to a water body where it is then purposefully used as a raw water supply for another water treatment plant. This occurs unintentionally in most rivers, since downstream water treatment plants use treated water discharged by upstream wastewater treatment plants.

Direct potable reuse refers to the use of reclaimed water for drinking directly after treatment, and, to date, has only been implemented in Africa.

Examples of non-irrigation permitted water reuse projects in Virginia are:

Hampton Roads Sanitation District's partnership with Giant Industries, Inc. to supply reclaimed water for cooling and other industrial processes at the Yorktown Refinery.

The Upper Occoquan Sewage Authority's production of highly treated reclaimed water for reuse within the Occoquan Reservoir to supplement the water supply and to improve reservoir water quality.

WATER RE-USE REGULATIONS

Introduction

The turfgrass and ornamental horticulture industries have grown as Virginia becomes more urbanized. The acreage devoted to high-value specialty crops that benefit from irrigation, such as fruits and vegetables, is also increasing. As demand for potable water increases, maintaining turf, landscape plants, and crops will require the utilization of previously underutilized water sources.

The regulation of reclaimed water production and use encourages both the supply of and the demand for reclaimed water. The benefits to suppliers of reclaimed water include greater public awareness and demand for reclaimed water and clear guidelines for reclaimed water production. Benefits to end users include increased public acceptance of the use of reclaimed water and a subsequent decrease in the demand for fresh water.

U.S. EPA Guidelines

There are no federal regulations governing reclaimed water use, but the U.S. EPA (2004) has established guidelines to encourage states to develop their own regulations. The primary purpose of federal guidelines and state regulations is to protect human health and water quality. To reduce disease risks to acceptable levels, reclaimed water must meet certain disinfection standards by either reducing the concentrations of constituents that may affect public health and/or limiting human contact with reclaimed water.

The U.S. EPA (2004) recommends that water intended for reuse should:

Be treated to achieve biochemical oxygen demand and total suspended solids levels of <30 mg/L, during secondary or tertiary treatment.

Receive additional disinfection by means such as chlorination or other chemical disinfectants, UV radiation, ozonation, and membrane processing.

Biochemical oxygen demand (BOD) is an indicator of the presence of reactive organic matter in water. Total suspended solids (TSS) or turbidity (measured in nephelometric turbidity units, or NTUs) are measures of the amount of organic and inorganic particulate matter in water. Some other parameters often measured as indicators of disinfection efficiency include:

- *Fecal coliforms, E. coli or enterococci:* The presence of these bacteria in water typically indicates the presence of pathogenic organisms associated with fecal contamination.
- *Residual chlorine:* The concentration of this disinfection chemical after a standard contact time measures effectiveness by inference.

PATHOGENS AND MICRO-CONSTITUENTS

Monitoring for specific pathogens and microconstituents may become a part of the standard testing protocol as the use of reclaimed water for indirect potable reuse applications increases. Pathogens of particular concern include enteric viruses and the protozoan parasites Giardia and Cryptosporidium, whose monitoring is required by the state of Florida for water reuse projects.

Micro-constituents include organic chemicals, such as pharmaceutically active substances, personal care products, endocrine disrupting compounds, and previously unregulated inorganic elements whose toxicity may be re-assessed or newly evaluated. Fish, amphibians, and birds have been found to develop reproductive system abnormalities upon direct or indirect exposure to a variety of endocrine disrupting compounds. Such microconstituents may have the potential to cause reproduction system abnormalities and immune system malfunctioning in other wildlife and humans at higher concentrations.

The impacts of the extremely low concentrations of these compounds found in wastewater effluent or reclaimed water are unknown. To date, there is no evidence that micro-constituents cause human health effects at environmentally relevant concentrations.

Some possible options for the removal of micro-constituents from wastewater are treatment with ozone, hydrogen peroxide, and UV light. These methods can destroy some micro-constituents via advanced oxidation, but the endocrine disruption activity of the by-products created during oxidation may also be of concern.

No illnesses have been directly associated with the use of properly treated reclaimed water in the U.S.. The U.S. EPA recommends, however, that ongoing research and additional monitoring for Giardia, Cryptosporidium, and micro-constituents be conducted to understand changes in reclaimed water quality.

VIRGINIA WATER RE-USE REGULATIONS

State regulations need not agree with U.S. EPA guidelines and are often more stringent. In Virginia, water reuse means direct beneficial reuse, indirect potable reuse, or a controlled use in accordance with the Water Reclamation and Reuse Regulation.

The Virginia Water Regulation and Reuse Regulation establishes legal requirements for the reclamation and treatment of water that is to be reused. These require ments are designed to protect both water quality and public health, while encouraging the use of reclaimed water. The Virginia Department of Environmental Quality, Water Quality Division has oversight over the Virginia Water Reclamation and Reuse Regulation.

The primary determinants of how reclaimed water of varying quality can be used are based on treatment processes to which the water has been subjected and on quantitative chemical, physical, and biological standards. Reclaimed water suitable for reuse in Virginia is categorized as either Level 1 or Level 2.

WATER REUSE: AGRONOMIC CONCERNS

Water quality must be considered when using reclaimed water for irrigation. The following properties are critical to plant and soil health and environmental quality.

Salinity Levels

Salinity, or salt concentration, is probably the most important consideration in determining whether water is suitable for reuse. Water salinity is the sum of all elemental ions (e.g., sodium, calcium, chloride, boron, sulfate, nitrate) and is usually measured by determining the electrical conductivity (EC, units = dS/m) or total dissolved solids (TDS, units = mg/L) concentration of the water. Water with a TDS concentration of 640 mg/L will typically have an EC of approximately 1 dS/m.

Salts in reclaimed water come from:

(a) elemental ions naturally found in water.

(b) ions retained in dissolved form after separation of solids during water treatment.

(c) any salts added during the water treatment process.

Most reclaimed water from urban areas is slightly saline. High salt concentrations reduce water uptake in plants by lowering the osmotic potential of the soil. For instance, residential use of water adds approx 200-400 mg/L dissolved salts. Plants differ in their sensitivity to salt levels so the salinity of the particular reclaimed water source should be measured so that appropriate crops and/or application rates can be selected. Most turfgrasses can tolerate water with 200-800 mg/L soluble salts, but salt levels above 2,000 mg/L may be toxic.

Many other crop and landscape plants are more sensitive to high soluble-salt levels than turfgrasses, and should be managed accordingly.

Concentration of Sodium, Chloride and Boron

Specific dissolved ions may also affect irrigation water quality. For example, irrigation water with a high concentration of sodium (Na) ions may cause dispersion of soil aggregates and sealing of soil pores. This is a particular problem in golf course irrigation since soil compaction is already a concern due to persistent foot and vehicular traffic. The Sodium Adsorption Ratio (SAR), which measures the ratio of sodium to other ions, is used to evaluate the potential effect of irrigation water on soil structure.

High levels of sodium can also be directly toxic to plants both through root uptake and by accumulation in plant leaves following sprinkler irrigation.

The specific concentration of sodium that is considered to be toxic will vary with plant species and the type of irrigation system. Turf grasses are generally more tolerant to sodium than most ornamental plant species.

Although boron (B) and chlorine (Cl) are necessary at low levels for plant growth, dissolved boron and chloride ions can cause toxicity problems at high concentrations. Specific toxic concentrations will vary depending on plant species and type of irrigation method used. Levels of boron as low as 1 to 2 mg/L in irrigation water can cause leaf burn on ornamental plants, but turfgrasses can often tolerate levels as high as 10 mg/L. Very salt-sensitive landscape plants such as crape myrtle (*Lagerstroemia sp.*), azalea (*Rhododendron sp.*), and Chinese privet (*Ligustrum sinense*) may be damaged by overhead irrigation with reclaimed water containing chloride levels over 100 mg/L, but most turfgrasses are relatively tolerant to chloride if they are mowed frequently.

Nutrient Levels

Reclaimed water typically contains more nitrogen (N) and phosphorus (P) than drinking water. The amounts of N and P provided by the reclaimed water can be calculated as the product of the estimated irrigation volume and the N and P concentration in the water. To prevent N and P leaching into groundwater, the Virginia Water Reclamation and Reuse

Regulation requires that a nutrient management plan be written for bulk use of reclaimed water not treated to achieve biological nutrient removal (BNR), which the regulation defines as treatment that achieves an annual average of 8.0 mg/L total N and 1.0 mg/L total P. Water that has been subjected to BNR treatment processes contains such low concentrations of N and P that the reclaimed water can be applied at rates sufficient to supply a crop's water needs without risk of surface or ground water contamination.

High suspended solids (TSS) concentrations may clog irrigation systems, and can fill pore spaces near the soil surface resulting in reduced drainage. Acceptable TSS levels will vary depending on the type of suspended solids and type of irrigation system. Generally, TSS levels less than 50-100 mg/L are safe for drip irrigation.

Free chlorine (Cl_2) is necessary for disinfection, but can damage plants at high concentrations (> 5 mg/L). Storage for a short time reduces the residual free chlorine concentration in water.

High or low pH is an indicator of presence of phytotoxic ions, and pH should be approximately 6.5 to 7, if possible.

High bicarbonate (>120 mL) and carbonate (>15 mg/L) levels can clog sprinklers and cause white lime deposits on plant leaves, and may increase soil pH and decrease permeability.

Heavy metals can be a concern in wastewater that has high industrial input, but such metals (for example, cadmium, copper, molybdenum, nickel, and zinc) are typically strongly bound to the solid fraction, or biosolids portion, of the wastewater and rarely are found in high enough concentrations to pose a reclaimed water quality problem.

Application Rates

The Virginia Water Reclamation and Reuse Regulations require that irrigation with reclaimed water shall be limited to supplemental irrigation. Supplemental irrigation is defined as that amount of water which, in combination with rainfall, meets the water demands of the irrigated vegetation to maximize production or optimize growth.

Irrigation rates for reclaimed water are site- and crop-specific, and will depend on the following factors.

1. First, seasonal irrigation demands must be determined. These can be predicted with:
   (a) an evapotranspiration estimate for the particular crop being grown.
   (b) determination of the period of plant growth.
   (c) average annual precipitation data.
   (d) data for soil permeability and water holding capacity.

   Methods for calculating such irrigation requirements can be found in the U.S. Department of Agriculture's National Engineering Handbook and in Reed et al. (1995). These calculations are more complicated for landscape plantings than for agricultural crops or turf because landscape plantings consist of many different species with different requirements.
2. The properties of the specific reclaimed water to be used, as detailed in the section above, must be taken into account since these may limit the total amount of water that can be applied per season.
3. The availability of the reclaimed water should also be quantified, including:
   - the total amount available.
   - the time of year when available.
   - availability of water storage facilities for the nongrowing season.
   - delivery rate and type.

WATER REUSE CASE STUDIES

Landscape and Residential Case Studies

State of Florida

Water reuse is actively promoted by the Florida Department of Environmental Protection since Florida law requires that the use of potable water for irrigation be limited. In 2005, 462 Florida golf courses, covering over 56,000 acres of land, were irrigated with reclaimed water. Reclaimed water was also used to irrigate 201,465 residences, 572 parks, and 251 schools. St. Petersburg is home to one of the largest dual distribution systems in the world. A dual distribution system is one where pipes carrying reclaimed water are separate from those carrying potable water. In existence since the 1970s, this network provides reclaimed water to residences, golf courses, parks, schools, and commercial areas for landscape irrigation, and to commercial and industrial customers for cooling and other applications.

Cary, North Carolina

The town of Cary is the first city in the state of North Carolina to institute a dual distribution system. The system has been in operation since 2001 and can provide up to 1 million gallons of reclaimed water daily for irrigating and cooling. The reclaimed water has undergone advanced treatment and meets North Carolina water quality rules. To date, there are over 400 residential and industrial users.

Bayberry Hills Golf Course, Yarmouth, Massachusetts

The Bayberry Hills Golf Course expansion is one of numerous water reuse projects in Massachusetts. It was initiated in 2001 as an addition to an existing golf course of seven holes irrigated with reclaimed water. These seven holes use approximately 18 million gallons of water per year, and water reuse was necessary since Yarmouth's water supply was already operating at capacity during summer months.

The reused water undergoes secondary treatment followed by ozone treatment, filtration, and UV disinfection. There are provisions for water storage during the nongrowing season. The water reuse project has reduced the nitrogen needed for golf course fertilization.

Case Studies of Agricultural Irrigation

Southeast Farm, Tallahassee, Florida

The Southeast Farm in Tallahassee, Florida, has been irrigating with reclaimed water since 1966. The farm is a cooperative between the city of Tallahassee, which supplies water, and farmers who contract acreage. Until

1980, the farm was limited to 20 acres of land for hay production, but has expanded since then to 2,163 acres. The irrigation water receives secondary treatment. The crops grown are corn.

In recent years, however, elevated nitrate levels have been found in the waters of Wakulla Springs State Park south of Tallahassee, which is one of the largest and deepest freshwater springs in the world. This has apparently resulted in excessive growth of algae and exotic aquatic plant species, causing reduced clarity and changes in the spring's ecosystem. Dye studies have confirmed that at least a portion of the nitrate comes from the Southeast Farm's irrigated fields, although studies are ongoing. As a result, in June 2006, the city of Tallahassee removed all cattle from Southeast Farm, eliminated regular use of nitrogen fertilizer on the farm, and implemented a comprehensive nutrient management plan for the farm.

Water Conserv II has been in existence since 1986, and is the first project permitted by the Florida Department of Environmental Protection for crops for human consumption. Over 3000 acres of citrus groves are irrigated with reclaimed water, in addition to nurseries, residential landscaping, a sand mine, and the Orange County National Golf Center.

No problems have resulted from the irrigation. The reclaimed water provides adequate boron and phosphorus and maintains soil at correct pH for citrus growth. The adequate supply of water permits citrus growers to maintain optimum moisture levels for high yields and ample water for freeze protection, which requires more than eight times as much water as normal irrigation.

Although, Water Conserv II had historically provided reclaimed water to citrus growers for no charge, the project recently began charging for water. It's unclear if citrus growers will continue to irrigate with reclaimed water, or whether it's emphasis will change to providing reclaimed water for residential, industrial, and landscape customers.

Bibliography

Agricultural Drainage Criteria. Chapter 17 in: H.P. Ritzema (ed. 1994), *Drainage Principles and Applications*, ILRI Publication 16, pp. 635-690. International Institute for Land Reclamation and Improvement (ILRI), Wageningen, The Netherlands.

Mollison, Bill, Permaculture: A Designer's Manual, Tagari Press, (1988). Increases in Porosity Enhance Infiltration and thus Reduce Adverse Effects of Surface Runoff.

Collinson, M. (ed.) *A History of Farming Systems Research*. CABI Publishing, 2000.

Davis, Donald R.; Riordan, Hugh D. (2004). "Changes in USDA Food Composition Data for 43 Garden Crops, 1950 to 1999". Journal of the American College of Nutrition, 23(6): pp. 669-682.

De Jong, M.H. 1979. Drainage of Structured Clay Soils. In: J. Wesseling (ed.), *Proceedings of the International Drainage Workshop*. ILRI Publication 25, pp. 268-280. International Institute for Land Reclamation and Improvement (ILRI), Wageningen, The Netherlands.

Friedland, William H.; Barton, Amy (1975). "Destalking the Wily Tomato: A Case Study of Social Consequences in California Agricultural Research". Univ. California at Sta. Cruz, Research Monograph 15.

General case studies of drainage methods and systems in agricultural land. Lecture note, International Course on Land Drainage (ICLD), International Institute for Land Reclamation and Improvement (ILRI), Wageningen, The Netherlands.

Wijdieks, J., and Bos, M.G., 1994. Pumps and Pumping Stations. In: H.P. Ritzema (ed.), *Drainage Principles and Applications,* ILRI Publication 16, pp. 965-1000. International Institute for Land Reclamation and Improvement (ILRI), Wageningen, The Netherlands.

Nosenko, P.P. and I.S. Zonn 1976. Land Drainage in the World. *ICID Bulletin* 25, 1, pp. 65-70.

Oosterbaan, R.J., H.A. Gunneweg and A. Huizing 1987. Water Control for Rice Cultivation in Small Valleys of West Africa. In: *ILRI Annual Report 1986,* pp. 30-49. International Institute for Land Reclamation and Improvement (ILRI), Wageningen, The Netherlands.

Predicting Soil Erosion by Water, a Guide to Conservation Planning in the Revised Universal Soil Loss Equation, U.S. USDA Agricultural Research Service, Agricultural Handbook No. 703 (1997).

Qorani, M., M.S. Abdel Dayem and R.J. Oosterbaan 1990. Evaluation of Restricted Subsurface Drainage in Rice Fields. In: Symposium on Land Drainage for Salinity Control in Arid and Semi Arid Regions, Vol. 3. Drainage Research Institute, Cairo, pp. 415-423.

Rao, K.V.G.K., D.P. Sharma and R.J. Oosterbaan 1992. Sub-irrigation by Groundwater Management with Controlled Subsurface Drainage in Semi-arid areas. International Conference on Supplementary Irrigation and Drought Management, Bari, Italy.

Saltini, A. Storia delle scienze agrarie, 4 Vols, Bologna 1984-89.

Watson, A.M. (1974). "The Arab Agricultural Revolution and its Diffusion", *The Journal of Economic History,* 34.

Watson, A.M. (1983). *Agricultural Innovation in the Early Islamic World,* Cambridge University Press.

Wells, Spencer (2003). *The Journey of Man: A Genetic Odyssey.* Princeton University Press.

Wickens, G.M. (1976). "What the West borrowed from the Middle East", in Savory, R.M. (ed.) *Introduction to Islamic Civilization.* Cambridge University Press.

Wolfgang Summer, Modelling Soil Erosion, Sediment Transport and Closely Related Hydrological Processes Entry by Mingyuan Du, Peiming Du, Taichi Maki and Shigeto Kawashima, "Numerical Modelling of Air Flow Over Complex Terrain Concerning Wind Erosion", International Association of Hydrological Sciences Publication No. 249 (1998).

Lu, Y.C., Watkins, K.B., Teasdale, J.R., and Abdul-Baki, A.A. Cover Crops in Sustainable Food Production,. Food Reviews International 16: pp. 121-157 (2000).

Index

W